WOMEN AND TRADE UNIONS

In memory of Alice Cook

Women and Trade Unions
A comparative perspective

JENNIFER CURTIN

Taylor & Francis Group
LONDON AND NEW YORK

First published 1999 by Ashgate Publishing

Reissued 2018 by Routledge
2 Park Square, Milton Park, Abingdon, Oxon, OX14 4RN
52 Vanderbilt Avenue, New York, NY 10017

Routledge is an imprint of the Taylor & Francis Group, an informa business

Copyright © Jennifer Curtin 1999

All rights reserved. No part of this book may be reprinted or reproduced or utilised in any form or by any electronic, mechanical, or other means, now known or hereafter invented, including photocopying and recording, or in any information storage or retrieval system, without permission in writing from the publishers.

Notice:
Product or corporate names may be trademarks or registered trademarks, and are used only for identification and explanation without intent to infringe.

Publisher's Note
The publisher has gone to great lengths to ensure the quality of this reprint but points out that some imperfections in the original copies may be apparent.

Disclaimer
The publisher has made every effort to trace copyright holders and welcomes correspondence from those they have been unable to contact.

A Library of Congress record exists under LC control number: 99072328

ISBN 13: 978-1-138-37052-4 (hbk)
ISBN 13: 978-1-138-37053-1 (pbk)
ISBN 13: 978-0-429-42797-8 (ebk)

Contents

List of Figures		vi
List of Tables		vii
Acknowledgements		viii
List of Abbreviations		ix
1	Introduction	1
2	Identifying Women-Inclusive Strategies	16
3	Australia	37
4	Austria	66
5	Israel	93
6	Sweden	118
7	Concluding with Comparisons	142
Appendix One		162
Appendix Two		165
Bibliography		166
Index		187

List of Figures

Figure 1.1	Female Union Density, 1960-1994	9
Figure 6.1	Increase in Women's Union Membership, LO and TCO	122

List of Tables

Table 1.1	Changes in Female and Male Trade Union Density	10
Table 1.2	Numbers (000s) and Percentage Increase of Female Trade Union Members in Selected Countries, 1950–1993	11
Table 1.3	Percentage of Women on Executive Committees in National Trade Union Confederations	13
Table 3.1	Distribution by Gender of Major Office Holders in Local Trade Unions, 1975 and 1995	44
Table 4.1	Women's Representation on the Praesidium in Selected Unions, 1993	73
Table 4.2	Women's Representation at ÖGB Congress, Various Years	74
Table 6.1	Percentage and Representational Ratio of Women in Upper Levels of LO	123
Table 6.2	Percentage and Representational Ratio of Women in Upper Levels of TCO	124

Acknowledgements

Many people provided me with assistance in the process of this research. First, my thanks go to Frank Castles and Barbara Sullivan for their intellectual guidance and support. Second, this work would not have eventuated without the contributions of the women unionists whom I interviewed and to them I am extremely grateful. Thanks go to Jelle Visser and Bernhard Ebbinghaus for providing me with data from the DUES data set, to Bo Rothstein, Michael Shalev, Gillian Whitehouse, Winton Higgins, David Peetz, Diane Sainsbury and Moshe Semyonov for feedback on early drafts, and to Gudrun Biffl, Bernhard Kittel, Wolfgang Pollan, Franz Traxler and Gary Chaison for their help with sources and clarification. Others who have given me encouragement, assistance and friendship include Shirin Ahlback, Christina Bergqvist, Heather Brook, Jenny Chalmers, Lorraine Elliott, Paul Grimes, Rolf Gerritsen, Andre Moore, Rebecca Stringer, Fiona Webster and my family. I would also like to mention Tony and Molly Beirne, Jenny Farley, Joyce Gould, Lois Gray, Beth Leslie, Gormley Miller, Robin Ingram, Ingrid Reischl, Zachary and Arza Sheaffer, Per Strand, Rose Ward and Birgit Weiss whose generosity and support were invaluable while I was researching abroad. Very special thanks is reserved for Craig Symes and Heather Devere. Finally, acknowledgement must go to Anne Keirby and Rachel Hedges of Ashgate for their patience, to Ruth Bader for assistance with formatting, and to the Swedish Institute for the Council of Europe Scholarship which greatly enhanced my research pursuits in Sweden. The book is dedicated to Alice Cook whose work first inspired me to pursue this topic. Alice took the time to discuss with me my initial thoughts and provided me with encouragement and access to sources and contacts, all of which have proved invaluable.

December 1998

List of Abbreviations

ACTU	Australian Council of Trade Unions
AS	Austrian Schillings
DUES	The Development of Trade Unions in Western European Societies Project, Mannheim Centre for European Social Research, University of Mannheim.
EEO	Equal Employment Opportunity
ETUC	European Trade Union Confederation
HREOC	Human Rights and Equal Opportunity Commission
ICFTU	International Confederation of Free Trade Unions
ILO	International Labour Organisation
KOM	Women and Men Working Together
LO	Swedish Confederation of Trade Unions
NSW	New South Wales
OECD	Organisation for Economic Co-operation and Development
ÖGB	Austrian Confederation of Trade Unions
SACO	Swedish Confederation of Academics.
SAF	Swedish Employers' Association
SSGCW	State Secretariat for the General Concerns of Women
TCFUA	Textile, Clothing and Footwear Union of Australia
TCO	Central Organisation of Salaried Employees.
TDC	Trade Development Council
UK	United Kingdom
US	United States
WTUC	Women's Trade Union Commission
WTUL	Women's Trade Union League

1 Introduction

Since the emergence of the labour movement in response to industrialisation, trade unions have had a mixed record on the representation of women workers. In the past, women have been excluded from membership, denied access to decision-making positions, and some trade unions have acted to reinforce rather than challenge women's inequality in the paid workforce.

Yet, from the 1960s onwards, women have become a permanent fixture in the paid labour force and, in many countries, women make up a substantial component of trade union membership. It is in this context that Cobble notes "the potential for forging a creative productive partnership between working women and unions is greater now than at any other time" (Cobble, 1993, p. 4). The aim of this book is to examine the extent to which such a "partnership" has been developed between women workers and trade unions. More specifically, I analyse how women trade unionists have sought to make trade union structures and policy agendas more inclusive of the interests of women workers in four countries: Australia, Austria, Israel and Sweden.

There has been a considerable increase in research concerning women over the last twenty years or so, and with it, the historical and contemporary situation of women in trade unions has emerged as an object of serious scholarly inquiry. Historical analyses of women and their interaction with trade unions rectify the previous invisibility of women's position within the labour movement (Collette 1989; Frances 1991; Milkman, 1985; Shute, 1994; Soldon, 1985; Street, 1994). Contemporary developments in the relationship between women and trade unions have also received increasing attention in the literature (Acker, 1994; Bergqvist, 1991; 1995; Briskin, 1993; Gardner, 1983; Lawrence, 1994; Pocock, 1995a; Pocock, 1997). With a few exceptions (see Cook, Lorwin and Daniels, 1984; 1992; Gelb, 1989; O'Donnell and Hall, 1988), this literature has not been comparative in nature; a gap this book begins to fill.

The continuing absence of women within the elites of political institutions has become an increasingly salient topic of late, both within the theory and practice of politics. Much of the focus of new democratic theorising and practice has been primarily on the absence of women in parliaments (Phillips, 1991; 1995; Sawer and Simms, 1993) and the bureaucracy (Eisenstein, 1991; Sawer 1990; Yeatman, 1990). Trade unions also need to be included in this debate since they play a critical role in the representation of workers' interests to both employers and governments. This book contributes to an assessment of democratic practice within trade unions by examining how workers' interests are defined and redefined and how women are provided with a voice in this process.

I have selected Australia, Austria, Israel and Sweden for a number of reasons. First, they exhibit several similarities (cf Przeworski and Tuene, 1970). In all four countries, a trade union movement exists which has encompassed a majority of wage earners, and has union confederations which are strong and centralised. All have close links to parties on the left. In Sweden, Austria and Israel, parties of the left have enjoyed a large electoral following and have participated as leading or equal partners in government for over 30 years. While this has not been the case in Australia, the Australian Labor Party did have an uninterrupted thirteen year period of majority government between 1983 and 1996, during which time an institutionalised relationship developed between union and party elites.

Second, Sweden, Austria, Israel and Australia have, at various times, all been labelled "corporatist". The term corporatism can be used to describe the institutional arrangements which allow for the effective participation of labour organisations in the formulation and implementation of policy across a range of key policy areas (Boreham and Compston, 1992, p. 146). Although there are numerous definitions of the concept, most definitions accept interest aggregation as a central feature of corporatism. There is a requirement for trade union elites to coordinate and limit the demands of their members in a way that will override sectional interests. In return they are granted a representational monopoly within the policy-making arena, which in turn can have a significant effect on final policy outcomes (Shalev, 1992, p. 6).

It is accepted here that political institutions such as the corporatist environment and the strength of trade unionism matter to the claims of women unionists. But just as weak unionism may constrain women from using unionism as a vehicle for change, so may strong unionism and institutionalised corporatist channels constrain women unionists from pursuing particular, more gender-specific, strategies.

While institutionally broadly similar, the four countries examined here represent variations of social-democratic corporatism. The comparison of Sweden and Austria may seem natural for a number of reasons (see Katzenstein, 1984; Kunkel and Pontusson, 1998), but the inclusion of Australia and Israel is not as intuitive. Australia's corporatist arrangements are less historically entrenched than the other three countries examined here, and have been bipartite in character (between state and unions) to the exclusion of business interests (Hampson, 1997; Matthews, 1991). Nevertheless, thirteen years of an Accord between the Labor Government and the centralised trade union confederation provided a dialogue around policy making previously unseen in Australia and offered unions a central voice during a period of declining union membership.

The choice of Israel could also be seen as peculiar in that union membership in Israel has been linked to membership of the union-controlled health fund, (not unlike the Ghent system of union-controlled unemployment insurance in Sweden). Furthermore, while corporatism has tended to be linked to strong economic performance, wage restraint, low unemployment and welfare reform, such outcomes have seldom eventuated in Israel's corporatist history. Yet the Israeli case provides an insight into the extent to which workers' interests are sectionalised, not only with respect to labour market position but also national and cultural identity and how such divisions influence the policy choices taken by corporatist elites. Focussing on the organisation and articulation of interests within each corporatist environment provides the context for an examination as to how such elites also seek to manage diversity according to gender.

The literature on institutionalised corporatism and public policy outcomes has often ignored the democracy deficit that is required for its entrenchment. Trade unions have seldom provided adequate representation of women at decision-making levels, from which corporatist delegates are drawn (Cook et al, 1992; Curtin, 1997). One consequence of this is, because of the fixed patterns of representation within corporatist arrangements; women are systematically excluded from these institutionalised elites (Bergqvist, 1991; Cockburn, 1997; Hernes, 1987; Lovenduski, 1986). Others argue the collaboration between economic organisations not only excludes individual women, but can also subordinate important issues of concern to women (Hernes, 1987; Hernes and Voje, 1980).

Furthermore, it is not always clear that the interests being represented by the elites continue to be the interests of rank and file workers. Schmitter states that the concept of interest intermediation allows for the possibility that interests may be generated from within the corporatist decision-making environment, independent of member preferences (Schmitter, 1981, p. 295). Others support the notion that conceptualisation and definition of interests occurs at the point of articulation (Pringle and Watson, 1992; Scott, 1990). If we accept that interests are often constructed not prior to interaction, but in the process of policy formation, then it becomes impossible to separate out what is to be represented from who is to do the representation (Phillips, 1995). This would reinforce the case for more women as representatives in the upper echelons of trade union movements.

With such criticisms of corporatism, it may seem strange to examine the utility these arrangements might have for women workers. However, there is nothing inherent in the nature of either unionism or corporatism to undermine their use as mechanisms to achieve gender equality in the labour market. Indeed, previous research suggests that if trade unions are possible vehicles of change for women workers, it would be in countries where trade unionism is strong and centralised and provided with representation in the policy-making arena (Cook et al, 1992; Ruggie, 1984; Whitehouse, 1992).

Research Parameters

Several questions are addressed in the book. What is distinctive about the strategies for change pursued by women unionists in each country? More specifically, I ask under what circumstances and around what issues have women trade unionists deployed class-based or gender-specific strategies in furthering the interests of women workers? I define class-based strategies as being derived from a specifically class-oriented ideology, which views the capital-labour relationship as primary. All workers are considered to have a common interest arising out of this relationship. Class strategies may range from strikes to formal involvement in the policy-making arena. Gender-specific strategies are those which invoke the notion of "woman" and often include separate organising within trade unions, utilising legislative measures and seeking to feminise union hierarchies. I also question how relevant the choice of strategy is to the

Introduction

history of women's inclusion and representation by trade unions and the political and cultural environment within which trade unionism has operated?

Primary research material was collected from interviews conducted with 50 women trade union officials (and five male trade unionists) working within the trade union confederations and in the head offices of national trade unions in Sweden, Australia, Austria and Israel (see Appendix One). A cross-section of unions was targeted to reflect the different proportions of women members, as well as various occupations and industries. Equality officers and/or women's officers were chosen as contacts since the interview questions revolved around what union policies existed or were being considered regarding issues relevant to women workers. The interviews took place between August 1994 and April 1995. Thus, my research draws primarily on the experience of women acting in positions that enable them to participate in both the identification and formulation of women's interests and strategies.

Also consulted were officials from parties of the left, government officials, academics, staff of international labour secretariats and international labour confederations, and people of interest who could provide further information and advice.

Such descriptive work is important because there remains much about women's representation within trade unions that we do not know. However, this has been placed within a specific conceptual framework and in this way avoids degenerating "into ad hoc description" (Castles, 1989, p. 9). I have therefore, sought to link the relevance of broad institutional and political configurations and discourses within each country with the articulated experiences of women trade unionists in the process of more micro-level representation (cf Peattie and Rein, 1983).

In addressing the questions outlined above, I interrogate the adequacy of existing models of corporatism and solidarity. I examine whether it is possible to re-conceptualise the ways we think about solidarity and collective action by women in trade unions. I argue that reference solely to conventional notions of solidarity based on class assumes the existence of a unified working class interest, subsuming the tangible differences that exist between workers. A similar criticism can also be directed at feminist approaches which view women's interests as fixed and unified, or where tangible differences between women are ignored and/or minimised.

The ways in which workers' claims are framed is necessarily selective and therefore exclusive of some interests. New claims for inclusion are formulated based on such exclusions, with alternative strategies and solidarities created in an effort to have these claims addressed. With each new claim and solidarity, the boundaries defining whose interests are included and excluded are redrawn. In this sense, the construction of interests and the formation of solidarities could be viewed as contingent rather than fixed.

Applying a comparative perspective is a useful means to explore the dimensions of contingent solidarities. In analysing how trade union women have articulated their interests and defined their plans of action across four countries, it becomes apparent a mix of gender-specific and class-based strategies have been adopted. The resultant mix is dependent on differences in political arrangements, historical and cultural contexts as well as on the organisational characteristics of the different national union movements. The ways in which women's inclusion and exclusion is constructed within these contexts necessarily has an impact on the utility of certain strategies.

For example, a similarity between the four countries is the early exclusion of women from participating in the labour force and joining trade unions. Women's eventual inclusion in both these arenas has often been marginal and secondary and, with respect to trade union hierarchies, continues to be so. However, despite this significant similarity, the ways in which these exclusions and inclusions have in turn, shaped and constituted the strategies employed by women in trade unions differ, both between and within countries.

While trade unions have not always acknowledged the ways in which gender intersects with class, women have not abandoned class-based strategies as a means for pursuing equality. Rather, in environments where the labour movement has considerable strength and is able to influence public policy making, there has often been an acceptance by women unionists that class-based outcomes can disproportionately benefit women who tend to be, for example, the majority of the low paid. There have also been explicit attempts by women unionists to gender the class politics approach by appealing to their identity as women, in an effort to make specific gains for women workers in addition to the overall class outcomes.

In this sense then, while corporatist structures are of considerable import to the strategies picked up by women unionists, the impact of such institutional arrangements is tempered and mediated by other forces including cultural or "discursive" traditions, the distribution of power and actors' perceptions of political choice.

There are significant practical implications of a study such as this. Although trade unionism is predicated on a collective identity and seeks to represent a unified working class interest, the findings presented here challenge this assumption. The collective actions of women may in some instances threaten the conventional solidarity of trade unions. Naming the gender-specific conditions that accompany women's participation in the labour market undermines the notion of a common work experience upon which trade unionism is based. Forming solidarities around the identity of "woman" also has the potential to destabilise the male, full-time worker norm that underpins trade unionism in the four countries examined here. Challenging this norm may then encourage trade union movements to view their members as workers with an increasingly diverse range of interests, which are flexible and fluid. Such a re-conceptualisation might serve as a stimulus for trade unions to become more representative of their membership.

Furthermore, in this period of globalisation, trade unions increasingly need to adjust to substantial changes to the environment in which they operate, including declining membership. Accepting, acknowledging and providing a voice for different groups of workers within trade unions therefore becomes increasingly necessary if unions are to continue to be viewed by governments and employers as representative of the working class in the public policy-making arena.

It has been suggested that women's presence in trade unions not only provides them with economic benefits, but also gives women access to important political skills and political elites and provides them with opportunities to influence the policies being demanded of governments (Lovenduski, 1986, p. 165). However, if women are to have the opportunity to influence the content of trade union agendas, trade union membership is a crucial pre-requisite. The remainder of the introduction provides an overview of the dimensions of women's trade union membership and representation across a number of countries, and is then followed by an outline of the book.

Women in Trade Unions: An Overview

In recent years, there has been increasing interest in the divergent development of trade union membership in western countries (Korpi, 1983; OECD, 1991b; Rothstein, 1992; Shalev and Korpi, 1980; Stephens, 1990; Visser, 1992; Wallerstein, 1989), but little of this has incorporated a gender dimension. Three reasons for this dearth of research spring to mind. First, the data are difficult to find and time consuming to collect. Indeed, gender-specific data is unavailable for Israel and so it is not included in this section. Second, women as a focus of study is relatively recent and largely a result of urging by the women's movement to include women in academic investigation. Finally, analyses of trade unions are often underpinned by a "labour versus capital" approach, with a view of the working class as a homogeneous group, while feminist analyses have often defined unions as male-dominated and inherently antagonistic to the interests of women.

When examining the development of women's unionisation over the last three decades several trends are evident (Figure 1.1). Despite the cross-national differences in rates of female unionisation, there has been a general upward trend in female union density over time. Between 1970 and 1980, in all but two of the ten countries for which data is available, (United States and the Netherlands), women showed an increase in unionisation. Over the period 1980–1989, a decline in women's union density is evident in six of the ten countries. Only Sweden and Canada show any continuing growth during this time while in Denmark and Germany there was little significant change. This reflects what has occurred with respect to overall union density during the same period (Neumann et al, 1989, pp. 6–9). Since 1989, female trade union density has declined in most of the countries included in Figure 1.1, with rises only apparent in Denmark and the Netherlands.

When comparing the decline in female union density to the patterns of male unionisation over the 1980–1989 period, Table 1.1 indicates that in all but two countries (Australia and Austria), female union density has declined less than male union density. In measuring the change in female unionisation over the whole period 1960–1989, it is apparent that in seven of the ten countries, women's union density has increased.

Figure 1.1 Female Union Density, 1960-1994

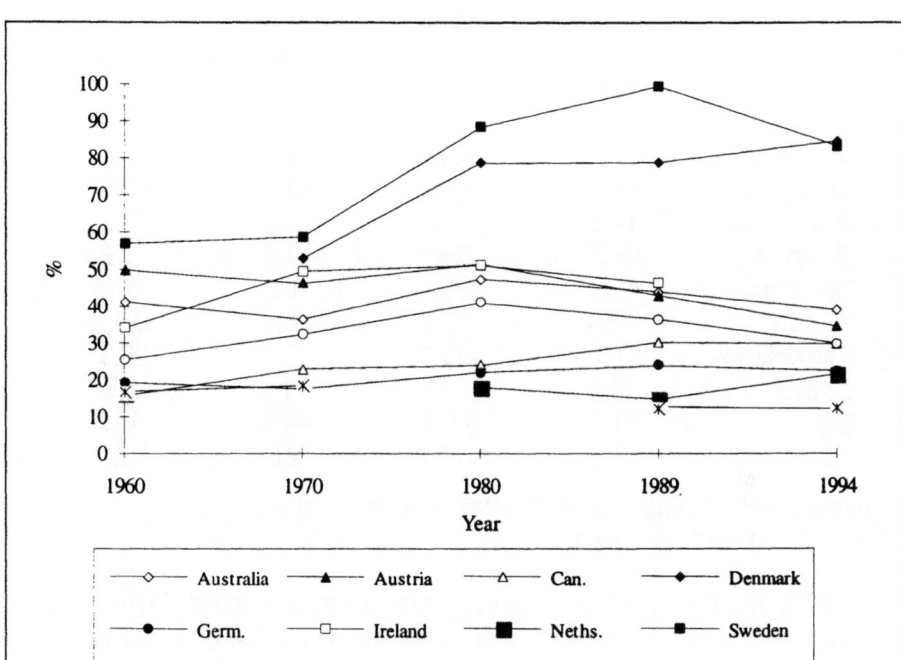

Sources: See Appendix Two.

In three of the four countries examined in depth in this book, several differences in growth trends are evident. In Sweden, female union density increased quite substantially between 1970 and 1980. During this same period, there was a large expansion in public sector employment in Sweden, with women accounting for 87 per cent of the growth in employment in health, education and welfare (Esping-Andersen, 1990, p. 201).

Table 1.1 Changes in Female and Male Trade Union Density

	Female change 1960-1989	Male change 1960-1989	Female change 1980-1989	Male change 1980-1989
Australia	2.7	-3.9	-3.5	-2.7
Austria	-6.9	-6.8	-8.5	-7.5
Canada	14.5	8.4	6.2	-4.5
Denmark	39.5*	0.4*	-2.5	-2.9
Germany	4.6	3.0	1.8	-2.9
Ireland	12.3	-3.4	-4.9	-14.8
Netherlands	-1.5	-11.2	-3.3	-9.2
Sweden	42.5	12.7	11.1	2.2
UK	11.1	-1.3	-4.5	-14.6
US	-4.4	-17.2	na	na

* represents the change from 1970-1989; na = not available.
Sources: See Appendix Two.

This is not surprising in that in every major European country, and in Canada and Australia, public employees are more likely to be unionised than their private sector counterparts (Rose, 1985, p. 40; see also Bakker, 1988; Kunkel et al, 1998; Rawson, 1988). The nature of public sector employment is such that in the past it has offered greater job security and exhibited lower turnover rates, making union membership, recruitment and retention more favourable (Visser, 1990, p. 51).

Women's union density in Australia decreased even more than their male counterparts between 1980 and 1989. While Australian women's labour force participation rates increased by 18 percentage points between 1973 and 1995 (OECD, 1996), much of this growth in women's employment was in the areas of retail, finance, recreation and community services rather than in public sector employment. In these industries, new jobs have largely gone to young part-time women workers, whom the union movement has been slow to recruit (Shute, 1994, p. 168).

In Austria, women's unionisation rates declined even more than in Australia, despite Austria being a country with moderately high union density. (In 1989, total union density in Austria was 55.4 per cent and

Introduction

female union density was 43 per cent). Furthermore, women's divisions have a long history as an integral part of the union movement and women have been represented by full-time staff at both confederation and national level (Cook et al, 1992, pp. 65–68). An interesting difference between Austria and other nations with moderately high union density is that Austria is a country with comparatively low levels of female labour force participation. Women's participation in the labour market in Austria remained almost stagnant for the thirty years up until 1990. Since 1990, the labour force participation of women has increased to 62.4 per cent in 1996, almost comparable with the rate in Australia. The low growth trend over the thirty years prior to 1990 was largely a result of minor increases in service sector employment during the 1970s, while public sector employment increased by only four percentage points during the same period (Scharpf, 1984, p. 267). Thus, the lack of service sector growth via public employment seems to have constrained the growth of female union density in both Australia and Austria.

Table 1.2 Numbers (000s) and Percentage Increase of Female Trade Union Members in Selected Countries, 1950-1993

Year	Sweden Number	% increase	Australia Number	% increase	Austria Number	% increase
1950	347.4		303.5		334.6	
1960	487.0	40.1	378.0	24.5	421.3	25.9
1970	753.5	54.7	564.1	49.2	418.7	-0.6
1980	1430.4	89.8	946.3	67.7	498.8	19.1
1990	1733.1	21.1	1205.2	27.3	512.3	2.7
1994/5	1799.2	3.8	1135.6	-5.7	501.6	-1.1

Sources: See Appendix Two.

Density calculations act as a control for labour force participation, obscuring the growth in the absolute numbers of women in trade unions. The data in Table 1.2 indicate that there has been an almost continuous increase in the number of women joining trade unions since the 1950s, the exception being in Austria between 1960 and 1970. Comparing Table 1.1

and Table 1.2, it appears that, in both Australia and Austria, the number of women union members has increased, but this increase has not kept abreast of the rate of increase in women's labour force participation in either country. As such, women remain a critical source of membership for unions in Austria and Australia.

Women's Representation in Trade Unions

Increases in women's trade union membership over the last thirty years have not led to a corresponding increase in the numbers of women in decision-making positions. In 1993, the European Trade Union Confederation (ETUC, 1994) conducted a survey of its affiliates to establish the current position of women in trade union hierarchies. Among the national confederations which responded, only two had female leaders (by 1994, this had increased to four): the French CFDT, the Belgian FGTB, the Swedish TCO and the Australian Confederation of Trade Unions (ACTU).

At the executive committee level the comparative position of women in national confederations is slightly better. The data in the Table 1.3 indicate there has been an increase or at least the maintenance of existing levels of women's representation in most of the countries listed. These improvements have required pro-active strategies, such as a commitment from trade unions to adopt policies to improve the position of women in the workforce and within unions (Trebilcock, 1991, p. 407).

An increase of women on the executive is evident in about half of the trade union confederations listed in Table 1.3. Several confederations have a system of reserved seats, which appears to ensure at least a minimum level of representation. In the cases of Australia, Italy and the United Kingdom, this strategy has served to increase the representation of women quite substantially. Such developments have focused on rule changes concerning the selection of officers and committee members, which is usually effected by adding seats rather than displacing the existing seat holders. This strategy has the immediate effect of increasing the numbers of women on boards and committees, but carries a risk that the women occupying the reserved seats will be regarded as token figures and excluded from important decision-making and collective bargaining (Trebilcock, 1991, p. 420).

Introduction

Table 1.3 Percentage of Women on Executive Committees in National Trade Union Confederations

Country & Confederation	% women 1981	% women 1993	% women members *	Special Policies
Austria OGB	14	8	31	R
Australia ACTU	0	29	33	R
Belgium FGTB	na	7	40	A
Denmark LO	12	14	49	none
France CGT	27	25	32	R+A
Germany DGB	7.7	13	32	none
Ireland ICTU	0	17	38	R
Italy CGIL	16.7	30	28	Q
UGIL	0	12	41	none
Netherlands FNV	0	19	22	none
Norway LO	6.7	25	42	A
Sweden LO	6.7	13	45	A
TCO	20	20	59	none
Switzerland SGB/US	8.7	16	13	none
UK TUC	13.7	31	36	R
US AFL-CIO	9	na	43	none

* various years in early 1990s
R = reserved seats, Q = quota, A = other measures, na = not available
Sources: ETUC (1983, 1994).

Although such strategies appear promising, the picture is still grim. The data in Table 1.3 reflect approximately 15 years of trade union advocacy of policies to promote women, yet in only six confederations does the number of women on executives come close to matching the proportion of female membership.

Outline of the Book

The remainder of the book is divided into six chapters. Chapter Two provides the analytical framework for the remainder of the research.

Because the focus of the research is on the representation of women workers' interests by trade unions, I begin with traditional and contemporary views on working class representation generally. I identify strategies that are derived from such perspectives and critically examine the assumptions that underpin this approach. This is followed by an examination of the various feminist arguments regarding the representation of women's interests. In juxtaposing these two broad sets of ideas, what I label "class-based" and "gender-specific" strategies become the two organising principles and evaluative mechanisms of the project.

In Chapters Three through to Six, I focus on the four countries in turn, Australia, Austria, Israel and Sweden. The aim of each chapter is provide an in-depth examination of the issues of concern to women workers and the strategies chosen by women unionists to address these concerns in each country. In each chapter, I seek to gain an insight into why certain strategies are considered more useful than others are by asking what is it about the particular claim and context that influences whether class or gender-specific strategies are most appropriate? The intention, then, is not to offer a causal explanation, but rather to identify the trajectory of choices made and the reasons why this might be so.

To this end, each chapter is divided into a number of sections. The first section offers a consideration of contextual factors, including the development of working class representation and the contemporary industrial relations setting. The strategic choices made by women trade unionists are constrained by both institutional arrangements and past choices and priorities. These are then mediated by the perceptions of the women themselves (Castles, 1989, p. 11; Scharpf, 1984, p. 260). As such, the organisational and discursive environment within which women trade unionists constitute their interests and formulate their collective actions requires examination.

The second section of each country chapter examines how the respective trade union movements have historically excluded and/or included women and the means by which women have sought inclusion. It reviews the representation of women in trade union hierarchies and the barriers that exist to restrict further entry by women into union structures. The third section concerns women's wages, with a particular focus on equal pay for women and women's predominance in low wage sectors in the context of the broader collective bargaining environment and trade union wage policy objectives. In the fourth section, women's working conditions are examined. These include the conditions or policies that

Introduction

facilitate women's labour-force participation as well as conditions of work on site. While the claims identified by women trade unionists vary across countries, in all countries, facilitating the mix of paid work and family responsibilities is an important issue for women trade unionists, as is equal employment opportunity and sexual harassment.

The cross-national similarities and differences in the strategies pursued by women trade unionists in their quest for labour market equality are explored in some depth in the concluding chapter. In particular, I identify and analyse what is unique about the utility of gender-specific and/or class-based strategies within a given country and, in doing so, examine the need for a re-conceptualisation of women's collective actions within trade unions.

2 Identifying Women-Inclusive Strategies

Introduction

Working-class action as manifest through trade unions has provoked a range of advocates and critics over the last century. While the strategies for working-class mobilisation as espoused by were revolutionary in character, they sparked continuous revision and debate. The contemporary social democratic approaches, which have resulted from this debate, view a democratic class struggle as more appropriate than revolutionary struggle in pursuing the interests of the working class.

Although these approaches differ in the class-based strategies they advocate, both rely on notions of conventional solidarity; that is, while there is an acceptance of the heterogeneity of workers' interests, the redefinition of these interests is seen as a necessary trade-off to secure outcomes. Furthermore, the interests of workers are viewed as given, concrete and fixed around the structurally defined core of capitalism.

Feminist critiques have highlighted the gender-blindness of the assumptions underpinning class perspectives and the way in which other identities are subsumed by class. These analyses have also identified how class approaches ignore the issue of intersectional and multiple identities and what this means for the ways in which workers interests are articulated and later redefined.

In this chapter I provide a brief analysis of these literatures and, from this, identify the various strategies available to trade unions to improve the position of workers. I provide some reflections on the class-based strategies that have resulted and explore the gender bias inherent in the assumptions underpinning much of the work on trade unionism. This leads to an examination of whether there is space for the representation of women's interests through such strategies.

In the second section of this chapter, I explore two different perspectives on the value of invoking the categories "woman" and "women's interests" as a way of organising for social change. The first position is that women as a group have a distinct set of interests derived from a number of different sources, but ultimately determined by their

Identifying Strategies

gender, providing a common ground from which women can seek representation. By contrast, in more recent feminist texts, this idea of "woman" has been contested and replaced with the notion that the category "woman" and "women's interests" are fluid, relational and constituted through interaction with others. As such, women are best seen as a volatile collective, thereby undermining the idea that there is an objective set of women's interests. Both perspectives have useful elements with which to analyse the gender-specific strategies used by women in trade unions. In the latter part of this chapter I focus on three strategies: the representation by women; the creation of women's spaces; and gendered legislative and labour market strategies.

Marxism, Social Democracy and Trade Union Strategies

Marx argued that the individual pursuit of interests is ineffective. Instead, a strategy of collective action was the only basis for the pursuit of better wages and working conditions and trade unions were viewed as a vehicle for securing such outcomes. Although Marx and Engels were not always consistent on the issue, they did believe that trade unions were potentially revolutionary organisations. The value of trade union action around economic issues was considered limited, primarily because unions were viewed as ultimately powerless against the economic forces of capitalism. Yet both Marx and Engels maintained that trade unionism challenged capitalism on a political front. Collective action was thus seen as both a means to a greater end and an end it itself. Such action allowed workers to move from being a mass of unorganised individuals with competing interests to become a group aware of their common interests able to engage in collective political struggle (Marx, 1955). Trade unions acted as "schools of war" and the strategies of strike action and of political protest were necessary strategies in bringing workers together as a unified class (Engels, 1950, p. 219).

Lenin had more to say than Marx did about trade unionism as a strategy for working class emancipation. He argued that the labour movement could develop trade union consciousness through economic struggle (made apparent through the conviction to combine in unions, fight employers and compel government to pass labour legislation). However, the "economistic" perspective behind such strategies meant that trade union economic objectives could only be sought out within the framework of capitalism (Lenin, 1902, p. 41). As such, the interaction of trade unions with the state was thought to undermine the growth of working class consciousness necessary for revolution.

Strategies of economic militancy and industrial action were, nevertheless, a requisite for obtaining improved wages and working conditions. Furthermore, because strike activity was considered a key element in the consciousness-raising process, classical Marxists were hostile to the institution of collective bargaining with its potential to demobilise workers' struggles (Lenin, 1902; Luxemburg, 1906). Gramsci, in particular, saw the growth of collective bargaining as enveloping trade unions in a myriad of rules and regulations and, as such, binding them to ongoing capitalist development (Gramsci, 1919).

Despite the opposition to reformism by classical Marxists, the onset of male and later female suffrage meant the parliamentary route to socialism became an option increasingly debated. Kautsky, similarly to Lenin, argued there were only limited gains to be made via economic struggle; in particular, insurrection and general strikes were deemed useless when utilised by a minority of the people. However, in contrast to Lenin, he maintained that democracy when coupled with freedom of the press, speech and organisation, was the shortest and least costly route to socialism (Kautsky, 1910, p. 121).

Bernstein, perhaps most famous for his articulation on the evolutionary route to socialism, also argued for democratic strategies rather than class conflict, maintaining that the labour movement should avoid confrontation and seek to bargain and compromise within the capitalist system. Combined, an organised labour movement and social democratic government could build upon piecemeal gains. In so doing, the resulting improvements in workers' social conditions would allow for the maintenance and recruitment of members, thereby strengthening and broadening the labour movement's organisational base (Bernstein, 1909; Gay, 1979, p. 229).

Contemporary social democratic analyses continue to focus on the mobilisation of power resources by the working class and its allies. This approach is clearly identified by Korpi (1983) and Esping-Andersen (1985) who have argued that while capitalism's resources exist within the market, labour's power advantage lies in its numbers (Korpi, 1983). To be effective, trade union strategies should involve developing a strong and centralised unionism for coherence and subordinating exclusive unions so that the bargaining advantages and disadvantages of each worker are socialised to the entire working class (Esping-Andersen, 1985, p. 33).

Universal welfare reforms and full employment, which endow all citizens with a greater capacity for participation within the political sphere, are considered to be critical to working class political strength. According to this school of thought, trade unions should act in conjunction with left-wing parties to ensure the presence of social democratic government through which such reforms are provided.

Drawing from the analysis of Korpi, Higgins (1985) argues that there can be no separation between the economic and political interests of unions; rather, all economic interests are inherently political. Higgins maintains the capitalist political program is one that cannot be fought against with strikes: recessions, economic policies which stimulate unemployment, and the general insulation of the market undermine workers' job security, wages and conditions. As a result, the class struggle is better fought in the political arena (Higgins, 1985, p. 357).

Higgins advocates a strategy of "political unionism" which focuses not only on wages and working conditions, but on challenging capitalist politics. He argues that political unionism rests on a broad definition of class conflict which incorporates "all manifestations of capitalist social power and economic control" and one that necessarily involves working class interaction with the state, employers and left wing parties in a proactive manner (Higgins, 1985, p. 364). This perspective sits in contrast to a narrowly-defined industrial unionism that is interested solely in improving workers' wages and basic conditions, usually through collective bargaining (Martin, 1975; Simms, 1987, p. 126). Political unionism, as espoused by Higgins, does not ignore collective bargaining as a strategy necessary for gains in wages and working conditions. But in virtue of its wider focus, political unionism has the potential to extend the legitimate scope of what are labelled trade union or industrial issues, and therefore what might be added to the collective bargaining and public policy agenda.

The involvement by trade unions in the political arena necessarily requires the formulation and implementation of a unified class interest. This interest is then represented through an institutionalised and centralised union presence in negotiations with the state (Dow, Clegg and Boreham, 1984). The term corporatism is often used to describe these institutional arrangements. While as a concept, corporatism remains contested (cf Boreham and Compston, 1992; Hampson, 1997; Higgins, 1985), a central feature in all definitions is a requirement that trade union elites coordinate and limit the demands of their members in a way that will override sectional interests. In return, trade union confederations are granted a representational monopoly within the policy-making arena and this in turn has a significant effect on final policy outcomes. Recent comparative analyses reveal that the involvement by centralised trade union movements in corporatist policy-making environments, combined with a left-wing government presence, is significant in explaining cross-national differences in economic performance, employment and welfare reform (Boreham and Compston, 1992; Boreham, Hall and Leet, 1993; Compston, 1992; Hicks, 1991; Korpi, 1983; Scharpf, 1984; Schmidt, 1982).

There are obvious differences in the strategies that can be derived from traditional and contemporary theories concerning working class mobilisation and representation. Yet despite these differences, both perspectives are similar in that they accept there is a need for trade union elites to coordinate and limit the demands of their members in a way that will override sectional interests in an effort to achieve conventional working class solidarity.

Rethinking the "Unified Class Interest"

While Marx said little about sex or gender fracturing class identity, what became known as the "woman question" was picked up and debated among early Marxist "feminists". Bebel (1904), Zetkin (1929) and Kollantai (1909) identified the existence of special "problems" faced by women, particularly with respect to the double burden undertaken in productive and domestic labour. Debate focused on how these interests were to be best represented; that is, as part of the class struggle or specifically as women's concerns. Ultimately, women's interests remained secondary to their class position as proletarians. While Engels viewed the participation of women in paid labour as a strategy for their emancipation, his emphasis on class necessarily assumed that once in the labour force, women were viewed simply as workers; assumed to share with working men a common class interest in overthrowing capitalism. Early social democrats argued for raising "the worker from the social position of proletarian to that of a citizen, and thus to make citizenship universal" through the provision of both political and economic rights (Bernstein, 1909, p. 147). But it is not evident that the notion of citizen was any less gender-specific than that of worker (O'Connor, 1993; Orloff, 1993; 1996).

The primacy of class has been challenged by a number of feminist thinkers. Jaggar (1988) argues that because classes are defined by their relationship to the means of production and the economic system determines all else, procreation, sexuality and child rearing practices which are taken to be part of the non-economic realm have attracted little analysis within traditional Marxism. It is argued that women's inequality cannot be explained without reference to the domestic and reproductive sphere and its interaction with the "productive" sphere (Ferguson, 1989; Hartmann, 1981; Jaggar, 1988; Vogel 1983).

It is also held that the category of worker within Marxism is "sex blind" as it obscures the sexual division of labour that operates on two levels: with respect to the interconnections between home and outside work, and within the paid workforce itself (Barrett, 1980, p. 8). In this vein, Pateman maintains that the notion of worker is sexually particular, "constructed on the basis of male attributes, capacities and modes of activity" (Pateman, 1986, p. 7). Although socialists may believe that a class revolution may bring universalism into being, fitting women into this universal undifferentiated framework assumes sexual difference is less than fundamental.

In general, class-based perspectives have ignored the way that society in general, and trade unions in particular, are structured by both class and gender. There has been little or no acknowledgment that "men and women experience class in different ways, and that the unities of class politics are disrupted by conflicts of gender" (Phillips 1987a, p. 12). This has implications with respect to whose interests are being represented as the (unified) working class interest.

The desire for a unified working class struggle was not reflected in practice during the late nineteenth century. Numerous studies have revealed the discriminatory policies of trade unions around the world. For many years, working women had to fight to establish their right to organise and to gain acceptance as workers. In the early days of unions, women were often excluded from the male unions, sometimes explicitly, sometimes through restrictions to apprenticeships and high membership fees (Balser, 1987; Drake, 1920; McBride, 1985; Qvist, 1985; Ryan and Prendergast, 1982; Shute, 1994).

The marginalisation of women and their interests was not necessarily an intentional choice made by the union movement (cf Milkman, 1990; Gardner, 1986). When craft unionism gave way to industry unionism, the latter lacking the structural bias toward exclusionism, this allowed for the organisation of large numbers of women, although they were not recruited as women (Balser, 1987; Gabin, 1990; Milkman, 1990). Cobble has detailed how various features of craft unionism, including sex segregation were actually embraced by women waitresses in the United States to organise collectively within a separate space (Cobble, 1990, p. 541). The unionisation of white-collar sectors also produced increases in the numbers of women unionised, but as an unintended consequence of seeking to increase the overall strength of the labour movement (Milkman, 1990, p. 101). Once it was realised that the issue of women workers would not go away, trade unions began to target women as potential members. However, this recruitment was slow to produce a gendering of class-based strategies.

Gendering Class Strategies

The masculine conception of worker and the notion of a unified class interest have had implications for the relevance of various trade union strategies for women workers. For example, some feminists have argued that industrial militancy around economistic demands for increases in wage differentials provides limited outcomes for women and primarily benefits well-organised groups of skilled and hence mostly male workers. While women unionists have undertaken militant action themselves (Balser, 1987; O'Farrell and Kornbluh, 1996; Soldon, 1985; Street, 1994), in general, occupational segregation has concentrated women in low paid and poorly organised jobs.

The strategy of collective bargaining is pivotal in gaining better wages and working conditions. Centralised wage bargaining in particular is significant in undermining gender-wage differentials (Ruggie, 1984; Whitehouse, 1992). Decentralised collective bargaining can be problematic for women's wages, since dominant groups are able to protect their differentials leaving other workers with less industrial muscle, including women, at the bottom of the wages hierarchy (Coote and Campbell, 1982; Phillips, 1983; Rowthorn, 1992). More generally, collective bargaining has tended to be limited in focus, with women's demands for equal pay or child care being defined as social issues requiring legal action. Legislative strategies have often been placed in contrast with the strategy of collective bargaining, since the former may interfere in what is seen as the domain of trade unions. Yet the distinction is not clear cut, as trade unions have often sought legislation on arbitration, occupational heath and safety standards and industrial democracy to enhance union demands (Acker, 1994; Phillips, 1983). Setting up collective bargaining and legislation as oppositional strategies causes problems with respect to many of the demands made by women, especially since the implementation of legislative measures may often depend on supporting institutions and policies which are derived from a collective framework (Whitehouse, 1992, p. 83).

The system of collaboration between organised interests, described here as corporatism, has primarily involved the representation of the collective interests of labour and capital. Workers are provided with a voice in the political arena, but this is predicated upon the homogenisation of the heterogenous demands of workers. Trade unionism is thus met with the "paradox that interests can only be met to the extent that they are partly redefined" (Offe and Wiesenthal, 1980, p. 79). The redefinition of interests is dependent on several factors including the processes of internal government, the interaction of membership and leadership and the struggles around which workers are mobilised (Gardner, 1986, p. 173). The extent to which women's interests are defined as industrial, are represented within the governing bodies of unions and are heard by leadership, remains variable (Cook et al, 1992; ETUC, 1994; ICFTU, 1991; Trebilcock, 1991). Offe himself argues that the process of conflict resolution between workers interests is often done at the expense of poorly organised, politically vulnerable groups (Offe, 1985, pp. 154, 227–228).

Political unionism has the potential to broaden its agenda well beyond the confines of wages and conditions to include issues such as child care and equal employment opportunity, which are not traditionally thought of as industrial issues. But feminist critics argue that the presence of women in trade union elites is required for these issues to be included on the union bargaining agenda (Curtin, 1997; Haavio-Mannila et al, 1985; Hernes and Voje, 1980; Phillips, 1991). Female representation is also important if, as Schmitter argues, the concept of interest intermediation allows for the possibility that interests may be generated from within the corporatist decision-making environment, independent of member preferences (Schmitter, 1981, p. 295).

Capitalism has never delivered a homogenous working class. Sectionalism has always been a part of trade union development: craft unionism, the emergence of white-collar unionism and public sector unionism has challenged the supposed unity of the larger labour movement. Marx and Engels were critical of the narrow outlook of craft unionism. They also denounced the system of division of labour within the working class arguing that divisions between workers with respect to skills, function, pay, conditions and status would further erode class solidarity (Marx and Engels, 1953; Hyman, 1971, p. 8–9). Similarly, Lenin,

Bernstein and Gramsci identified the potential for sectionalism, acknowledging that workers may identify themselves and their interests in a variety of ways: with a section of their class or with the working class as a whole. In this sense, the "woman question" has been no different.

Kelly (1988) argues that it is important to think about sectionalism (and difference) not in terms of overcoming or suppressing it, but providing it with a voice so that workers will realise their sectional interests are compatible with socialism. Similar arguments could be made with respect to gender and other subjectivities, which are constantly being formulated. If articulation of difference is encouraged, rather than suppressed, trade unions might become more encompassing of women and other groups and would be able to facilitate a process whereby different groups of workers recognise their common interests.

Feminist criticism does not dispel the need for class-based strategies, since the salience of class continues to exist. Rather, feminists engaged with a politics of class and other differences have suggested the need for a flexibility which recognises the historical specificity of any situation and the possibilities to which it gives rise. In this vein, strategies and solidarities are not fixed, but are based on subjective understandings of existing circumstances. This perspective has the potential to destabilise the conventional notion of solidarity upon which trade unionism is based. This approach is discussed more fully in the following section.

Feminism and Trade Union Strategies

Identifying Women's Interests

In her article "When are women's interests interesting", Sapiro argues that women as women should be considered as a group with a set of representable interests. In addressing this issue, Sapiro maintains that the term "women's issues" most often refers to public concerns that impinge primarily on the private (especially domestic) sphere of social life and particularly those values associated with the family and caring for children. She suggests that the division of labour within the home, the differential impact of law and public policy on women, and the socioeconomic differences between women and men, indicate that women do have a distinct and shared set of problems worthy of representation (Sapiro, 1981, pp. 703–704).

Sapiro also notes that having different interests is not the same as saying that women are conscious of these differences or that women define themselves as having special interests requiring representation. In other words, Sapiro is arguing that women have certain objective interests derived from their unequal economic and social position. She states that representation or a response to these interests will only come when women become aware of these interests and overtly define them as political interests warranting attention (Sapiro, 1981, p. 704).

Diamond and Harstock agree that women share common interests across class boundaries, and that these are objective interests which may not be recognised by women themselves (Diamond and Harstock, 1981, p. 717). Drawing on psychoanalytic theory they concentrate on the division of labour in private life as the source of commonality between women which "grows from women's life activity of producing and sustaining human beings" (Diamond and Harstock, 1981, pp. 718–719). From this position, Diamond and Harstock argue that only women can represent women when invisible problems affecting the lives of large numbers of women require political identification.

Jonasdottir has drawn from both Sapiro and Diamond and Harstock in an effort to reassess the usefulness of the concept of interest. She too argues that women are a valid interest category. However, Jonasdottir suggests that the social contrapositions outlined by Sapiro are too narrow and a focus on women versus the state should be replaced by a focus on women versus men, or sex/gender versus sex/gender. Jonasdottir asks us to see women as more than another interest group, but as one part in an historically determined, antagonistic relationship to men (Jonasdottir, 1988, p. 47).

In terms of representation of women, Jonasdottir maintains women have an objective political interest in building up and controlling as sex/gender a concrete presence or attendance in the political system. She argues that although women and men may have interests in common, women should be represented as women, politically visible and empowered to act as women, since their interests will often be different to those of men (Jonasdottir, 1988, p. 53).

There is some acknowledgment of the differences between women by these authors. Race, class and ethnicity are highlighted as factors which "mediate this common female experience" (Diamond and Harstock, 1981, p. 718) and such differences "fragment strategy development amongst women" (Jonasdottir, 1988, p. 55). Fundamentally, however, proponents of this perspective argue that there continues to exist an objective set of interests for women as women.

Rethinking Women's Interests

More recently, some feminist theorising has moved away from assuming that "woman" refers to a set of universal commonalities and interests, a shared oppression and that a unified feminist strategy will attend to all women's needs (Calhoun, 1995, p. 9). The focus has shifted from a politics of gender to a politics of difference. This challenge arose from within feminism, with criticisms made by women of colour and other groups of women, whose identities and interests were ignored, marginalised or subsumed under the universalising category "woman" (Nicholson, 1990; see also Dill, 1983; Hooks, 1984). A feminist politics of unity served to generate and reinforce borders, dichotomies and exclusions rather than representing and encompassing all women.

A second challenge has arisen from a general questioning of the modernist project of universalist assumptions and theories. Feminists in this camp argue that the varying identities of women are constructed and constituted through language and discourse (Pringle and Watson, 1992, p. 64; Scott, 1990, pp. 134–135). Rather than seeing women as a unified and fixed category, they maintain that the "woman" category is relational; woman is only knowable in so far as she is similar to, different from or complementary to man, making "women and their interests virtually unrepresentable except in relation to a masculine norm" (Pringle and Watson, 1992, p. 68). While feminism has played an important role in revealing that there are no generic "men", it follows from this that there can be no generic "woman". In other words, dissolving the essential and universal man necessarily leads to the dissolution of the essential woman (Harding, 1991, p. 17).

While the opposition of male/female constructs particular exclusions and inclusions, it also serves to obscure the differences among women in behaviour, character, desire, subjectivity, sexuality, gender identification, and historical experience (Scott, 1990, p. 143). Butler argues that the minute the category of women is invoked as describing the constituency for which feminism speaks, an internal debate invariably begins over the descriptive content of that term. Thus, every time the specific content of what is "woman" is defined, there is resistance and factionalisation amongst those who are supposed to be unified by such articulation (Butler, 1992, pp. 15–16).

Gatens argues the strategy of invoking an identity of womanness is one that has unwelcome effects because of the manner in which institutionally encoded essentialisms in turn play an active part in the construction of female subjects. Invoking an identity of womanness could lead to the further oppression of women (Gatens, 1996, p. 78). Yeatman has also suggested that identity, which is the referent for the interest concerned, is made to appear as though it precedes politics (Yeatman, 1993, p. 236). Appealing to the category "woman" may mean that women end up participating in the fixing of their interests in a way that becomes a controlling mechanism, a fixed exclusion or inclusion, with detrimental (policy) consequences.

The Sears case is an oft-cited example of the negative consequences of invoking fixed gender differences (Bacchi, 1990; Gatens, 1996; Milkman, 1986; Scott, 1990). In the United States, the Equal Employment Opportunities Commission (EEOC) charged the Sears retailing company with sex discrimination in their hiring practices. The Sears defence argued that fundamental differences between women and men, resulting from culture and socialisation, had led to a lack of interest by women in commission sales work. The defence maintained that sexual difference and not discrimination could explain the hiring patterns of Sears. The EEOC representative argued that Sears' hiring practices reflected inaccurate and inapplicable notions of sexual difference (Scott, 1990, p. 139). The judge accepted the Sears argument that the differences between women and men were real and as a result "discrimination was redefined as simply the recognition of 'natural' difference" (Scott, 1990, p. 141), entrenching within the United States legal system an essentialised perception of women.

As a case in contrast, Sullivan has evaluated feminist strategies which focused on achieving sex equality through the use of de-gendering strategies, with particular reference to the passage of sex discrimination legislation in Australia. Sullivan argues that in seeking to de-gender the public sphere, feminists may unwittingly encourage a de-politicisation of issues particularly relevant to women's public and private lives, since it is women who are required to forfeit their sexual specificity. In this way, the "lived experience of a female body", which can involve abortion, pregnancy, childbirth and child rearing, may no longer be considered relevant to the public sphere (Sullivan, 1990, pp. 174, 184). For example, women demanded the outlawing of discrimination on the grounds of pregnancy, but without mandatory maternity leave provisions in place. This implied women would have "only the same rights as men, regardless of some major differences in needs and concerns" (Sullivan, 1990, p. 186). In this sense, strategies of de-gendering only de-gender the feminine aspects of the public sphere, leaving the explicit masculinity of public sphere intact.

In order to avoid the encoding of the category "woman" as either essentially different or the same as "man", some feminist theorists have preferred to understand women not as a fixed or unified category. They reject the view that women simply know their material and other interests, or have fixed objective interests of which they are unaware. Rather, women's interests are seen to be actively constructed in the process of engagement with other actors. Women form conceptions of their interests in the process of articulation and interaction and therefore these interests are unstable, fluid and momentary (Pringle and Watson, 1992; Yeatman, 1993), as are the solidarities women form around these interests.

These alternative accounts of women's collective actions highlight the multiplicity of differences that may influence the grouping of women. The emphasis is shifted from how women's interests are best represented to the specificity of the process through which women constitute their interests and strategies and the contingent and specific nature of the claims themselves. In this way it becomes possible to take account of how the political strategies put into place by women unionists rest on analyses of the usefulness of certain arguments in certain discursive contexts, without invoking absolute qualities for women or men (cf Scott, 1990).

While viewing women and their interests as constantly in flux, neither pre-given nor universal, there nevertheless remain pragmatic political reasons for thinking about women as groups with interests (not a single group with interests). Riley suggests medical discoveries regarding the prevention of cervical cancer is an example of a valuable outcome resulting from invoking women as a group with special needs (Riley, 1988, p. 98). Scott too has argued that there are times when it makes sense for mothers to demand consideration for their social role or for women in paid work to demand a revaluation of the status of what has been socially constructed as women's work (Scott, 1990, p. 144).

However, it does not follow that motherhood equals womanhood or that women workers epitomise womanhood (Scott, 1990, p. 144). In other words, we should not reduce everything related to women to their womanness, but accept that women can be very differently positioned, thus making the continuity of woman as subject unreliable (Riley, 1988, pp. 2–3). So when women come together as a group, that they are women will not be the only factor which unifies them; there are other locations which give them affinity (Young, 1994, p. 737).

History has already provided us with many examples that indicate the difficulties that come with viewing women's interests as objective and fixed. There have often been opposing groups of women seeking to represent what they claim to be the interests of women: those who have argued for and against sex-based protective legislation, both of which have been claimed as feminist strategies (Cott, 1987). Contrasting arguments regarding the interests and nature of women were made in the fight for women's suffrage (Riley, 1988), while contemporary feminist perspectives have been divided into liberal, socialist and radical, all of which claim to know and represent the interests of women.

To not accept women and their interests as predetermined means debates over what constitutes women's issues, as opposed to other kinds of issues, cannot be resolved by references to clearly understood and agreed upon differences between one's gender and other experiences through which women might be situated. In this sense there can be no theoretical agreement on what "women" are and what women's issues and interests will be (Ang, 1995, p. 58). Feminism instead becomes concerned with embracing the "inherent shakiness" of the term "woman", which exists prior to its political deployment (Riley, 1988, p. 98), and developing a flexibility in understanding these deployments.

It is possible that the notion of contingent or temporal solidarities is a useful tool for interpreting women's collective actions. It provides a means of analysing gender-specific strategies in a way that avoids essentialising the concept woman and their interests. It allows for the examination of women's agency in the process of the (re)formulation of interests and strategies through which women seek to have these interests addressed.

This perspective could provoke a reinterpretation of the numerous alliances made between middle class women and working class women in the late nineteenth century around issues of unionism, working conditions and suffrage in the United States. Many middle class women had taken an interest in the working conditions of women at the time when an increasing number of women were entering paid work, but labouring under intolerable working conditions (Drake, 1920; Dye, 1980). However, the alliance dissolved when suffrage became the primary interest of middle class women. This dissolution could be interpreted as an inability to integrate the goals of feminism with those of unionism. It could also be argued that such a dissolution was not a failure as such, but rather a change in the formulation of interests resulting from the interactions not only between the two groups of women, but also with other actors. In this sense, the solidarity between working and middle class women can be conceived as contingent, constituted by a variety of influences and discursive contexts, which are not stable but in flux.

It does remain possible to talk of women's interests. In fact, this is a crucial strategy open to women in that it names the particularity of existing and assumed universal categories. Invoking women's interests requires awareness that reference is not being made to all women, but to groups of women who have come together in the process of forming their interests. In the remainder of this section, I illustrate how, viewing women's interests from this perspective, changes our interpretation of the variety of gender-specific strategies undertaken by feminists. In doing so, I focus on three gender-specific strategies: the representation of women by women; the construction of separate spaces for women; and, gendered labour market and legislative strategies.

Gendering Representation

One feminist strategy has been to argue that women's interests need to be represented by women. Phillips (1994, 1995), like Sapiro (1981) before her, suggests that specific interests and needs that arise from women's experiences would not be adequately addressed in a politics dominated by men. However, unlike Sapiro, Phillips argues that challenges to ideas about an objective set of interests shared by all women, do not undermine, but strengthen, the case for increasing the number of women representatives. If women's interests are varied, fluid, or still in the process of formation, it is difficult to separate out what is to be represented from who is to do the representation. Representation in this situation is about the formulation of identities and interests as well as how they are represented. As a result, there is a stronger case for more women as representatives to help define areas of concern and construct appropriate policies (Phillips,

1994, p. 15).

With respect to the Australian femocrat strategy (that is of feminists entering the bureaucracy as feminists), Pringle and Watson argue it was recognised that femocrats were not giving voice to pre-given interests. Rather these interests were constructed during the process of interaction and articulation within the policy-making context (Pringle and Watson, 1992, p. 60). While this meant that conflicts occurred over whose interests were being represented, there was little denial that such representation resulted in a range of positive policy outcomes for women (Sawer, 1990).

To date, there is limited evidence to suggest that women are more likely than men to bring women's issues forward when in representative positions in trade unions (Heery and Kelly, 1988). One reason is because a critical number of women are yet to hold decision-making positions within most union movements. Certainly, the election of women will not ensure the representation of all interests. However, as Phillips has argued "different experiences do create different values, priorities, interests" (Phillips, 1991, p. 65) and democratic process should allow for the representation of these different interests via political presence.

Male dominance of trade unions, often both at membership and executive level, has meant that it is men who have tended to define the interests taken up by trade unions. Whether male unionists can represent the interests of women workers without awareness or comprehension of what those interests are is questionable. In this sense, it could be argued that women are needed within leadership positions to provide awareness and to allow for women's interests to surface, thereby altering the discursive contexts through which women's interests are constituted.

It is impossible for women in union hierarchies to represent the interests of all women. As Gatens argues, there are real limits to empathising with, and gaining an understanding of, the specific and total context of the lives of those seeking representation. A practical solution, suggests Gatens, may be one where women are represented at all levels of legal, social and political life (Gatens, 1996, p. 141). Including women from a range of occupations or industries, as representatives within union hierarchies, would at least ensure a broad range of working women's interests received a voice.

Institutionalised Separate Spaces

A second gender-specific strategy is that of separate organising by women. Women-only unions were established in several sectors including the textile and clothing industry and amongst waitresses, laundresses and retail clerks (Balser, 1987; Boston, 1987; Dye, 1980; McBride, 1985; Meyerowitz, 1985; Street, 1994). Towards the end of the nineteenth century reformist umbrella organisations were also created whereby women activists sought to encourage trade unionism amongst women. (Boston, 1987; Dye, 1980; Drake, 1920; Lewenhak, 1977; Soldon, 1985). These organisations resulted from alliances between working class and middle class women who saw themselves as both feminists and unionists. The women in these organisations believed that women of all classes working together could organise women into trade unions and persuade the labour movement to integrate women into its ranks (Dye, 1980, p. 2).

Brown argues that a new feminist politics requires the cultivation of political spaces for posing and arguing about feminist political norms and for developing a discourse on justice. She suggests such political spaces are scarcer and thinner today than in previous times (Brown, 1991, p. 79). Yet, at least within trade unions, there has been an increasing (rhetorical) acceptance and legitimacy given to separate organising by women and an institutionalisation of structures to facilitate this process over the past fifteen years. This has included: women's conferences, committees, departments and officers; reserved seats on executive bodies; proportional representation; education for women workers; and, consciousness raising through networks (Briskin, 1993; ETUC, 1994; Gabin, 1990; ICFTU, 1991; Lawrence, 1994; McBride, 1985; Quataert, 1985; Sapiro, 1981; Soldon, 1985; Trebilcock, 1991).

Brown argues that while these spaces require elements of definition and protection, they cannot be "clean, sharply bounded, disembodied or permanent ..... they would be heterogeneous, roving, non-institutionalised" (Brown, 1991, p. 80). However, it does not necessarily follow that the institutionalisation of separate spaces for women within trade unions constrains women unionists. Brown's position seems to assume that it is the institution rather than the voices spoken within the institution, which is important. Yet, if women's networks and committees within trade unions allow for continuing and varied discussions on what strategies should be pursued to improve the lot of women workers, this will be useful in the process of formulating and representing women's interests.

It is impossible to claim that separate spaces either succeed or fail by virtue of being separate. The ability of women trade unionists to have their demands heard and addressed is dependent on a complex set of contextual circumstances, including the governmental structure of the union hierarchies. Nevertheless, it is women's agency that has provided women with political space within trade unions and women have agency within this space. Cook maintains that where women

> have an organisational home within the unions - formal or informal, existing by union statute or custom, independent or dependent - they eventually seek ways to gain political skills, educate their male colleagues, and claim their representational rights (Cook, 1984, p. 19).

Although separate spaces for women may be institutionalised at various points in time, institutionalisation in itself should not be viewed as negative. Just as women's interests and claims are viewed as dynamic, so are the discursive contexts within which they are formulated. Agendas change, participants change and these spaces may become a window of opportunity for women to alter the discursive frameworks through which women's claims are constituted.

Legislative and Labour Market Strategies

As outlined earlier, recent feminist theorising maintains that invoking the identity of women in the formulation of strategies can result in the rigidification of sexual difference that is then taken to represent the essential nature of women. Gatens is critical of "essentialized conceptions of female and male sexualities that, if encoded in the law, will entrench conservative and destructive ... notions of male and female embodiment" (Gatens, 1996, p. 78).

Early attempts to regulate women's working conditions often resulted in women arguing for protective legislation which, for example, exempted them from night work and from working while pregnant. In the first half of the twentieth century, the International Labor Organisation also advocated conventions protecting women (Henry, 1923). Put in context, legislative regulation was often the only means by which women's working conditions could be improved, since many female occupations were non-unionised and were therefore not covered by the rules of collective agreements. Such regulations were often supported by both liberal and social-democratic feminists (Anderson, 1992; Evans, 1977).

Protective legislation did allow for the signification of women workers as less able than their male counterparts in a variety of working environments. Similarly, the institutionalisation of the family wage principle, often with the support of working class women, has contributed to the representation of women as transitory labour force participants whose labour value is secondary to that of men's. Even with the massive influx of women into labour markets since the 1960s, which for many feminists was to be the answer to women's inequality, their predominance in a limited number of occupations and in part-time work indicates how even economic activity constructs woman as other, unskilled and subordinate.

Over time these "encoded" representations of women have become contested, with women in trade unions demanding the removal of protective legislation and paternalistic clauses in collective agreements. Women workers have made claims for equal pay, either through the wage bargaining system or by enactment of legislation and have sought the reclassification of women's skills. In many of these instances, the category "woman" has been invoked as part of a strategy for change.

Interpreting gender-specific strategies as inherently leading to rigidification implies that the results of such strategies are fixed and in turn, not open to contest. Yet as Butler argues, as soon as the interests of women are named as such, a process of normalisation and exclusion occurs (Butler, 1992, p. 16). This process creates new interactions between those included and excluded. Further interest and identity construction takes place and alternative claiming strategies are built, perhaps around a renegotiated notion of "woman". Such exclusions are not problematic if the ultimate goal is not one of an all-inclusive feminist strategy. Rather, it may be more useful to interpret legislative and labour market strategies as modest feminist strategies which continually redraw boundaries between women, with the outcomes as part of a claiming process and not ends in themselves.

Conclusion

Despite various feminist attempts to rescue Marxism for feminism, critics have argued that the key concepts of Marxist theory are not gender-neutral, but based on a male view of the world that excludes women's needs and experiences. A similar criticism can be made of social democratic ideas. Phillips has argued that a politics of equality based on class tends to direct its energies to the spheres that are occupied by men; women are expected to fit into slots devised for men. While some needs may be met through this approach, other needs that differ to those of the dominant group are ignored or subsumed. Equality in this sense may mean women shaping themselves to a world made for men (Phillips, 1987b, p. 19).

In this context, the class approach is portrayed as an either/or situation for women. That is, women cannot seem to achieve class equality without becoming like men. Yet, we cannot ignore the fact that women have interests both as women and as workers and, as such, trade unions, as class-based organisations, are potentially useful in representing women's interests as workers. Women unionists may choose to embrace class strategies when outcomes are perceived to benefit both men and women or as a tactical decision to gain support from their male counterparts.

It remains important not to assume that women are a homogenous group. By doing so, feminists become as reductionist as those they criticise. Women have needs, interests and concerns that arise from being women workers, concerns that may or may not coincide with the interests of male workers. There are differences between women who work in terms of class, race, age, ethnicity, parental status, and so on. There are also differences between women who do and do not undertake paid work. These work-related differences between women may be greater than gender differences.

Nevertheless, invoking the category "woman" has often been a strategy used by women in trade union politics. Gender-specific strategies have been advocated by both feminist academics and practitioners alike in their campaign to make trade unions address the many concerns of women who undertake paid work. How such strategies eventuate is "always determined by the historical context in which they operate" (Yeatman, 1995, p. 42; see also Cook, et al 1992; Scharpf, 1984). How best to conceptualise the process of identity formation through the collective actions of women has been the subject of much interest and debate amongst feminist theorists.

What is apparent is that tensions exist between class and gendered explanations of the position of women workers, tensions that permeate the analysis of the relationship between women and trade unions. I have not sought to resolve these tensions at a theoretical level. Rather, I have suggested that the salience of class remains, but that other differences also exist, not parallel to class, nor in a hierarchy with class or gender as primary, but rather in a state of flux, ever-changing, intersecting, and very much conditional on a particular historical context. This means accepting that conflicts between sectional interests will always exist and may defy incorporation.

A number of questions arise from this examination. Under what circumstances and around what issues have women trade unionists employed class and gender strategies in furthering the representation of issues for working women? What factors have an impact on the choices made by women trade unionists? How relevant is the history of women's inclusion and representation by trade unions, the institutionalisation of women's interests, the political cultural environment within which trade unionism operates, to the choice of strategy made by women in trade unions? More generally, how useful might it be to reconceptualise strategies and solidarities as flexible and changing, depending on the particular historical and discursive context? These questions will act as a guide in examining the strategic choices made by women trade unionists in Australia, Austria, Israel and Sweden.

3 Australia

Introduction

Class politics in Australia has been "labourist" in its orientation, focusing primarily on the needs of wage earners in terms of both economic and social security. In satisfying these needs, trade unions have relied heavily on the mechanisms of the state, particularly those of compulsory conciliation and arbitration. However, it was not until 1983, with the election of a Labor Government, that a "consensual corporatist" framework was established between the Australian Council of Trade Unions (ACTU) and the Labor Government. Within this framework wage and social wage policies were negotiated in line with the overarching macro-economic agenda (Gerritsen, 1986).

This chapter explores how women in trade unions have sought to have their interests represented in the context of state regulation and more recently, corporatism in Australia. The chapter does not deal with the new industrial relations regime established under the conservative government elected in 1996. What becomes evident here is that while trade union rhetoric has often been explicitly masculine and exclusive of women, women trade unionists have been able to utilise industrial mechanisms to further the interests of women workers, both with and without the support of their male colleagues. Solidarity with male unionists has fluctuated depending on the claim. In addition, women unionists have sought out separate political spaces for themselves within trade unions, within which new claims and strategies have been formulated. It appears that women in trade unions, like their sisters in the women's movement (Sawer, 1990; Sullivan, 1994), have taken a pragmatic approach to the pursuit of change, utilising the mechanisms already in existence, but supplementing this strategy with explicitly feminist discourses and policy platforms.

The Labour Movement in Australia

Working class ideology in Australia involved the adoption and adaptation to Australian conditions of political ideas from overseas as well as incorporating values originating from the specific Australian experience. The ethos of mateship, which focused on egalitarian principles, solidarity and fellowship, was picked up in the 1880s by trade unions of unskilled and semi-skilled miners, shearers and waterside workers (Archer, 1992, pp. 381–382). Collectivist "new liberal" ideas, which had replaced earlier espoused notions of *laissez-faire,* encouraged the state to play a central role in assisting and empowering its citizens (Macintyre, 1989, p. 11). This notion of state involvement was not new. As a settler society, the Australian state was considered crucial to national development, required to provide much of the infrastructure of economic development such as roads and railways and became a large employer of labour. As an employer, the government was expected to set an example with respect to wages and working conditions (Macintyre, 1989, p. 11).

In a comparative perspective the most striking feature of the labour relations environment in Australia is the extent to which government has sought to regulate the system. Compulsory conciliation and arbitration was established at both state and federal (Commonwealth) level, with industrial tribunals having powers to settle disputes and enforce decisions

The *Conciliation and Arbitration Act* (1904) led to substantial trade union development in the early twentieth century Australia. While trade unions had existed in Australia since the 1850s, under the 1904 Act, trade unions were explicitly recognised through registration, and the operation of the system was both formally and effectively dependent on their participation. All registered unions could compel their employers to negotiate before an industrial tribunal and thereby obtain wages and conditions comparable to those which stronger unions had gained through direct negotiations (Martin, 1975, pp. 5–6).

One of the most famous rulings was the Harvester Judgement of 1907, whereby the Arbitration Court ruled that a fair wage must be based on need and not on either profit or the market value of labour. The minimum wage was set as the amount by which a (male) worker could support his wife and three children in frugal comfort (Macintyre, 1985, p. 55). This decision was underpinned by the assumption that tariffs and restricted immigration provided employers with enough protection to pay wages according to need.

This basic wage became the foundation component of all award wages until the 1960s. The second component of award wages was the margin for skill, which recognised differences between occupational classifications. Within this component, the principle of comparative wage justice was incorporated, whereby tradesmen in general would receive similar wages. In 1967, a "total wage" concept replaced the previous wage setting process, undermining the family wage concept and opening the way for equal wages to be paid to men and women (Gardner and Palmer, 1992, pp. 323–329).

The dominant philosophy of the trade union movement has not been one of revolution but of "labourism". The objective was to obtain a combination of strong unionism and the Australian Labor Party in government to facilitate the management of the economy in a way that benefited wage earners. This philosophy underpinned the development of Australia's welfare state with the primary premise being wage security rather than social security. Castles (1985, p. 102) has coined the phrase "wage-earners welfare state" to best describe the way in which the principle of a living wage set the foundation for social policy development in Australia. The latter could be considered residual rather than universal in nature due to the provision of wage guarantees.

The craft origins of trade unions in Australia led to the formation of large numbers of unions. General and industry unions also developed over time, with over 300 unions in existence for most of this century (Archer, 1992, p. 384). This large number of disparate trade unions thwarted the creation of a peak union organisation until 1927, when the ACTU was formed. However, its coverage was far from universal and until the late 1970s represented only blue-collar workers. The white-collar peak organisations, the Australian Council of Salaried and Professional Associations and the Council of Australian Government Employee Organisations amalgamated with the ACTU in 1979 and 1981 respectively.

The creation of one large peak council in the early 1980s meant binding agreements between the ACTU and governments and/or employers and covering all wage and salary earners, were a possibility for the first time (Carney, 1988, p. 67). In February 1983, an Accord was created between the ACTU and the Australian Labor Party (which later that year became the Government). Prompted by continuing stagflation of the 1970s, the Accord process followed the labourist tradition of maintaining the emphasis on wage earner security, but with additional focus on wage restraint. This was backed up with tax reform and increases in the social wage in the form of state sponsored medical insurance, increased family allowances and a government subsidised superannuation scheme. There were a number of revisions of the Accord, with Mark VIII released in May 1995. Despite the arguments as to whether this bipartite agreement benefited workers (cf Hampson, 1997; Manning, 1992; Stilwell, 1986), the Accord continued to provide the framework for policy making at a macro level until the election of a conservative Coalition Government in 1996.

In addition to the Accord, there were three other major developments in Australian labour relations in this period. In 1987, the ACTU published *Australia Reconstructed*, which outlined the Confederation's strategy regarding the reality of increasing unemployment, inflation and external indebtedness. A significant feature of this report was the promotion of the concept of "strategic unionism". This concept involved unions moving "beyond the narrow focus of wages and conditions" and developing through the ACTU centrally coordinated goals and integrated strategies for full employment, labour market programs, industry policy, productivity, industrial democracy, social welfare, and taxation (ACTU/TDC, 1987, p. 169). This was followed by another ACTU report in 1987, *Future Strategies for the Union Movement*, which amongst other things emphasised the need for industry-based unionism. The most immediate outcome of the latter report was the reconstruction of unions through substantial amalgamations, with the number of unions decreasing from 326 in 1986 to 56 in 1995, with a view to an eventual 20 super unions (Singleton, 1995).

The second development was the move toward a more decentralised wage bargaining structure. Between 1987 and 1988, the two tier wages system was introduced whereby all workers received a flat rate increase and further increases of up to four per cent could be negotiated between unions and employers in return for concessions on efficiency and productivity (Gardner and Palmer, 1992, p. 337). The *Industrial Relations Act* (1988) replaced the *Conciliation and Arbitration Act* (1904) and, while it provided a framework for continued conciliation and arbitration, there was an emphasis on increased flexibility in the means for settlement and a lessened emphasis on arbitration. In this way, the scene was set for moves toward enterprise bargaining, backed by further legislative changes in 1993. Both the ACTU and the Labor Government actively pursued enterprise bargaining although for different reasons. The Government hoped enterprise bargaining would enhance economic growth and productivity, while the ACTU saw it as a means of "appeasing the employers' desire to promote greater efficiency and productivity" (Peetz, 1995, p. 20). In the shift to a more decentralised system, the award structure was retained to protect minimum wages and conditions for workers not covered by agreements.

The third major change in Australian unionism has been the decrease in membership. Since the 1920s union membership has fluctuated with downward tendencies in the early 1930s and again, during the late 1950s and 1960s. However, the overall rate tended to remain above 50 per cent. Membership rose again in the 1970s, which has been attributed to compulsory unionism and union growth in the public sector (Peetz, 1990, p. 221; Rawson, 1978, pp. 39–40). However, union membership has declined throughout the corporatist period reviewed here, dropping from 48.3 per cent in 1982 to 41.6 per cent in 1988 and to 31 per cent in 1997 (ABS, 1998; see also Hampson, 1997).

While the interview material in this chapter relates to the period before the arrival of the conservative Coalition Government in 1996, several points are worth noting. Under the *Workplace Relations Act* (1996), Australian Workplace Agreements have been introduced, whereby workers may be expected to sign an individual contract and forfeit award coverage. These new forms of workplace agreements will be monitored to ensure they match the existing award conditions (which themselves have been considerably refined). The Industrial Relations Commission continues to exist but its powers have been curtailed and the legal recognition of trade unions has been weakened in terms of rights of entry and representation. Thus the new environment is substantially more deregulated than the 1983–1996 period covered here.

Women's Representation in the Australian Union Movement

Various feminist writers have argued that the labourist tradition in Australia has embodied an ethos of mateship, which has strongly encouraged male bonding and enhanced the exclusion of women (Lake, 1986; Sawer and Simms, 1993, p. 183). Lake maintains that, in the late nineteenth century, sections of the trade union movement were strongly influenced by the idea that wage labour undermined manhood. Socialism would enable working men to retrieve their male status, but until socialism was achieved, "workers could assert their masculinity through trade unionism" (Lake,

1986, p. 54). Lake suggests that the preoccupation with manhood has permeated union culture and defined the union movement as inherently masculine (Lake, 1986, p. 55).

Late last century, women were seldom encouraged by men to undertake paid work let alone become active participants within trade unions and those women who did work were concentrated in factory and domestic jobs (Ryan and Prendergast, 1982, p. 267). This occupational segregation was aggravated by the activities of male unionists who fought successfully to exclude cheaper female labour from the better-paid male crafts. There is debate as to whether this exclusion by male unionists can be attributed to sexism, with men defending their privileges against women, or class, in that workers were protecting themselves against employers' attempts to erode male wages (cf Frances, 1991). Women who wanted to unionise were forced to do so separately. In 1882, the first women's union, the Victorian Tailoresses Union, was created and, after 1890, more women's unions were established, some of which were restricted to a single occupation, while others spanned several occupational groups (Ryan and Prendergast, 1982, p. 267).

Few of these unions survived into the twentieth century and those that did were gradually subsumed into unions encompassing both male and female workers. Ryan and Prendergast argue that the arbitration system put in place in 1904 stifled the continued development of women's unions. Registered unions gained the sole right to represent employees in their particular industry or occupation and women usually lacked the precise coverage of a distinct occupational or industry group required by the courts. In New South Wales, domestic workers were excluded as an occupation eligible for registration, thus prohibiting union representation in this area of work where women dominated (Ryan and Prendergast, 1982, p. 268).

Despite the demise of women's unions, there continued to be pockets of activity from women within the union movement. Campaigns for equal pay occurred in the 1920s with the Council of Action for Equal Pay established in 1937. Women of the left were also active in the Union of Australian Women (established in 1946). However, it was during the 1970s that more concrete links were established between the women's movement and trade unions. Groups such as the Women's Action Commission, the Women's Trade Union Commission and the various Working Women's Centres came together to produce objectives and guidelines for the trade union movement to address the needs of working women (Booth and Rubenstein, 1990, pp. 124–126). A Working Women's

Charter was drawn up, which was then adopted by the ACTU Congress in 1977. Following the adoption of the Charter, the ACTU Women's Committee was established to ensure the goals of the Charter were implemented by the movement.

Within the Charter, emphasis was given to the need for women workers to "be actively encouraged by trade unions to stand for elected office to ensure that union executives are fully representative of all union members" (cited in Deery and Plowman, 1991, p. 294). Although this goal was set in 1977, in 1989 Bill Kelty, Secretary of the ACTU stated that,

> the Australian trade union movement cannot pretend to be representative of women if we have within the ranks of Congress and union leadership far fewer women than is warranted (Kelty, 1989).

More recently, in the report *Unions 2001,* the issue of women's role and voice again was highlighted as essential for unions, with particular emphasis given to increasing women's involvement at every level of the organisation (Evatt Foundation, 1995, p. 61).

Little systematic data exists concerning the representation of women within the various levels of union structures. Small studies have been undertaken to gauge the extent of women's under-representation. The general indication is that while the number of women in decision-making positions has increased over the last 20 years, women remain disproportionately under-represented (Donaldson, 1991; Martin, 1975; Nightingale, 1991; Pocock, 1994; Ryan and Prendergast, 1982; Wilkinson, 1983; WTUC, 1976).

At national level, in 1976, there were no women on the executives of two of the major union confederations, while the Australian Council of Salaried and Professional Associations had two women out of eighteen. By 1995, 26 per cent of the ACTU executive were women. A substantial part of this increase resulted from the establishment of three affirmative action positions in 1987. At state level, reserved places for women have also been created on the executives of Trades and Labour Councils in four of the eight states and territories.

While still few in number, women are however, becoming increasingly obvious in the upper echelons of the union movement in Australia. In 1983, Jennie George became the first woman on the ACTU national executive and in 1987 became the first woman assistant secretary on the same body. The presence of several female national secretaries and three women occupying the affirmative action positions have also increased the visibility of women on the ACTU executive. In early 1994, the feminisation of the upper echelons of the union movement made the media headlines (Loane, 1994, p. 13; Wilson, 1994, p. 9). The most recent significant achievement in this regard is the election of Jennie George as ACTU President in September 1995.

Table 3.1 Distribution by Gender of Major Office Holders in Local Trade Unions, 1975 and 1995

	Women Branch Presidents		Women Branch Secretaries	
	1975-76	1995	1975-76	1995
Victoria	4% (3/74)	30% (7/27)	4% (1/25)	22% (12/54)
NSW	1% (1/100)	5% (1/21)	3% (3/102)	17% (10/59)
Queensland	0% (0/28)	6% (1/18)	3% (2/40)	15% (6/41)
Tasmania	0% (0/24)	6% (1/17)	3% (2/58)	15% (6/39)

Sources: 1975 figures from Ryan and Prendergast, 1982; 1995 figures from ACTU, 1995a.

Although there exists a consensus on affirmative action strategies, initiation and implementation at lower levels has been the responsibility of individual unions. Pocock notes that it is the full-time elected union officials, particularly union secretaries, who shape union strategies, priorities and methods. Thus, she argues, that the absence or under-representation of women in these positions may be detrimental for the "public face of unionism" (Pocock, 1995a, p. 14). The data in Table 3.1 indicate the changes in women's representation in decision-making positions at branch level over the last twenty years.

While the percentage of women presidents has increased, the actual number of women in these positions has not increased at all in New South

Wales (NSW) and by one in Queensland and Tasmania (a likely result of amalgamations). Larger increases have occurred with respect to branch secretaries, particularly in Victoria and NSW.

The inflation of the percentage representation is a result of the amalgamation process, which has reduced the number of available official positions. Elsewhere amalgamations have been cited as detrimental to levels of female representation (Bergqvist, 1991; Pocock, 1995a), yet it appears that women have been able to maintain a representative presence within some branches during the amalgamation process in Australia.

It has also been suggested that recent amalgamations "offer unique opportunities for unions to start with a clean slate and build up structures that are more responsive to women's needs" (Nightingale, 1991, p. 19). The process has included the creation of new constitutions and several amalgamated unions have sought to address the issue of women's representation by writing specific rulings into the constitution guaranteeing women greater representation. For example, the Australian Services Union has a female Vice-President elected by women members and a National Affirmative Action Officer, while the Australian Education Union's rules provide for 50 per cent female representation at their National Council. The ACTU also has a target of obtaining 50 per cent women's representation at all levels of the union movement by the year 2001. However, more research is required before these examples are accepted as the rule rather than the exception. In South Australia, 80 per cent of unions surveyed were in the process of amalgamation, but only 25 per cent were adopting measures to improve women's representation in the new union (Pocock, 1995a).

In addition to the dearth of women in decision-making positions, women remain under-represented at lower levels of the union hierarchy. In 1975 only 3 per cent of the delegates to the ACTU Congress were women. This increased to 13 per cent in 1983 and 17 per cent in 1987. By the 1997 Congress, 201 of the delegates were women: 29 per cent. Estimates suggest an increase in women's share of full-time union positions from less than 5 per cent in 1971 to about 11–12 per cent in 1985, although women predominated in the appointed rather than elected positions (Pocock, 1995a, p. 8). With respect to industrial officers (who participate in direct negotiation with employers), recent figures for South Australia indicated 41 per cent were women and 28 per cent were women in Victoria (Pocock, 1995a, p. 14). Several unions were seeking to recruit young people, both men and women, as organisers, in an effort to provide both men and women workers with a view of youth and women in the union movement. With the move towards enterprise bargaining, the involvement of more women in negotiation has been seen as increasingly important. One interviewee concluded that without women negotiators it was "unlikely that women's special needs will be addressed, unless there are some very enlightened men present".

Having women in high profile and powerful positions within the union movement was considered by women unionists to be a necessary, but not a sufficient, condition to further the participation and representation of women. While women leaders did not guarantee that women's issues would be dealt with, women's increased visibility could change members' perceptions of unions and undermine the dominant images of the ACTU as a "bastion of male superiority" and controlled by "out of touch men". Women's visibility was also thought to have implications for recruitment in that it would give women workers a feeling of association with the union movement.

Dismantling the Barriers

In recent years, research investigating what prevents women from participating more fully within trade unions indicates that women have negative feelings about participating in the internal governance of unions and lack the confidence to become more involved. Sometimes there was little encouragement from within unions to change this situation (Griffin and Benson, 1989; Pocock, 1994).

Family responsibilities and a lack of child care were considered by women unionists to be impediments to women's participation in trade union activities. In recognition of this, some unions have varied their meeting times and have provided child care and a meal at evening meetings. Several women unionists noted that often women did not see themselves or their occupation as being one with industrial muscle. Such perceptions were thought to deter not only participation but also membership. In addition, women shop stewards and organisers continued to face sexism from male organisers in their own unions, in other unions, as well as from employers. This included regular "baiting" in management meetings, being "bad-mouthed" on site or more covert harassment, such as the withholding of relevant union information.

Union education was emphasised as a means by which women could overcome these obstacles. The Working Women's Charter recommended that where necessary positive discrimination in favour of women attending courses should be exercised to redress the gender imbalances. Within a number of unions, training courses have been designed to target women members, shop stewards and consultative committee representatives. Such courses have dealt with a variety of issues ranging from consciousness raising and developing skills such as assertiveness, minute taking, nominating for elections and negotiating. In addition, the Trade Union Training Authority (recently abolished) provided specialised courses for women on a regular basis.

The Anna Stewart Memorial Project has facilitated participation by women in union activities. This project has allowed women to come out of their jobs, fully paid for two weeks, to work with their union and gain experience with industrial issues. This was financed by individual unions and so participation was ultimately dependent on funding. However, many women unionists viewed the project as a positive mechanism in encouraging women to become more active in union activities.

There was also significant concern within the union movement at the decline in union membership in Australia. Women's unionisation rates have decreased less than men's, but continue to be less than men's. The ACTU executive has prioritised the issue of recruitment, as have a number of unions. While not all unions saw women as a major source for recruitment, some women unionists believed this view would change as male unionists accepted that the traditional areas of union coverage were shrinking. The growth sectors in the economy such as finance, tourism, hospitality are industries where there continues to be a high proportion of non-unionised female employment.

These growth sectors include large numbers of casual and part-time workers - workers which unions have not traditionally targeted. Part-time workers have, more recently, been targeted by some industries, but this has tended to be at large work-sites. Reaching part-time and casual women workers in small work sites remains a key concern.

Gender-Specific Strategies

Women in the Australian union movement have, over the last two decades, been quite explicit in identifying the representation of women in gender-specific terms and have adopted strategies that reflect this. Women's committees and caucuses began to appear in a few unions in the early 1970s, but now exist in many unions at national, state and branch level.

The committees were thought to facilitate the participation of rank and file women in union activities, providing women with an environment which was comfortable and where they could meet other union women. In some male dominated unions, women's committees were the only forms of representation and participation to which women had access. Informal networks have also grown up within and across unions.

At branch level, committees tended to be run by rank and file women (which in itself was seen as a training mechanism), and were used to provide additional training. Women's committees also provided a forum in which otherwise marginalised issues were raised, discussed, and policy recommendations formulated. Many of these committees fed into women's conferences where policies were finalised and forwarded to the ACTU National Executive and Congress. Union policy statements on women workers, and women's position in unions are now common, but the impetus for change in these documents, and their supplementation with affirmative action programs has been the result of the activity of women's committees and women's conferences.

The committee system was cited as an important tool in the implementation of policies and in monitoring how union decisions had a differential impact on women. Most women unionists acknowledged that few men overtly block strategies to increase women's representation. Rather it was inactivity and discouragement on the part of men which was most likely to stall implementation. As a result, women's committees had become crucial in encouraging women to put themselves forward for nomination at elections, providing women already in such positions with support, and continuing to remind union executives of their obligations with respect to women's policy.

More recently, specific women's officers have been appointed within some unions. In addition to a job description of policy formation, recruitment and changing union culture, women's officers act as a focal point for women's committees and collecting and disseminating information. In turn, women's committees give the women's officers contact with women at a grass roots level; a necessary link for the identification of issues requiring attention. In this sense, women's committees have acted as an accountability mechanism for the women's officers.

At Confederation level, the ACTU Women's Committee was established in 1977. Women from a number of different unions are represented on this committee and its function is to ensure that the goals of the Working Women's Charter are taken up and implemented by the union movement. There have been mixed feelings as to whether the Committee has had an impact on ACTU policy. The organisational culture of the ACTU is such that committees are seldom formally integrated into the decision making process. In addition, the Women's Committee is the only ACTU Committee without its own budget, thereby limiting both its resources and the extent to which it was seen as a powerful forum.

Despite these drawbacks, the Committee has provided women with a legitimate connection to the ACTU power brokers and women unionists maintained that it has contributed to changing the consciousness of the ACTU Executive. Similar comments were also made with respect to the affirmative action delegates. While these three women may have no direct impact on the agenda-setting process, their presence in a predominantly masculine environment "pricks their conscience" and can "provide a different flavour to the way meetings are run, moving the image away from the grey cardigan old-style male trade unionist". This in turn has encouraged and facilitated the inclusion of issues, such as women's representation, parental and family leave and equal pay, on the ACTU's policy agenda.

An increasing number of women unionists were focusing on the strategy of affirmative action to recruit more women into industry and into unions. The ACTU target of 50 per cent women on the executive by 2001, and the various targets set by trades and labour councils, have set the tone for individual unions to follow. A number of unions have affirmative action plans in place, such as the Australian Services Union with its target of proportional representation at all levels by 2003 and the National Union of Workers' target of 20 per cent women officials by 1998. Other unions accepted the need for affirmative action but were still debating the form this should take. While affirmative action remains a controversial strategy in several (mostly male-dominated) unions, many women unionists believed that without it change would occur too slowly.

An important incentive for unions to undertake affirmative action is provided by the *Affirmative Action Act* (1986), whereby any union with more than 100 employees must develop an affirmative action program and submit an annual report to the Affirmative Action Agency. From 1997, employers who have met certain criteria need only submit a report every three years (Affirmative Action Agency, 1997). With the amalgamations that have taken place, more unions are bound by this law. While there is an acceptance that no one strategy alone would solve the problem of representation and recruitment, women unionists have looked to "affirmative action strategies to achieve the appropriate balance".

Representing Diversity

Although women-centred strategies were common, acknowledgment was made of the differences that exist between women in the Australian union movement. Women, like their male colleagues, were divided factionally between right and left, and in some cases this was exacerbated by the amalgamation of unions representative of opposing factions. Differences were evident between public and private sector women, with gains made in the public sector not always flowing on into the private sector. As a result, large gaps still exist in wages and conditions between women in these two sectors. A blue/white-collar division was also apparent, particularly with respect to inter-union committees. In some instances blue-collar women felt white-collar perspectives dominated the definition and prioritisation of issues to be pursued, with a focus on issues such as parental leave and equal employment opportunity, that did not "recognise the reality of blue-collar women's experience". However, the increasing presence of women representing blue-collar occupations on the ACTU Women's Committee was considered to be important in encouraging a diverse group of women unionists to share ideas and experiences, thus facilitating an awareness of the differing interests of women workers

More diverse representation, in terms of gender and ethnicity, has been achieved within the Clothing Division of the Textile Clothing and Footwear Union (Victorian Branch), where there has been significant change over the last ten years with respect to full-time union officials. In 1994, almost all officials were shop-floor women from non-English speaking backgrounds. It was noted that having representatives who reflected the nationalities, cultures and languages of the workers allowed for a better capacity to work with membership in ways that involved understanding and acknowledging difference. Within the Vehicle Builders' Division of the Metal Workers' Union in Victoria, migrant workers were well represented as shop stewards, facilitating the dissemination of union information to workers from different cultures.

Since the 1970s, strategies focused on the gender-specific have been numerous and their advent has not been unrelated to the increasing presence of a visible and vocal women's movement. Special women's courses, women's committees, caucuses, conferences and networks have burgeoned. Such political spaces have been considered important as support mechanisms and as forums for policy development and implementation. Ensuring that these spaces have at least semi-formal links with the mainstream trade union decision-making channels has also been important in promoting and facilitating solidarity with men in order to gain support for women's claims.

Women's Wages

In Australia, a man's right to work was given precedence over a woman's and this was reflected through a wages system that paid a man a family living wage, based on his need to provide for a wife and children. Married women's participation in the labour force was for many years viewed by workers, trade unions and governments alike as being as a result of economic circumstance. It was not until 1967, that the marriage bar for female public servants was abolished and 1977, that the Arbitration Commission ruled the dismissal of women on the grounds of marital status equated to sex discrimination. Furthermore, it was only after considerable lobbying from women trade unionists that the ACTU explicitly affirmed the right to work for anyone, man or woman, who chose to do so (Hargreaves, 1982; Ryan and Conlon, 1989).

Over the last twenty years or so, the participation of Australian women in the labour market, both married and single, has continued to increase. Between 1973 and 1995, women's labour force participation rates increased from 47 per cent to 65 per cent. Much of this increase was the result of growth in service sector employment, which went from 57 to 72 per cent of civilian employment. During the same period, part-time employment increased from 11.9 to 24.8 per cent (OECD, 1991a; 1996).

Despite this activity, women's wages have remained lower than have men's. For the decade from 1981, women's average earnings for full-time ordinary hours of work were between 81 and 83 per cent of men's. By 1991, this gap had narrowed further, with women earning 84.5 per cent of their male counterparts. However, the gap was significantly wider when such factors as part-time work, overtime and over-award payments were taken in account. Furthermore, recent research suggests that with the shift to enterprise bargaining, the gender-wage differential has begun to widen (Bryson, 1994, p. 186).

Using the Industrial Relations Commission

In Australia, women's wage inequality was made explicit through several arbitration rulings handed down by the Industrial Relations Commission. The establishment of a family wage in 1907 reinforced the notion that women were only to work if single. In 1912, it was established that where women performed "men's work" equal wages were to be paid so that the earning capacity of men was not threatened. Otherwise women were granted 54 per cent of the male rate of pay, which increased to 75 per cent in 1950.

While there were numerous campaigns around the issue of equal pay, it was between 1969 and 1974 that substantial improvements were made in women's wages, largely as a result of considerably lobbying by women's groups both within and outside of the union movement. The Equal Pay Case of 1969 introduced the concept of equal pay for equal work, but because of the sex segregated nature of the paid workforce it was difficult to argue that women and men were performing equal work. As a result, only 18 per cent of female employees benefited from the decision. In response to this anomaly, a new principle of equal pay for work of equal value was adopted in 1972. Wage increases based on this principle were introduced in three uniform steps over the next three years. A 30 per cent shift in the female-male award wage ratio occurred between 1969 and 1976 (Gregory and Daly, 1990).

Utilising the test case strategy to achieve equal pay has only proved successful when the claim did not challenge the accepted mode of wage fixation. For example, in 1972, the Commission exempted the Male Minimum Wage from its equal pay decision because it contained a "family component" which women were not able to claim (Ryan and Conlon, 1989, p. xv). In 1974, the equalisation of minimum wages was introduced, overriding the previous exemption. In 1986, the ACTU test case on behalf of nurses regarding the introduction of a comparable worth concept was rejected by the Industrial Relations Commission because it sought to introduce a basis for wage fixation that would potentially affect relativities between all workers, not just between women and men.

By contrast, in 1989 the National Wage Case decision included the introduction of the Minimum Rates Adjustment. This process was to ensure that "rates for classifications throughout awards are related appropriately on the basis of relative work value" (Equal Pay Unit, 1992, p. 1). In this way, Minimum Rates Adjustments were an acceptable alternative to comparative worth, fitting within traditional notions of wage fixing. A significant example of using the Minimum Rates Adjustment process to rectify the historical undervaluation of women's work was the Australian Capital Territory and Northern Territory child care workers' case presented between 1987 and 1990. The Industrial Relations Commission eventually ruled that a child care worker level three, with one year's experience, was equivalent to the metal/building industry tradesperson, on the basis of the level of competence and training required (Equal Pay Unit, 1992, p. 4). In addition to a considerable wage increase, the decision allowed for an increased recognition of professionalism in the industry.

In 1992, the Human Rights and Equal Opportunity Commission, reported that the difference in over-award payments reflected practices which constituted direct and indirect discrimination on the basis of sex (HREOC, 1992). While the introduction of supplementary payments and Minimum Rates Adjustments between 1988 and 1991 compensated many women workers who did not receive over-award payments, these were not enough to overcome the discrepancies in the female-male pay ratio (ACTU, 1995b, p. 32).

During 1995, the ACTU gathered material for an equal pay test case which focused on inequities in over-award payments, to which women workers had less access primarily because they have been employed in less strategic areas of employment. Several of these claims were settled out of court between particular unions and employers. The test case strategy has also been applied within industries, with the Clothing Union winning a case in 1987, which allowed outworkers to have same rights to pay and conditions as those working in factories.

Several women unionists argued that relying solely on test case rulings "does not encourage a grass roots understanding" of the struggle around issues of pay and conditions, in that the verbal struggle made through submissions and the witness box did not contribute to the "ever-important consciousness-raising of workers". Nevertheless, women unionists saw the test case approach as effective in addressing systemic discrimination and in establishing new minimum standards on a national basis which flow on into awards.

Award Restructuring

In Australia, wages and working conditions are generally set out in awards made by industrial tribunals, which are legally binding. Awards play a significant role in extending and maintaining industrial benefits for workers and provide the primary safety net for workers. However, in areas such as home care, child care, and outwork awards have, until recently, been non-existent. Several women unionists highlighted that putting awards in place to provide decent wages and conditions was their primary goal. Maintaining these awards was also cited as crucial, particularly in the current political and industrial relations environment.

In 1988, the ACTU won a decision from the Commission to remove discriminatory provisions in awards. This was significant in that many awards had different wages and classifications for women, restrictions on women working overtime, shiftwork, or with dangerous machinery and heavy weights (Donaldson, 1991, p. 111). Section 150A of the *Industrial Relations Act* (1993) strengthened this decision by requiring the Industrial Relations Commission to review awards every three years to ensure they were non-discriminatory. Several women's officers within unions made reviewing all award provisions their priority: a substantial task as some industries had over 200 awards.

In addition, in 1988, a process of award restructuring was set in motion whereby awards have been simplified and classifications broadened. Award restructuring was seen by some as offering possibilities for women, in terms of recognising and reclassifying women's skill, providing access to skill related career paths and redesigning jobs in less sex-stereotyped ways (Henry and Franzway, 1993, p. 135). In seeking to facilitate such possibilities, the ACTU produced a set of guidelines for unions to recognise the issues especially important for women in restructuring awards (ACTU, 1990).

For some industries, such as banking, this has been detrimental to women workers who predominate in jobs which have been downgraded (see also Pocock, 1995b). However, for other women workers, reclassification has actually meant an increase in the number of grades to better reflect their varying degrees of skill and often an increase in wages. A top-level machinist is now recognised as equivalent to a tradesperson, while a grade three clerical worker is ranked alongside a class one fitter or a truck driver. In the past, the definition of skill has been an important factor in justifying lower pay levels for women. Linking "women's jobs" to trades was considered an important step in overcoming the under-valuing of many occupations. Women unionists also sought to harness the concepts of career structure and professionalisation to improve the promotion and wage prospects for women, particularly in teaching and nursing.

Within male-dominated industries, undermining the traditional views of skill remains a problem. Strength and stamina are still considered the important qualities in heavy industry environments. Gender segmentation continues to exist within these industries and, as a result, combating pay inequity is seen as inherently connected to combating gender segregation. This has been partially achieved through workplace reform within the vehicle building industry. A move away from the Taylorist mass production model to a job-rotation system has enabled workers to partake in a wider variety of jobs and provided them with greater control over their work. While the reform was not sought from a gendered perspective, as it was seen to benefit all workers, it was thought to have the potential to have an impact on the gendered division of labour within male-dominated industries. To date, the rotations have led to an increase in women's skill acquisition and some increase in wages.

Countering Decentralisation

During the mid-1980s, the ACTU began to shift the focus of wage fixation away from the Arbitration (Industrial Relations) Commission to collective bargaining. However, it was the move to enterprise bargaining in the 1990s which represented the most significant change in the wages system since the development of awards in 1907, and one which women unionists considered to be the biggest threat to women's wages and conditions. Studies indicate that the more decentralised the wage system, the wider the gender gap between male and female earnings (O'Donnell and Hall, 1988; Ruggie, 1984; Whitehouse, 1992). Since the inception of enterprise bargaining several studies have been undertaken analysing the impact of workplace bargaining on women, the findings of which have been mixed (Stephen, 1995). In 1992, the Department of Industrial Relations found that women and part-time workers were less likely than men and full-time workers to be covered by a workplace wage agreement. In female-dominated workplaces, employees were less likely to obtain wage increases as productivity increased (Evatt Foundation, 1995, p. 90). Similar results were found in a NSW study of 345 enterprise agreements (NSW DIRETFE, 1993). While ACTU figures suggested that women's wages kept pace with average wage rises, this was only where agreements had been concluded (ACTU, 1995b).

Jennie George, President of the ACTU, argued that enterprise bargaining was a form of "managed decentralism" because the award system continued to underpin enterprise bargaining. Indeed, maintenance of awards was considered by several women unionists as a crucial strategy for securing at least basic wages and conditions for those unable to conclude agreements. The *Industrial Relations Act* (1993) also provided several safeguards for women, through compulsory consultation with "special interest groups", new equal pay provisions, the award review process and continued access to conciliation and arbitration.

However, despite the award safety net, several women unionists argued that there existed considerable differences in capacity between unions to partake in enterprise bargaining, since it was a resource-intensive and time-consuming process. In smaller workplaces and sectors which were industrially weak and were not highly unionised, the employers' ability to undercut costs by cutting wages and conditions has been accentuated. Such disparities in bargaining power between unions have the potential to undermine worker solidarity and increase the gap in both wages and conditions between groups of workers.

In several large banks, enterprise bargaining has enabled employees to have some power over regulating their own work hours and work days as well as increased access for women to structured training programs. Large retail employers were also working with unions over enterprise agreements to eliminate inconsistencies across states, restructure awards, incorporate penalty payments into wage rates and extend the spread of hours, all of which are considered by the union to be beneficial to employees. Women unionists in less powerful unions have focused primarily on preserving benefits already achieved.

With the introduction of enterprise bargaining came an explicit commitment to training as part of the requirement to increase productivity. However, while the jobs and skills of organised workers were usually well defined and linked to formal training structures, in other industries where unions were industrially weak, traineeship courses were not given equal weighting and recognition. In addition, research indicates that full-time workers predominate in the acquisition of training, while part-time, casual, non-English speaking and lower-status workers (many of whom are women) were less likely to be represented in structured forms of training (Smith and Ewer, 1995). Despite these difficulties, women unionists saw accredited training as a necessary strategy for increasing women's economic equality but argued that such training should be linked with affirmative action and equal employment policies and monitored accordingly (Henry and Franzway, 1993; Smith and Ewer, 1995).

The new emphasis on productivity has also encouraged concession bargaining, enabling conditions to be traded off for wage increases. In this sense, protecting gains made in the areas of equal employment opportunity (EEO) and occupational health and safety had become a priority for several women unionists. There had been some successes in this area with many employers creating EEO programs and committees. However, for a number of women unionists the priority of maintaining wages and job security for their workers was higher than the provision of EEO initiatives.

Several women argued that trade unions which have primarily focused on the needs of male workers in the past need to rethink this position, especially as male-dominated unions have more industrial strength and set the scene for other unions to follow. Teaching men to see "women's issues" as mainstream industrial issues, relevant to men as workers, and requiring effective representation at the bargaining table, was also seen as crucial. To this end, considerable work was required to educate unionists generally, and male industrial officers specifically, of the differential impact of bargaining outcomes on women and men. Training courses were being provided in a number of unions to change the attitudes of unionists and workers. Guidelines on the importance of seeking provisions for family leave and child care during negotiations have been produced and women's officers continue to monitor the process.

Women within the trade union movement have been most adept at using the state-regulated system, particularly the test case mechanism, to pursue better wages and conditions both within an individual industry and with respect to equal pay across all sectors. The 1972 equal pay decision was particularly important in reducing the gender-wage differential. Women unionists have also used the process of award restructuring to remove discriminatory clauses from awards and to reclassify women's skill levels, thereby providing women workers with access to better wages. The increased emphasis on training that followed the shift to productivity-based bargaining in 1993 led to strategies focused on enhancing access to training for women workers. Finally, the introduction of job rotation within male-dominated industries was supported by women as having the potential to provide women with multi-skilling and ultimately higher wages. All of these mechanisms were initiated as class-based reforms, but have been seen by women trade unionists as having the potential to increase the wages of women and have, accordingly, been harnessed and imbued with gender specificity to provide particular benefits to women workers.

Women's Working Conditions

Labourism in Australia has an orientation toward wage earner security and welfare provision based on need. To this end, universal welfare provision has not been seen as an important priority, with policies instead designed to alleviate poverty and promote income redistribution (Castles and Mitchell, 1993, p. 94). Welfare provision has also reflected a traditional belief in a male breadwinner model in which women were secondary participants in the labour market and up until the mid-1980s, a woman was eligible for support from the state by virtue of her dependent status as wife, widow or mother.

While maternity leave had been legislated in 1973, this was limited to providing federal public servants with paid leave. In 1979, working women won twelve months unpaid maternity leave in a test case before the Federal Arbitration Commission. This ruling applied to all women working under federal awards, although the provisions had to be inserted into each federal award on application by individual unions. Women received protection against sacking or demotion as a result of being pregnant and, for some women in the private sector, this was seen as an important achievement, despite it being unpaid.

During the mid-1980s, there occurred a change in the rhetoric and direction of welfare policy, with pensions being redefined as parental or individual allowances, rather than in terms of being a wife or mother. Bryson argues this represented a reconstruction of women as workers as well as mothers, moving beyond the "legitimate dependent" status (Bryson, 1994, p. 191). This redefinition was reflected in the strategies employed by women trade unionists, with the ACTU commencing a test case on Parental Leave in 1989, claiming one year of unpaid parental leave for fathers. Three weeks of this was to be available to fathers at the birth and the remainder available up to the child's second birthday. The case was successful and the Commission provided 52 weeks leave for a parent (ACTU, 1991).

More recently, the test case strategy has been used in conjunction with ILO Convention 156, which the Government ratified in 1990 after substantial lobbying from the ACTU and women's organisations. This Convention calls for governments to implement policies that cater for the needs of workers with family responsibilities. The ACTU ran a test case during 1994 seeking the provision of five days special family leave. The Commission ruled that there was to be an aggregation, extension, and more

Australia

flexible arrangement of existing leave entitlements. More specifically, access to sick and special leave was to be available to provide care for sick family members. Other facilitative provisions were introduced: one week of annual leave could be taken in single days; employees were allowed to make up time for time off; and could take unpaid leave to care for sick family members (Australian Industrial Relations Commission, 1994, pp. 38–41). However, these latter provisions were to be negotiated at enterprise level, highlighting the importance of having a gender perspective represented at the negotiation table.

There have been mixed reactions as to whether this test case was a success. The ACTU saw it as a such, while others viewed it as a disappointment since no extra leave was provided. In addition, several public sector unions had awards with more favourable conditions, which women unionists would have to fight to maintain. Nevertheless, in general, test cases were considered an effective means by which issues could be raised and an excellent means of providing conditions that had not previously been achievable.

Women had also made some gains through the involvement of the union movement in the Accord process. While the ACTU advocated that paid maternity leave for all women workers be recognised as a basic necessity for achieving equality for women in the workforce, this was considered too difficult to win industrially in the private sector. Instead, the Accord context enabled the ACTU and the Government to negotiate a maternity allowance for women, regardless of whether they were in the workforce. In 1995, a means tested maximum allowance of $816 was introduced which provided women in the private sector with a minimum form of paid maternity leave. This was not a comparatively generous provision and maintained the labourist view of state support according to need. However, the initiative was lobbied for and strongly supported by many of the unions covering private sector workers and was considered to be a significant gain for women. Several women unionists also felt that the social wage outcomes of the Accord, such as a state-funded medical insurance scheme, an eight per cent real increase in pensions and an increase in family allowances for low income families had been of benefit to women workers.

Through the Accord relationship, improvements were also secured with the expansion of the number of federally-funded child care places from 50,000 in 1983 to 190,600 in 1993 (Brennan, 1998). The child care cash rebate introduced in 1994 aided all working parents who needed to pay for care in order to undertake paid work. Other forms of government support for child care included fee relief for low-income families and subsidies for the operating and capital costs of some child care centres.

Yet, despite the increase in places and rebates, most women unionists suggested that access to affordable child care remained a problem for many of their women workers. Some of the larger unions with progressive bargaining agendas were able to include child care provisions in their enterprise agreements. Within the vehicle building industry, where enterprise bargaining has been in place for some time, paid maternity leave was agreed to in principle, while family leave arrangements and some child care provisions had been accepted by several large companies. However, for most women unionists the key strategy in the area of child care had been to continue to lobby the Labor Government for funding of places, as well as industry initiatives to encourage more employer-provided child care. The Accord process was useful for such lobbying but with the arrival of the new conservative government many of these gains have been eroded.

The New Flexible Workforce?

Traditionally, trade unions in Australia have fought to protect full-time jobs, viewing the use of casual or part-time workers as a threat to the best interests of both employees and unions. Over the last twenty years, the number of part-time jobs has increased substantially and women have predominated in what part-time work has been available, at present making up 81 per cent of the part-time workforce. It is only recently that unions have begun to see this work as legitimate and unionisation rates of part-time workers remain low.

Three quarters of all part-time workers are concentrated in three industries, community services, wholesale and retail, and recreational and personal services (Donaldson, 1991, p. 91). These are all industries in which women predominate. Some trade unions covering these industries have had safeguards for part-time workers built into award provisions, as well as entitling these workers to *pro rata* award conditions and wages. Award restructuring and enterprise bargaining has facilitated an increased emphasis on permanent part-time work, as opposed to casual work. While such a move may provide gains for these workers, early research suggests that, during the negotiation process, care must be taken that this work is not just casual work renamed (Whitehouse, Boreham and Lafferty, 1995).

Despite the ACTU-driven emphasis on permanent part-time work, the more casualised sectors of the workforce continue to grow. Low paid, low status, part-time work continues to exist in hospitality, cleaning and other service-based occupations; organisation of which is difficult because of worker mobility and shift work. Casualisation within banking, retail and the tertiary sector of education has increased and there has also been a substantial increase in outwork in the clothing, clerical and home-based care occupations. The nature of outwork is such that these workers have been difficult to organise, receive very poor wages and often face intimidation from employers. Where awards cover these workers, these have been difficult to enforce.

In 1994, an information campaign was run by the Textile, Clothing and Footwear Union, resulting in a report entitled *The Hidden Cost of Fashion*. The campaign identified an estimated 330,000 outworkers in the clothing industry in Australia. The campaign sought to provide outworkers with a greater awareness of their rights and the problems associated with outwork were given substantial publicity (TCFUA, 1995, pp. 22–28). The union has also continued to build networks between the union and ethnic community groups, as well as negotiating with industry groups to implement and enforce codes of conduct for those employers hiring outworkers.

More generally, women unionists have investigated ways of effectively identifying and communicating with part-time, casual and outworkers, with a view to increasing their levels of unionisation and facilitating the process by which unions can enforce the rights of these workers. While enterprise bargaining may have undermined the ability of weaker unions to "piggy back" on the gains made by stronger unions, recent research does show that unionisation is important in protecting and, in some cases, enhancing the conditions of work (Boreham, Hall, Harley and Whitehouse, 1996, p. 62). In this sense, the recruitment of those in part-time and casual work is crucial for both unions and workers.

Sexual Harassment

ACTU policy has been that all employees should work in an environment free from sexual harassment. However, sexual harassment was still considered by women unionists to be a problem for many women workers. Most commented that there was a continuous need to remind both unions and employers of the existence of sexual harassment and to provide both groups with strategies for dealing with it. Several unions had adopted comprehensive policy positions on sexual harassment, much of the initiative for which had come from women's committees within the unions.

Education was a key strategy in implementing policies on sexual harassment. Union organisers, officials and shop stewards were targeted through training programs. Information on sexual harassment and methods for dealing with complaints were integrated into mainstream training courses and complemented with specialist courses. In addition, multilingual booklets were published to inform members of their rights and the avenues through which complaints could be pursued.

Trade unions have provided employers with procedural guidelines for dealing with sexual harassment. Women unionists were also pushing for explicit policies and procedures to be adopted and implemented through the enterprise bargaining process. Some employers had begun to take their role in this process seriously and understood their obligations for involvement. This change was thought to have resulted from a combination of continuing pressure by unions for policy changes, as well as recent highly publicised cases against employers. Teaching union officials to view sexual harassment as an industrial issue was considered necessary in the new enterprise bargaining environment, particularly if specific measures were to become an integral part of an agreement.

Legislation exists to guard against unfair dismissal and discrimination on the grounds of sex. However, utilising the legislative mechanism requires the worker to make an official complaint that is then taken to court. Some women unionists felt this form of action compounded the problem and instead placed the emphasis on providing unionists with the skills to provide mediation at the workplace.

Women's officers and women's committees have become a crucial means of monitoring the issue and ensuring the implementation of preventative strategies. Posters and campaigns have aimed at encouraging male workers to police the behaviour of colleagues, thus setting in place an internal peer-group monitoring process. Publicity through union publications has also been used to let women know about cases won by their fellow members, thus encouraging them to feel more confident about reporting harassment. Women unionists emphasised that to be seen to be dealing with sexual harassment effectively was necessary not only in upholding the rights of workers, but also for unions to be seen as relevant to women workers.

Many of what in the past have been labelled "women's issues" have gained credence as industrial issues in Australia. Equal employment opportunity, family leave and policies for combating sexual harassment are now working conditions for which trade unions are expected to bargain. In addition, the wage/social wage trade off that came with the Accord provided women trade unionists with the opportunity to broaden what was seen to be part of the social wage, in this sense making policies which facilitate women's labour market participation part of the mainstream union agenda.

However, trade unions have been slow in adapting themselves to the changing demographics of the labour market. Women still make up a large number of potential union members, many of whom are in part-time work. Indeed part-time work has increased considerably over the last two decades and, over the last ten years or so, the number of outworkers has also expanded. While women trade unionists were pursuing a variety of strategies, to at least stay in touch with these workers, this is an area that will continue to be a challenge for Australian trade unions.

Conclusion

The Australian labourist tradition is one in which class has been inherently linked to ideas of masculinity and mateship. Within the union movement, women were initially excluded and, even when included, unions remained "a product of a distinctive culture of male solidarity" (Aitkin cited in Shute, 1994, p. 167). Today, despite the increasing number of women in the paid labour force and overt feminist activity, several women unionists argued that women continue to see trade unions as masculine institutions.

The links between maleness and class have permeated both wage and social policy. Bryson argues the development of the welfare state in Australia can be seen as an expression of male class politics (Bryson, 1992, p. 161). Through the arbitration system, male workers were provided with a family wage based on the needs of a married man with a family. In this way, the position of women was officially rendered different to that of men and women's exclusion from the paid labour force was officially reinforced (Bryson, 1995, p. 49). Even with welfare provision, the assumption of women as dependent on a husband remained in place (Bryson, 1995, p. 69).

There has been an explicitly masculine aspect to the class discourse in Australia, which has been reflected in wage and social policy outcomes. In response, women's struggle against exclusion within the trade union movement has been undertaken in a gender-specific manner, embracing the notion of a "woman's interest". The insistence on gender-specificity has had an impact on both the identification of issues and the means by which women unionists have sought to have these issues addressed. Strategies of separate organising were first expressed early this century with the formation of women's trade unions and are now apparent with the increasing number of women's committees, conferences, networks and officers. This mode of organising has been crucial in providing women with their own form of solidarity within the union movement. More recently, there has been an emphasis on the importance of increasing the presence of women at all levels in trade unions, most evident through the creation of affirmative action delegates.

The separate presence of women has also led to the politicisation of concerns of explicit interest to women, which have then reached the union movement's bargaining agenda. The issues of sexual harassment, parental leave and equal pay have begun to gain currency in the mainstream industrial arena. In this sense, women's representation as women has been critical in undermining the male-dominated agenda-setting process of the broader union movement and strategies to further improve this representation are increasingly including affirmative action. To some extent, this strategy reflects previous feminist strategies for the representation of women's interests within the bureaucracy (Curtin and Sawer, 1996; Sawer, 1990; Sullivan, 1994).

Although women have organised separately, they have nevertheless looked to the arbitration system to have their needs met as workers. While the national test case of 1907 set highly restrictive boundaries for women at the time, subsequently women have been able to use this strategy to redraw these boundaries. Achievements in the areas of equal pay, maternity and parental leave and other conditions have been made in this way. Furthermore, the *Sex Discrimination Act* (1984) has set standards to which awards must adhere, while affirmative action legislation adopted in 1986 has required trade unions to report on the representation of women within their own ranks. In this way, legislation has supplemented the industrial relations system in encouraging both unions and employers to implement gender-equity reforms.

It is not surprising that, with the recent unprecedented changes to the environment within which Australian trade unions operate, maintenance of the award system and national wage cases have remained a substantial issue for women workers. Enterprise bargaining, although still underpinned by awards, threatens many of the previous gains made through a centralised

Australia

negotiation system. To some extent women unionists were still reacting to these changes, seeking protection through special provisions in the amalgamation process and upgrading award conditions. This is not an unusual strategy: women often make gains during times of economic expansion and attempt to preserve them in times of recession (Pocock, 1995a, p. 2). However, the move toward enterprise bargaining and the further deregulation of the industrial relations system under the Coalition Government continues to favour those with the most bargaining power, that is, full-time workers in industrially strategic positions, a minority of whom are women.

4 Austria

Introduction

Austria is often cited as a corporatist success story. During the 1970s, when many countries were suffering the side effects of economic crisis, in Austria inflation was contained, unemployment remained low and economic growth continued. At a political level, the corporatist policy making arrangements have been accepted as legitimate and have remained largely unchallenged (Katzenstein, 1984). The labour movement has played a significant role in the creation and resulting outcomes of this corporatist framework. Analysing how this framework has had an impact on the representation of women's interests as workers is the purpose of this chapter. In particular, I examine how the historical precursors to corporatism, and the corporatist context itself, has contributed to the formulation and articulation of women's interests by women trade unionists and the strategies that have been harnessed to further these interests. In doing so, I identify a tendency toward gender-specific solidarities, albeit in a way that has not disrupted the consensus-oriented politics of Austria. Yet, what appears to be a rather moderate approach taken by women trade unionists has begun to create tensions over the entrenched norms of women's labour force participation in Austria.

The Labour Movement in Austria

During the nineteenth century, the conservative Hapsburg regime applied repressive measures in an effort to contain working class organisation. The association of workers was forbidden until 1868 and, even after 1870, the workers' movement was still subjected to harassment by state authorities (ILO, 1986, p. 24). Despite this, the number of trade unions multiplied in the second half of the nineteenth century, but were disparately organised and espoused either Christian or Social Democrat ideas (Ströer and Sweeney, 1988, p. 129).

The development of social policy in Austria in the 1880s enhanced this conservative/socialist split within the labour movement. The aim was to preserve stability and social order, while mitigating the excesses that capitalist advancement imposed upon farmers and workers (Esping-Andersen and Korpi, 1984, p. 179). Social provision was also explicitly designed to undermine the organisation of the emerging industrial working class and was imposed in a way that institutionalised divisions between groups of workers. Manual workers were separated from salaried employees, with the latter receiving substantially greater privileges.

Nevertheless, the socialist platform in Austria, labelled Austro-Marxism, viewed state involvement in the development of social policy as an important means of persuading the working class of the reformist possibilities under capitalism (Esping-Andersen et al, 1984, p. 191). Ideologically, Austrian socialists rejected both Bernstein's revisionism and Bolshevik revolutionism, viewing themselves as standing between the two; rhetorical revolutionaries committed to class struggle, but also dedicated to maintaining political unity and achieving pragmatic reforms (Lafleur, 1978, p. 217). It has been argued that this dualism continued to persist in that radical party statements were often at odds with the moderate approach actually adopted by the Social Democrats (Sully, 1982). This reformist ideology had a profound influence on Austrian trade unionism, distinguished by its rejection of violent action and with an emphasis on moderation and compromise between labour and the state and, later, capital (ILO, 1986, p. 26).

The reformist orientation of the union movement was disrupted several times between 1920 and 1945: by a conservative authoritarian regime in 1933; civil war in 1934; and the *Anschluss* in 1938, when independent trade unionism ceased to exist. However, after 1945, consensus and co-operation became key features of Austrian politics. The willingness of the socialists to co-operate with former political and economic rivals was influenced by the tragedies of the inter-war period and by a desire for independence from allied occupation (Sully, 1988, p. 57). What resulted was a "grand coalition" between the two major parties between 1945 and 1966 and a social partnership which has involved institutionalised co-operation between labour, business, agriculture and government around all key aspects of economic and social policy (Guger, 1992, p. 346).

However, despite the institutionalisation of labour representation in the social partnership, the equally strong presence of the right in the electoral arena of politics has undermined the potential for a hegemonic social democratic presence in Austria. Indeed, it was not until the formation of a one-party Social Democrat government in 1971 that reform of the status-oriented social insurance system occurred, with 1979 being the year when conditions in key areas of social protection were equalised between workers and salaried employees (Esping-Andersen et al, 1984, p. 193).

The Austrian Federation of Trade Unions (ÖGB) founded in 1945, united former members of Christian, Socialist and Communist Unions. Representation of the different parties is provided internally with the parties drawing up lists for elections to the executive of the ÖGB. There are now 14 national trade unions, which are subdivisions of the ÖGB, with the ÖGB alone being endowed with legal authority. The structure of the ÖGB is highly cohesive and centralised, accentuated by the presence of presidents with "strong personalities" who have remained in office for long periods of time (ILO, 1986, p. 28). This centralisation is supplemented by organisational unity with the ÖGB covering all sectors of the economy: public, private, and primary, secondary and tertiary sectors.

At the local level, the work council is the source of employee representation; there are no shop stewards. If a workplace has five or more employees, a work council must be established if the workers so desire. Councils are elected by proportional representation for a period of four years. In multi-plant enterprises, each work council is entitled to elect a number of its councillors to a central enterprise work council (Cook et al, 1992; Traxler, 1992, p. 274). While work councils are independent of trade unions, there is, in practice, substantial overlap. More than 90 per cent of work councillors are estimated to be union members and the use of work council elections by trade unions to determine representation provides for a highly integrated system. Work councils have become "the backbone of the unions, providing them with organisational essentials such as collecting dues, explaining union policy, and ..... in recruiting members" (Traxler, 1992, pp. 281–282).

In addition to trade union representation, workers have their interests protected by the Chamber of Labour, membership of which is compulsory (unlike trade unions). Established by law in 1920 in response to long standing demands by trade unions for bodies similar to those already in existence for employers, there is a Chamber of Labour in each of the nine Austrian provinces and a single uniting body at federal level. At the political level, all proposals for legislation at local, provincial and federal level must be submitted to the Chamber of Labour (as well as to the Chambers' of Business and Agriculture) for expert appraisal before being considered by the appropriate legislature.

Although the membership and leadership of the Chamber of Labour and the ÖGB often overlap and the two organisations cooperate on many issues, they do have different functions. The ÖGB is responsible for collective bargaining, while the Chamber provides training, cultural activities, legal advice for workers and statistical and technical information to trade unions (ILO, 1986, pp. 28–33; Traxler, 1992, p. 270). The existence of two networks of labour organisations, representing the interests of workers to the government and employers, is unique to Austria.

Austria has been labelled the most corporatist of states, since the members of the social partnership, the Chambers' of Business, Labour and Agriculture and the ÖGB, play a significant role in regulating the labour market, planning the social security system and coordinating trade policy (Milner, 1994, p. 120). There are considerable links and influence between the ÖGB and the Social Democratic Party with many senior union leaders being members or ministers in parliament and business has equally strong links with the People's Party on the right (Gerlich, 1992, p. 133). The integration of the four major players with their associated political parties both strengthens their authority over members and guarantees them representation in parliament and government (Gerlich, 1992, p. 138; Traxler, 1992, p. 277; see also Sweeney, 1988; Tálos and Kittel, 1996).

Although the government has no formal place in the social partnership, cabinet ministers and state secretaries often take part in meetings with the economic interest groups (Compston, 1994; Gerlich, 1992). Governments have tended to formulate economic and social policy within parameters set by the social partners, and often obtain the partners' consent prior to implementation (Compston, 1994, p. 127). Exclusion of populist movements from the policy-making process has been intentional in an effort to maintain social cohesion in the immediate post-war period and, since this time, the social partnership has proved considerably durable in this regard.

A key feature of the partnership is its informality. A small number of officials, who know each other well, attend meetings where compromises are negotiated. It is argued that such informality is necessary for the successful operation of the consensus mechanism by creating "a climate of great mutual respect and understanding" (Gerlich, 1992, p. 137; see also Traxler, 1992). It is taken as given that the issues and options discussed are only those on which compromise and agreement are possible. Unacceptable alternatives are seldom raised in this forum (Gerlich, 1992, p. 137; ILO,

1986, p. 63).

Thus, class politics in Austria in the post-war period has been more about class consensus than class struggle, with strikes and lockouts seldom pursued. The social partnership and its intimate links with the parliamentary arena have provided labour with an opportunity to participate in the economic and social policy-making process continuously since 1945. Yet class politics has been conservative, with status-oriented social policy and broad economic inequalities sanctioned by the left in partnership with the right.

Women's Representation in the Austrian Union Movement

The Hapsburg Empire was Catholic, conservative and authoritarian but it took a somewhat inconsistent position regarding the rights of women. Women were granted considerable legal powers over their own property and, in 1848, the property franchise explicitly included women, although it pertained to only a small number, since most women lost their property rights on marriage (Bader-Zaar, 1996, p. 61; Evans, 1977, p. 93). In contrast, a law of 1867 banned women in Austria from joining or forming political associations.

Prior to 1914, all attempts by women to have this law repealed were unsuccessful and this influenced the demands women's associations could make, since too radical a program would result in the dissolution of their organisations (Evans, 1977, p. 94). As a result, women's organisations tended to focus on a wide range of reforms including vocational training, pension rights and health insurance which were acceptable to the authorities (Anderson, 1992, p. 37; Evans, 1977, p. 95).

The employment conditions of women did become a focus for women's organisation with the creation of the Vienna Women's Employment Association which, amongst other things, campaigned for the admission of women to jobs in the postal and telegraph service (Evans, 1977, p. 93). Toward the end of the nineteenth century, the representation of the interests of women workers took a variety of forms. Middle class women in paid work created self-help organisations to combat discrimination in the workplace. Women excluded or ejected from membership in existing unions established their own, with the Association of Women Teachers and Governesses set up in 1870 and the Association of Women Postal Officials created in 1876. In 1901, the Union of Working

Women was founded to represent women officials in banks, railways, insurance and legal offices, as well as secretaries, typists, commercial employees, shop workers, seamstresses and tobacco sellers (Anderson, 1992, pp. 35–37).

Another middle class women's initiative was the General Austrian Women's Association founded in 1893, which was not confined to any one concern but encompassed many issues, including women's suffrage and the employment conditions of working class women (Anderson, 1992, p. 39). In particular, the Association was committed to the reform of regulations concerning domestic service (Anderson, 1992, p. 76).

For working class women, the 1867 law made it difficult to organise separately from the Social Democrats. Social Democrat leader Victor Adler was openly opposed to a separate women's movement and advised women not to risk violating the Law of Association by engaging in political action independent of the Social Democrats (Evans, 1977, p. 166).

Working class women had extended their labour force participation into industry in the 1890s and this was further stimulated by the advent of World War One. Male workers considered this participation to be unfair competition and responsible for the lowering of wages. To avoid confrontation, socialist women looked to join their male colleagues in trade unions and working women were entitled to membership in the Chamber of Labour established in 1920 (Lafleur, 1978, pp. 237–238).

Within the Social Democrat Party, the rhetoric emphasised class over sex as the driving force for social change, with women's emancipation to follow socialist revolution. Most socialist women subordinated their demands and their interests to party policy and party unity, exemplified by Social Democrat women in Austria abandoning the call for women's suffrage in 1906 to concentrate on the fight for universal manhood suffrage (Bader-Zaar, 1996; Lafleur, 1978). Prior to this, women had been unable to get party backing for a women's organisation or the creation of women's clubs. After manhood suffrage was granted, women threatened to break away and so the Social Democrats and trade unions, fearful of losing the women altogether, allowed for the establishment of official women's organisations (Evans, 1977).

In 1925, the Vienna Chamber of Labour entrusted Käthe Leichter, a socialist feminist, with creating a department concerned with women's work. Leichter began collecting survey data on the poor position of domestic workers and industrial outworkers. She used this material to push demands for improved working conditions, more factory inspections and equal pay. In the process, Leichter made contact with women union activists, thereby establishing a link between the top echelon of women unionists and the head of the women's department in the Chamber of Labour, a link which still exists today (Bei, 1990; Lafleur, 1978).

By 1934, women workers in Vienna made up 26.4 per cent of trade union membership. Despite this presence, trade unions did little to alter the impression that women were unwanted in the workplace. Generally, there was little effort made to integrate women workers or to accord them positions in their organisations either as work councillors or as delegates to congress (Gruber, 1991, p. 153). Women's divisions existed at both national and confederation level within the trade unions and the Chamber of Labour, but these were not intended by male trade unionists to be divisions with any power (Cook et al, 1992, p. 64). This gender-specific means of inclusion was not viewed as a challenge to the primacy of class politics, but rather was a means by which the "woman question" could be absorbed and remain subordinate to issues of class.

Separate women's divisions continue to be a feature of the Austrian trade union movement. The structure of the ÖGB, created in 1946, included the creation of a women's department. Today the ÖGB's Women's Division has input into the making and amending of legislation concerning the status of women and so acts as a link between women workers and policy makers. The Division also provides a multitude of services to encourage the further representation of women workers and their interests.

In 1994, the ÖGB Women's Division had three officials and three support staff. While it did not have its own budget, requests for funds from the ÖGB Executive were rarely refused. The Division has organised annual conferences with approximately 50 women participants from the various trade unions attending. Every four years a larger conference with over 200 delegates is held, where issues are debated and policy directives are drawn up for presentation at the ÖGB Congress which follows immediately.

Officials of the Women's Division regularly travelled to the regions to talk with union women and run workshops. Such contact was referred to as "a consciousness-raising exercise". Women were encouraged to pass on issues of concern and this process was thought to help the women themselves become "aware of their problems". The head of the ÖGB Women's Division saw meeting with women members as crucial in gaining an understanding of major issues and informing women workers of their rights.

Over time, the number of women's divisions has increased and they are now replicated at both national and provincial level within most of the 14 national trade unions and within the various branches of the Chamber of Labour. In a manner similar to the practice of the ÖGB, small conferences and workshops were held throughout Austria by a number of these divisions to maintain links with women workers. More recently, the divisions have been used to facilitate networks of women so as to increase the dialogue and communication between women and their representatives. This strategy was considered important for those groups of women that were otherwise isolated or unorganised. Again, the information gathered from these women was seen as vital for the divisions' involvement in trade union policy making.

Table 4.1 Women's Representation on the Praesidium in Selected Unions, 1993

Union	Praesidium	Female Membership
Public Service	0% (0)	42%
Textile	40% (2/5)	70%
Hotel	50% (2/4)	75%
Private Sector	14% (2/14)	43%

Source: Interviews.

The existence of women's divisions guarantees at least minimal female representation on the executives of individual unions, since the division head is usually an ex-officio member. However, in none of the four national trade unions with close to, or over, 50 per cent female membership (Table 4.1), does women's representation at the executive decision-making level (the Praesidium) reflect the proportion of membership.

In 1993, there were two women out of ten at the highest level of the ÖGB, one of whom was the head of the Union for Salaried Employees in Private Employment, and the other the head of the ÖGB's Women's Division. Women were 31 per cent of ÖGB membership in 1993, 17 per cent of officials assisting senior leadership in policy making, 38 per cent of ÖGB committee membership and two of these committees were chaired by women (ETUC, 1994, pp. 30–31). Similar patterns are evident within the upper echelons of the Chamber of Labour. All women workers are members of the Chamber (42 per cent) but, in 1989, women only made up 10 per cent of the General Assembly and 12 per cent of councillors in the provincial Chambers (SSGCW, 1991, p. 42).

At the ÖGB Congress, although the percentage of female representation has almost doubled over the last twelve years (Table 4.2), representation remains poor in comparison to female membership. While women receive guaranteed representation on union executives through the representation of women's divisions, no reserved places exist at Congress. Women's presence at these occasions was considered critical since it is at both ÖGB and national trade union congresses, held every four years, where overarching policy platforms are decided.

Table 4.2 Women's Representation at ÖGB Congress, Various Years

Year	% Women
1979	7.6
1983	10
1987	10.3
1991	14

Sources: 1979, 1983, 1987 figures from SSGCW (1991, p. 41); 1991 figure from ETUC (1994, p. 28).

The representation of women as negotiators on collective bargaining committees varied according to trade union. There appeared to be few women negotiators in the unions representing public servants, private sector white-collar employees and those in the metal industry. Within the garment section of the Textile Union, 98 per cent of the workers were women and almost all negotiators were also women. In the textile section, where membership was evenly split between men and women, negotiators were predominantly men. Within the banking industry, the female section head within the union had made a conscious effort to encourage more women to join negotiating teams. Largely as a result, in 1994, three of the seven representatives on their negotiating team were women.

Austria

Dismantling the Barriers

Several women unionists argued that women often lacked the confidence to involve themselves in a political environment dominated by men. Where women had a large majority in a workplace, for example in the garment industry, there was little difficulty in encouraging women to stand for election. Where there were equal numbers of men and women, it was more likely that men were elected. Even when women were elected at shop-floor level, a number of interviewees claimed that women did not have the same opportunities as their male counterparts to rise through the ranks of the union.

Confidence was regarded a vital prerequisite to cope with the often unsupportive environments women union officials faced. One woman noticed in meetings of the ÖGB, where all the other secretaries were male, that the "men did not appear to take her as seriously as they took themselves". Another woman commented that "sometimes you get the feeling you are doing something important and serious but sometimes it feels just the contrary".

Family responsibilities were seen as major barriers to women's participation in trade union activity. Union officials had long working hours and child care facilities in Austria were considered inadequate to facilitate the mix of family responsibilities and trade union politics. Many women felt they did not have enough time to take on the extra responsibilities of a being a work councillor.

In 1982, the ÖGB Women's General Council adopted a nine point resolution in an attempt to overcome these barriers. The nominated strategies included motivating more women to stand as candidates, seeking measures to promote women from positions of work councillor and increasing the number of women delegates to Congress. Women's sections at various levels had facilitated the development of support networks and encouraged women to see their representation as an important issue. Women unionists were also continuing to fight for increased child care and were calling for men to take more responsibility for unpaid work in the home to allow women to play more of a role in trade union activities.

Most women's divisions provided training courses to help women overcome their fear of participation. Women were taught public speaking, time management, supervision and research skills. One women unionist noted that over the last ten years of running such courses, significant differences in the behaviour of women negotiators were apparent. Where "women used to cringe at the negotiating table, now they are talking the men down".

Promoting Women's Representation

Quotas and affirmative action strategies for increasing the numbers of women in executive positions have been discussed in the Social Democratic Party and within trade union circles, but have been loaded with negative connotations. Within the ÖGB, the implementation of quotas had been debated but was not acceptable as a policy objective. Instead, women unionists were trying alternative strategies to increase the number of women elected.

For example, the female head of the Banking Section within the Union for Salaried Employees in Private Employment had actively sought out women for placement on negotiating teams and this had proved successful. She maintained that

> women work councillors know the problems women face from their own experience and so of course it is absolutely necessary to have them on the bargaining teams, especially in the bank where over 50 per cent of employees are women.

Within the Public Service Union, women officials argued for a policy whereby official places vacated through resignations or retirements were to be filled by women. Reactions to this strategy were mixed and the interviewee acknowledged that, even if it was accepted, changes in the numbers of women would be slow.

The women unionists with whom I spoke all argued categorically that without women as representatives or women's divisions, they doubted issues of most concern to women workers would be addressed. Women officials from the Union for Salaried Employees in Private Employment noted that having a woman head, who was also a member of Parliament (which is a common feature of corporatist intermediation in Austria), had meant women's issues had received higher priority than it previous years.

The consensus and compromise which results from the social partnership between the state, the Chamber of Labour and the ÖGB has been described as the result of "a kind of gentlemen's agreement". The male presidents of the Chamber of Business and ÖGB have dominated the scene for almost 25 years (Gerlich, 1992, p. 137). While it is claimed that such corporatist arrangements have proved successful in terms of maintaining economic and political stability in Austria (Boreham and Compston, 1992, p. 146), they have also been successful in excluding women (amongst others) from influencing and participating in the public decision-making process. This stems from the limited influence of outside interest groups and the failure of women to reach the upper echelons of the movements involved in the social partnership (cf Neyer, 1996, pp. 108–109).

Women have created their own informal networks to work alongside the corporatist process. Women in trade unions, the Chamber of Labour, the government and the bureaucracy meet to discuss issues as they arise, with such meetings organised with a phone call. Women from the various national trade unions also meet regularly to compare problems and strategies. These networks were considered vital for the dissemination of information and the coordination of joint campaigns and mobilisation of the social partners. Although women unionists felt they could influence members of the social partnership, this was not to be seen as a substitute for increasing women's representation in the corporatist arena.

Women's Wages

During the 1950s, Austria had a comparatively high rate of labour force participation, primarily as a result of post-war reconstruction (Biffl, 1996). In 1960, female labour force participation in Austria was 52.1 per cent, surpassed only by Japan and Finland (Schmidt, 1993, p. 182). However, over the last 30 years, the female labour force participation rate in Austria (like its German-speaking counterparts) stagnated, with the rate at 53.5 per cent in 1990 (OECD, 1995).

There are several significant factors that have contributed to the long period of stagnation in women's labour force activity in Austria. To begin with there has been far lower growth in Austria's tertiary sector than elsewhere in the OECD, while the industrial sectors have remained relatively large. Austria's industrial sector is dominated by small and medium-sized specialist firms, which are characterised by jobs, skills and sub-cultural patterns, arguably resistant to the recruitment of women (Schmidt, 1993, p. 194). Public sector employment as a share in total employment rose from only 14.1 per cent to 18.5 per cent between 1970 and 1979. The same pattern is evident in community, social and personal services, the share of which in total employment only increased by one percentage point (from 23 to 24 per cent) between 1972 and 1980 (Scharpf, 1984, p. 267). In 1995, women's labour force participation had risen to 62 per cent, no doubt a result of a recent five per cent growth in service sector employment and a similar percentage point growth in part-time work (OECD, 1996).

In terms of wage inequality, women wage and salary earners on average earn 70 per cent of what their male counterparts earn. This figure takes account of women in part-time work. Women are over-represented in the low wage earner category, with 26 per cent of female blue and white-collar workers earning less than the minimum wage, while only eight per cent of men are in this category (Wolf and Wolf, 1991, p. 20). There are also a considerable number of women foreign workers whose earnings are lower still (SSGCW, 1991, p. 52). While corporatist arrangements in Austria have led to economic growth and low unemployment, they have led to neither an increase in female employment nor a decrease in the gender-wage differential.

The Collective Bargaining Process

The central instrument of Austria's social partnership has been the Parity Commission for Wages and Prices, wherein the framework for wage agreements is negotiated, linking incomes policy with state economic policy. Within this environment, the ÖGB's position has been to pursue full employment by promoting economic growth and wage restraint. While the focus on productivity as a basis for wage policy development helped keep unemployment comparatively low, a solidaristic wage policy has not been forthcoming, with substantial wage differentials evident between sectors (Traxler, 1992; 1994). The Austrian trade union movement instead argued that redistribution through wage policy would lead to lower investment, reduce long-term productivity growth and ultimately lower real wage increases (Guger, 1992, p. 35).

Collective bargaining takes place nationally, regionally and locally in Austria. The ÖGB, as a member of the social partnership, is involved in the general coordination of wages and employment. However, this is not the level where actual wage increases are decided upon; only where the initiation of negotiations is approved (Katzenstein, 1984, p. 47). Although, in a formal sense, the power to engage with employers in collective bargaining lies with the leaders of the ÖGB, the vast majority of collective agreements are concluded at the sector level, between the relevant section of the Chamber of Business and the appropriate trade union (Traxler, 1992; 1994). The autonomy of individual trade unions in this respect suggests that too much emphasis should not be placed on the high degree of centralisation of bargaining in Austria (Guger, 1992, p. 348). By 1986, over 1500 collective agreements were in force, 180 of which were framework agreements, while the remainder were agreements which supplemented the framework and wage agreements. The wage rates tended to be minimum rates and it was not uncommon for higher wages to be paid, with the negotiation for higher rates often undertaken by local work councils (Anon, 1992, p. 25).

The general wage policy orientation taken by the ÖGB focusing on productivity rather than wage solidarity has had an impact on the gender-wage differential since many women workers are concentrated in a limited number of economic branches within sectors. Women make up over 50 per cent of those employed in clothing, leather, retail, restaurant, personal services, health, education and household services (Biffl, 1996, p.144). In all these occupations except health, women wage and salary earners received less than the median female wage across all economic branches (Wolf and Wolf, 1991, pp. 23–25).

Within sectors, differences in wage outcomes also exist, exacerbated by the large number of collective agreements in existence. For example, while one woman unionist felt much had been achieved in terms of wages for women working part-time in the banking industry, the same could not be said for women in the insurance or savings and loans companies. In this sense, consistency in wage gains across jobs within a sector could not be guaranteed.

Because the wage bargaining system is decentralised, women unionists argued that addressing the gender-wage differential had to occur at lower levels; in particular, an increase in the numbers of women on sub-national bargaining committees was required. Although in theory, the ÖGB concludes all collective agreements, because this does not happen in practice, there is little scope for the ÖGB to estimate the impact of high-low wage sector outcomes on women workers or demand corrective measures in this area. Furthermore, although there has been rhetorical support for reducing the gender-wage gap at ÖGB Congress (Gruber, 1991, p. 153), there has been little action taken by the national trade unions which negotiate sectoral wage agreements (Cook et al, 1992, p. 149).

Although separate collective agreements for men and women

workers have long since been abolished, within collective agreements the criteria used to classify occupations into wage groups have proved linguistically problematic. For example, there is no male equivalent in the German language for the job titles seamstress and embroiderer, so these are immediately recognisable as jobs designated for women. Nor is there a female equivalent in German for such jobs as electrician, mechanic or driver (Metzker, 1980, p. 246). Job descriptions of "light" and "heavy" also existed, with "heavy" jobs being ranked higher than those entailing mental demands, indirectly reinforcing notions of gender-specificity (Cook et al, 1992, p. 161; Metzker, 1980, p. 243).

Open discrimination within collective agreements is now outlawed as a result of the *Equal Treatment Act* (1979) and, in 1994, the Supreme Court ruled that the distinction between "light" and "heavy" work constituted a form of indirect discrimination. However, gender-specific job titles may still exist within smaller agreements, since it is only the wage schedule that is updated each year, with renegotiation of the whole agreement occurring less often. The Equal Treatment Ombudsman revealed that agreements made by some firms have provided male workers with private insurance for themselves, their wives and children, while women were entitled to receive insurance only for themselves. A few women have approached the Equal Treatment Office with requests to review their contracts before being signed. More generally, most women unionists felt increasing the numbers of women negotiators, and/or educating male negotiators on how these issues have an impact on gender-wage differentials were necessary strategies to combat such discrimination.

Occupational segregation was also considered critical to the issue of equal pay for women. Several women noted that, as a result of the continuing occupational segregation, the issue for the future would be pay equity. Comparisons of women's work and men's work needed to be undertaken, with a substantial revaluation of the work undertaken by women. While some individual comparisons had been made within individual trade unions, to date no confederation-wide policy on pay equity has been adopted.

Women's predominance in low wage occupations has also focused women unionists' attention on the issue of raising minimum wages. Minimum wages are set economy-wide and several women unionists noted that their trade unions were generally able to negotiate more than the minimum for their workers, although this strategy was not available to all women unionists. The Metal Workers' Union set the new minimum standard for each bargaining round and in 1994 this was raised by a third. By contrast, the woman official from the Hotel, Restaurant and Personal Service Workers' Union lamented that just achieving the previous minimum target had taken much hard work during negotiations.

A number of women unionists expressed concern about the large number of women who earned less than half the monthly minimum wage. Employers who hired cleaners or other workers under contract often encouraged women to work only a few hours per day. This has meant that while the women paid no tax, they were also ineligible to receive social security benefits, including pensions and no accrual of benefits occurred. A number of unionists believed many women workers were unaware of this potentially detrimental outcome. As from 1993, employers were required to reveal how many casual workers they employed, but this had achieved little. The main strategy to date, has been the lobbying of Ministers by women unionists to allow these workers access to benefits.

The low (and inconsistent) minimum wage cannot be addressed through minimum wage legislation since in Austria wages remain the sole responsibility of the trade unions and employers. Rather, women unionists had sought to address the issue through further negotiation with employers. During this process, discussions around the minimum wage were not couched in terms of "women's" wages, but were argued as being necessary for both men and women, thereby defined as a general union issue.

Also of concern to women unionists have been the different qualifying conditions for pay rises. This sort of discrimination arose when women required a longer period of service than did men to secure promotion. While this form of discrimination was becoming less explicit, the relevance of longevity of service to wage increases was considered to have an impact on the gender-wage differential. Within the Union for Salaried Employees in Private Employment for example, every two years workers receive two wage increases, one of which is bargained for, the other which is an automatic incremental increase based on length of uninterrupted service with the company. This system advantaged men, who tended to have long periods of uninterrupted labour force participation.

In 1994, officials within the Industry Section of the Union for Salaried Employees in Private Employment sought to revamp the way in which wage increases were allocated, whereby larger increases were to be made to younger workers, with smaller increases being made according to length of service. This was to involve condensing the wage scales, so that there were more groups vertically and less horizontal positions. The change to wage policy was driven by the problem that, as a result of increasing levels of qualifications, younger people entering companies were eligible to start on the same scale as workers who had been there 20 years.

This new wage system was pursued not because of a major concern with women's pay, but because of the entrance of increasing numbers of young highly qualified workers. It has become apparent to several women unionists that such a system would also help women workers, since if women started on a higher salary earlier, before interrupting their careers, then on their return to the labour market these women would be able to restart on a relatively high salary. It also had the potential to make women's salaries more comparable with men's and so encourage fathers to take up a share of the parental leave.

Legislative Strategies

Although collective bargaining tends to be the realm where wages are determined, Austria does have a long history of defining specific labour rights and conditions in law and applying them through established enforcement bureaucracies (Cook et al, 1992, p. 36). The principle of equal pay was introduced into the ÖGB constitution in 1958, but legislation in the area did not come about until the passage of the *Equal Treatment Act* (1979) (Steinberg Ratner, 1978, p. 31).

This legislation prohibited any discrimination on the grounds of sex in the fixing of wages. It became illegal to advertise jobs using gender-specific language. An Equal Treatment Commission was set up to deal with all questions relating to discrimination in wage fixing. Employers, work councils, trade unions or an individual worker could apply to the Commission for an investigation into both the provisions of collective agreements and/or individual cases of discrimination. The Commission could also initiate its own investigations (SSGCW, 1991, p. 45).

Despite the good intentions behind the creation of the Equality Commission, it was evident by 1990 that few women were prepared to seek redress by these means. In the 11 years from 1979–1990, only 18 cases were taken before the Commission. The Equality Ombudsman noted that while some men suggested that women's failure to use the Commission showed they were not suffering discrimination, she argued "it was quite apparent that this was not the case. No-one really believed that the grievances did not exist".

As a means of better implementing the legislation, the position of Equality Ombudsman was created in 1991, whereby women could receive both advice and representation. Since 1991, over 500 requests for advice have been received per year since 1991. In 1994, the Equal Treatment Office provided representation for approximately fifteen cases per year, most of which were usually precedent-setting cases in areas of income and promotion.

The Equality Ombudsman suggested that informing women workers of the outcomes of cases was an important strategy in that women would then be in a position to make more demands of their trade unions, thereby stimulating change at the institutional level. Ultimately, it was hoped women would take up their grievances at the firm level through their work councils. The Equal Treatment Office had prepared material to aid work councillors and negotiators in this process.

Although separate wage scales no longer exist, the payment of different wages according to gender-specific titles and the distinction between light and heavy work has implicitly guaranteed different wages for women and men. In the late 1970s, trade union women exposed the discriminatory nature of collective agreements but arguably, because of their lack of influence within the collective bargaining sphere, pursued legislative remedies, specifically through the enactment of the *Equal Treatment Act* (1979).

Initially, the Equality Commission's creation in 1980 was seen as helping to achieve "a breakthrough in the implementation of the equal treatment rule at all levels of labour law and in all fields of working life" (Metzker, 1980, p. 253). However, in itself, it proved inadequate and has required institutional reinforcement through the creation of the Equality Ombudsman's Office in 1991. Even with this improved implementation mechanism, by 1994 there had been little systematic change in the gender-wage differential.

Other Strategies

Another important issue for women's wage equality was equal access to training. Several women unionists were making women's access to education and training an issue in work council elections. Promotion was dependent on ongoing vocational training and was especially important for women, since in many cases they had the same qualifications as their male counterparts, but began their career in lower positions.

Within the insurance and parts of the banking industry, income inequalities tended to become apparent after women had been in the job five years and the Equality Ombudsman argued this was related to access to in-firm training. Employers made the decisions as to who received training and access tended to be easier for men, who then received wage increases and promotion. She noted that often women paid for their own training, but this was not always considered by employers to be as worthwhile as in-firm training. More generally, the Equality Ombudsman also maintained it was important for women to have the issue addressed since, once their male counterparts had received the training, the resulting income inequalities "became irrelevant because the employer can argue that the wage difference was a result of the man being better qualified".

Within the public service, there had been a push by the women's division for increased training for women who were located in clerical jobs. With the typing pool and secretaries becoming almost redundant, retraining these women and providing them with a broader skills base was considered necessary for their own personal career development and to increase their chances of earning further wage increases. The women's officer made several field trips to Germany to identify the best means by which to undertake such retraining and small group discussions were being held with the relevant Ministers. By 1994, positive responses from government officials had been forthcoming, although detailed plans for increases in access to training were still in the early stages.

In conclusion, it is apparent that the lack of commitment to equality in wages emanates from the top of the corporatist hierarchy. The trade union confederation in Austria, although both economically and politically strong, has not pursued a solidaristic wage policy, but has instead sanctioned an inegalitarian wages structure, which has led to the creation of high and low wage sectors, with women predominating in the latter. Thus corporatist political arrangements in Austria have favoured a wages policy which advantages already powerful groups of mostly male workers.

Wage bargaining is decentralised so the ÖGB is largely powerless to demand that gender-wage differentials be addressed in contract negotiation. National trade unions have shown little commitment to the cause of equal pay and to counter this, women trade unionists have sought to increase the number of women negotiators on bargaining teams. Increases in women's representation were considered doubly important in Austria since the overarching framework of consensus meant that all gains had to be obtained through negotiation, with militant or industrial class action virtually non-existent.

Combining Work and Family Responsibilities

Historically, both Catholics and Social Democrats in Austria have sought protective measures for working women, with the latter arguing that their support for protective legislation was based on "protection for woman as mother. .... This lies not only in the interests of women but is significant for the whole proletariat" (Lafleur, 1978, p. 237). The motivation to protect women as mothers has continued to permeate policy development in Austria.

Austria's long history of maternity leave provision has been achieved by legislative means with trade union support. The first reforms in 1885 were initially the result of a desire to protect pregnant women workers. After the Second World War, women in trade unions and trade unions themselves lobbied for the *Maternity Protection Act* (1957), which provided most women workers with six months maternity leave, extended to 12 months in 1960. In addition, trade unions were successful in having outlawed the employment of pregnant women six weeks before and after childbirth. Later the entitlement to leave was backed up with protection against dismissal until four weeks after resuming work (Krebs, 1975, pp. 274–275). Some unions had been able to bargain for benefits beyond those provided by law (Cook et al, 1992, p. 13).

The *Parental Leave Act* (1990) provides the opportunity for either (employed) parent to take or share leave. Protection from dismissal applies to fathers and mothers and a fixed allowance is provided for 12 months. This was a step away from the previous legislative definition of parental responsibilities as solely the province of women. However, because the payment for leave was a fixed amount, rather than a percentage of previous earnings, there has been little financial incentive for fathers to leave work and take up parental responsibilities.

In 1991, maternity leave was extended to two years and in 1994, arguments were put for increasing maternity leave to three years. Support for extending maternity leave was forthcoming from men in the labour movement and the government, but most women unionists believed men supported it more for conservative reasons rather than for progressive ones, since extended maternity leave provisions would encourage women to stay longer at home. A number of women unionists had vigorously opposed the extension of maternity leave provisions, fearing it would further restrict women's employment opportunities.

Women trade unionists did succeed in having the period of maternity leave count toward pension entitlements, but they were concerned that unpaid family responsibilities did not count, disadvantaging many women who chose to stay at home beyond the two years maternity leave provision. To qualify for a full pension, 15 years of labour force participation has been required. In 1992, new legislation was passed which provided women with a deduction of four years per child. Now a woman with one child need only work eleven years to qualify. This pension reform was part of an "equality package" and was very much a product of lobbying undertaken by women in the various trade unions, women from the ÖGB and the Chamber of Labour, and the Minister of Women's Affairs. Several interviewees commented that considerable effort was required to encourage male ministers to accept women had interests as workers and not only as mothers. Much use was also made of the media, with the united stance taken by women from the various organisations on this issue publicly highlighted.

The emphasis on motherhood and the provision of benefits for women workers to stay at home and care for their children has allowed the issue of child care to become less of a priority for governments in Austria, while trade union leadership has not seen it as a major concern. In 1990, the Ministry of Women's Affairs acknowledged there were considerable shortages in pre-school child care places: 85 per cent of all creches and 64 per cent of child care centres were located in Vienna, with very little access to child care available in the regions (SSGCW, 1991, p. 15). Firms seldom provided child care and in general it was considered the government's responsibility. In this sense, child care was not taken to be an industrial issue and so was not discussed in the collective bargaining process. Women unionists also suggested that maternity leave was considered by policy makers to be a cheaper option than child care and was one that did not disrupt the status quo.

The issue of child care has been linked to the hours of schooling in Austria. Primary school hours are eight in the morning until lunch time and several women unionists noted there were considerable problems in finding child care for the remainder of the day. The limited availability of part-time work also acted as a disincentive for women to continue their labour force participation. Women unionists have lobbied the government to increase the hours of school to a full day since the early 1970s, but to date have met with little success.

Support for child care has been further complicated by two factors. First, although the federal government is charged with supplying funds for child care centres, the establishment and administration of these centres is undertaken by the Lander (or provinces). Most of the Lander had conservative administrations that have been slow to embrace the idea of extra-familial child care. In the early 1990s, the federal government offered a financial contribution to the Lander for increased child care and the education of kindergarten teachers. Disagreements between the two levels of government regarding control over where the funding would be targeted meant no outcome was possible.

Second, in 1994, as a result of a coalition government between the Conservatives and Social Democrats, the Social Democratic Minister of Women's Affairs, when seeking initiatives on child care, had to liaise and obtain consent from the Conservative Minister for Family, Youth and Education. While the two had regular discussions on the issue, little progress was made.

In isolation, Austrian maternity leave benefits appear progressive. However, when viewed in tandem with the inadequate provision of child care facilities, the motivations for continued extensions of leave are somewhat ambiguous. They seem less about providing for women as workers and more about reinforcing the role of women as mothers, making both maternity leave and child care social rather than industrial issues.

Part-time Work

In Austria, the growth in part-time work has been minimal. In 1973, part-time employment made up 6.4 per cent of total employment and this had risen to only 9.1 per cent in 1992. In 1975, 14 per cent of women in the labour force worked less than 35 hours per week, while 86 per cent worked full-time (Steinberg Ratner, 1978, p. 15). By 1987 this had risen to 16 per cent and had increased to 20 per cent by 1990 (Wolf and Wolf, 1991, p. 13). In 1996, 28.8 per cent of women in the labour market worked part-time.

The lack of growth (until recently) has been attributed to the low share of service and public employment in total employment compared to industrial employment ratios, where men outnumbered women. Nor has industrial employment been open to part-time working arrangements in the past (Schmidt, 1993, p. 190). Trade unions in Austria have continued to resist increases in this type of employment and instead have pursued generalised working time reductions for all workers, supplementing this with bargaining for wage increases to support a single income family (Schmidt, 1993, p. 196).

Interestingly perhaps, is the fact that women unionists in Austria have continued to follow the conventional union arguments against the development of part-time work, albeit imbuing this position with a gender perspective. While women acknowledged that part-time work would allow women to better juggle work and family, part-time work was considered to have a number of disadvantages. Part-time workers were expected to be more productive in fewer hours of work than full-time workers and were viewed as difficult to organise. There was also a fear that part-time work would be detrimental to the careers of women, reducing their chances of promotion and would lead to losses in pension payments.

An alternative to part-time work being proposed by women in the labour movement in Austria was the reduction of working hours for all employees to 30 hours per week. This strategy was put forward by the Minister of Women's Affairs in the early 1980s, but at that time was dismissed by many women trade unionists. The strategy recently applied to achieve the change had been incremental in its approach, whereby several unions sought to have the working week reduced to 35 hours, with the support of most women unionists.

Although not encouraging of part-time work as a labour market strategy, women unionists in Austria were fighting to improve the conditions of those in part-time work and to provide them with the same rights as full-time workers. In the banking industry, women unionists have managed to negotiate for the provision of better parental leave payments for both full and part-time workers than were granted by law. Better conditions were also being sought for women who work from home in the metal industry and several women representatives were working to provide better access to social security for women who worked very few hours per week. However, a number of women unionists recognised the difficulties of regulating such work, and acknowledged they were not always successful in achieving parity for part-time workers with respect to overtime rates and other conditions.

Equal Employment Opportunities

Austria has a history of "protecting" women workers from night work. In

1950, Austria ratified the ILO Night Work (Women) Convention and by 1972, the *Night Work (Women) Act* applied to almost all women workers aged eighteen and over (Krebs, 1975, p. 275). Trade unions, with the support of women, had always supported the restriction of women's participation in night work, since the protection of women workers was viewed as an effective means of regulating their working conditions (Andersen, 1992, p. 66). Protection was considered a blessing for low paid women who got "little or no help in the home from their husbands" (Krebs, 1975, p. 275).

There has been increasing opposition to the prohibition of women working at night over the last ten years, with arguments concerning equal employment opportunity for women taking on a new salience for women within the trade union movement. Such prohibitions have restricted women's access to rotating shiftwork and arguably have curtailed women's possibilities for promotion. Under special circumstances women could get permission to work from ten in the evening until midnight, but this only occurred on a very short-term basis.

Austria's admittance to the European Union in 1995 required a commitment by the Austrian Government to overturn the prohibition on night work for women in line with new ILO and European standards. In response to this move, the ÖGB called for unions to suggest what changes to working conditions should be included in the redrafting of the legislation relating to night work.

Women officials put together a substantial list of demands including: shortening night shifts without reducing the penal rates; an increase in the number of breaks during the shift; more vacations; earlier access to pensions; and the provision of hot meals and on-site health services. Women unionists noted that although the change to night work legislation was seen by many men as a women's issue they were trying to recast the issue as a general one, focusing on the importance of good night work conditions for all workers, both men and women.

Becoming a member of the European Union has had an impact on the working conditions of women in other spheres. The issue of sexual harassment has been more explicitly addressed, with broad guidelines being set by the Ministry of Women's Affairs, which were then specified through precedent setting cases heard by the Equality Commission. A spokesperson from the Ministry of Women's Affairs maintained that it was unlikely that such progress would have eventuated if Austria had not joined the European Union.

A pamphlet informing workers of procedures to follow and the reasons why sexual harassment is unacceptable behaviour was designed by the women's officer for public service employees, and distributed to all unions by the ÖGB. There has also been considerable discussion around the issue of sexual harassment in Parliament, in the workplace and in the media.

Prior to 1992, women were expected to retire between the ages of 55 and 60, while the male retirement age was between 60 and 65. However, a Constitutional Court ruling found the unequal pension age discriminatory and a legislative amendment was sought (Falkner and Tálos, 1994, p. 59). Women in trade unions and the Ministry of Women's Affairs argued that as a result of raising the age of retirement for women, women, in turn, required better working conditions, if they were to stay longer in the labour force. The broad set of demands which were then proposed by women unionists and the Minister of Women's Affairs became known as the "Equality Package" and again involved an adaptation to corresponding European Community rules (Falkner and Tálos, 1994, p. 59).

Married women's labour force participation has not been strongly encouraged in Austria, evident through the lack of both demand side (the availability of part-time work and growth in public sector employment) and supply side policies (child care provisions, individual taxation). While generous maternity leave benefits exist, these have been promoted for natalist and protective reasons rather than through a desire to increase the employment of married women. Lately however, Social Democratic women trade unionists have begun to challenge this norm of marginal labour market status by refusing to support the increase of maternity leave from two to three years, arguing that it is detrimental to both the career and wage prospects of women workers. In this sense, women trade unionists have sought to undermine the rigidifying process often associated with gender-specific strategies.

Changes to working conditions such as child care, measures against sexual harassment and parental leave have not been addressed by trade unions in the industrial arena, but have been dependent on women's divisions lobbying and negotiating with the state. This indicates the narrow agenda of contemporary trade unionism in Austria. While new government policies on such issues were discussed with the social partners, open union support for demands around issues of concern to women workers were not always forthcoming. The fact that strong (male-dominated) industry unions continue to control the ÖGB bargaining agenda, combined with the lack of interest in stimulating an increase in women's labour force participation, could account for this lack of interest. It remains to be seen if European Union membership has any ongoing influence in altering corporatist attitudes to women's issues as workers.

Conclusion

Austria has been labelled as displaying an inherently conservative form of class politics (Esping-Andersen et al, 1984). After 1945, the Social Democrats became participants in a social partnership with business, and linked themselves with the conservatives in a grand coalition at the parliamentary level. The corporatist environment was one marked by consensus and compromise. With this came a forfeiting of trade union rights to militant action, and a freezing of the status quo, with the Social Democrats, albeit initially the weaker partners in the relationship, sanctioning the maintenance of status-based financial rewards and welfare benefits. This, combined with the linking of wage agreements to productivity and economic growth, rather than to a solidaristic wage policy, has undermined the potential of class politics to embrace universal notions of equality.

This conservative stance has had an impact on the position of women. Notions of women as mother and wife were already embedded in Austrian culture and the renewed emphasis on consensus and maintenance of the status quo allowed these norms to become rigidified. As a result, women's entry into the labour market did not become part of the transition to social democracy. There has been a continued emphasis on maternity benefits, but these have not been supplemented with child care policies, thereby reinforcing women's role as mother. In addition, the collective bargaining agenda narrowly defines what are industrial issues, with women's claims largely defined as social issues requiring remedy through legislation.

It is in this context that Benard and Schlaffer (1984, p. 72) argue that the linkage of women's issues with social democracy in Austria was a "fateful development". They maintain that the desire for political unity and consensus has suffocated any possible radicalisation of women's demands (Benard et al, 1984, pp. 72–73). The social partnership has been dependent on the encompassment of interests within the trade union movement, whereby the heterogeneity of workers' interests have been redefined as a unified class interest. This has influenced the way women have organised their interests as workers. In 1945, women's divisions were reinstituted as the primary means of representing women and their interests. These divisions have provided women workers with at least some voice in the decision-making arenas of trade unions and opportunities to lobby the government and social partners through the appropriate channels. However, this institutionalisation has not disrupted the requirement for political unity or challenged the existing system of decision-making.

Furthermore, there exists an agreement not to raises issues that would be controversial or unacceptable to any of the social partners. While the corporatist decision-making environment remains male-dominated, it is likely that these customs will continue to exclude the possibility of gender equality becoming a topic for consideration within this forum.

While women trade unionists have not directly challenged the consensual and conservative form of class politics evident in Austria, they have appealed to their identity as women in seeking a focal point for collective action. For many years this choice brought with it the reinstatement of women as "other" in terms of their role in the paid workforce. More recently however, women trade unionists, while continuing to use gender-specific strategies, have begun to challenge and redefine the conception of women's labour force equality. In particular, women have sought to expose as potentially rigidifying the existing night work restrictions and proposals for increased maternity leave. In this sense, the gender-specific solidarities employed by women trade unionists in Austria are in the process of being redrawn and politicised.

5 Israel

Introduction

Israel displays several features that enable it to be labelled corporatist. The major union confederation is encompassing in its scope of membership, it is both strong and centralised with an associational monopoly and it has always had intimate links with the party of the left. However, the mix of socialist and Zionist ideas, which underpinned trade union development, has led to a unique brand of worker representation, which has in turn affected the way in which Jewish women workers in Israel have formulated their claims and solidarities.

In this chapter, I identify how Jewish women have sought recognition of their demands as workers through institutionalised inclusion within the labour movement. What becomes apparent is that the broader solidarity created around national Jewish identity, both rhetorically and organisationally by the labour movement overshadows the gender-specific solidarities constituted by women around a variety of claims. Indeed, Jewish women's interests as workers have been largely marginalised by the trade union movement and this has been even more so for Arab-Israeli women and women from the occupied territories.

In 1994, the Israeli Labour-Coalition lost control of the major trade union confederation for the first time since its creation in 1920. Following this, a substantial restructuring has been taking place within the confederation, with considerable repercussions likely for membership levels. This chapter focuses on the period before January 1995.

The Labour Movement in Israel

The labour movement in Israel is quite different in origin, ideology, structure and functions, to the models of unionism which exist in both Australia and Europe. In the late nineteenth century, discussions regarding the "Jewish problem" linked the idea of creating a new Jewish society to notions of a classless society (Levin, 1978, p. 385). The vision was of a Jewish state based not on private property rights, but on the principles of cooperation and egalitarianism. These ideals were most explicitly manifest through the establishment of kibbutzim (Levin, 1978, p. 445).

In pre-state Israel, workers (who were predominantly in agricultural work) were not mobilised around traditional class and political struggles, but around a combination of both socialist and Zionist ideals (Shalev, 1992, p. 30). These factors had an impact on both the structure and the functions of the labour movement, with the trade union confederation not only representing the interests of workers, but also involving itself in building the economy and providing health and some welfare services.

The Histadrut, founded in 1920, translates as the General Federation of Trade Unions. As in the case of ÖGB in Austria, workers are recruited directly by the Histadrut and are then assigned to a trade union. This direct membership system, combined with the establishment in 1940 of a trade union department within the Histadrut, has provided centralised and institutionalised control over union finances, executive and committee appointments and trade unions at the local level (Shalev, 1992, p. 169).

There are approximately 40 national trade unions in Israel (Histadrut, 1993). These unions are organised by industry for manual workers and by occupation for professional workers. While labour councils provide the Histadrut with representation at the local level, Grinberg argues that the dominance of the Labour Party in labour council elections has stifled internal democracy and has undermined the legitimacy of the local labour council as representative of rank and file workers (Grinberg, 1991, p. 63). In addition, there exists a strong degree of detachment between the Histadrut's unions and the rank and file membership. It is only the workers' committees, which exist at the shop floor level, that directly represent the interests of rank and file workers. These are not an organic part of the Histadrut, and delegates are elected independently of the political parties (Grinberg, 1991; Shalev, 1992). However, because union officials are elected from lists put forward by political parties, workers committee representatives who seek promotion into the Histadrut hierarchy are dependent on their status in the party, not their service to the rank and file.

The Histadrut does not only involve itself in trade unionism. It also supplies social welfare and economic services, including education, housing, culture, banking, insurance and sport. In particular, its involvement in and administration of the Sick Fund guarantees its membership, since access to these health services comes only by being a Histadrut member (Arian, 1989, pp. 33–35). The Fund offers primary health care services to a variety of non-paying members such as students, pensioners and housewives. As a result, while 75 per cent of all wage earners were members of the Histadrut in 1990, the latter representing approximately 85 per cent of workers in the negotiation of collective agreements, actual trade union membership was only around 30 per cent of the wider Histadrut affiliation (Shalev, 1992). By 1995, trade union density was estimated at 23 per cent (ILO, 1997). The Histadrut itself has not been dependent on organising workers to provide itself with a membership base and in many sectors workers remain unorganised (Grinberg, 1991). The Histadrut's breadth of membership has however, provided it with a substantial capacity for political mobilisation which was critical to the Israeli Labour Party's long-term governmental hegemony from 1948 until 1977 (Grinberg, 1991; Shalev, 1989; 1992).

The role of the Histadrut has been as much about nation building as about representing labour. In pre-state Israel, the Histadrut involved itself in economic activities that would not have otherwise attracted a capitalist investor and is now a major employer in its own right. While the Histadrut's role in state building was redefined after the establishment of the state of Israel in 1948, in 1986, Histadrut firms were continuing to generate 27 per cent of the country's industrial product (Arian, 1989, p. 35). Thus, unlike other OECD countries, the economy in Israel is divided into three sectors: the government sector (comprised of the military, public services and state-owned enterprises), the private sector and the Histadrut sector (Izraeli, 1994, p. 307).

The overlap of the Histadrut's economic and trade union functions manifests itself in the collective bargaining sphere. Histadrut representation of workers' demands is constrained by its interests as an employer. This contradiction in functions has often diminished the incentive for the Histadrut to centralise and control wage demands, thereby undermining the development of a unified working class interest (Horowitz and Lissak, 1989, p. 129; Shalev, 1992, p. 30).

It is important here to note the differential status of Arab-Israeli citizens and Palestinians who live in the occupied territories of the Gaza Strip and the West Bank. Arab-Israeli citizens are entitled to Histadrut membership, whereas Palestinians are not. However, even for Arab-Israelis, affiliation and participation within the Histadrut has been dependent on the level of threat Arab workers have posed both economically and politically. In the years prior to 1948, Arab workers were in greater demand than Jewish immigrants as the former were cheaper to hire and more productive. After 1948, an alliance between worker pioneers and organised Zionism provided the means by which Arab workers were excluded from both jobs and workers organisations in Jewish sectors (Grinberg, 1991, pp. 62–63; Shalev, 1992, pp. 64–69).

The labour movement promoted the connection between labourism and Zionism to protect itself from alliances between Jewish and Arab trade unionism. By 1927, the Histadrut accepted some Jewish-Arab joint trade union activity but this was not actively encouraged. After 1948, Arab workers proved less of a threat politically (many had left after the declaration of the state of Israel) and economically (after World War Two there was an substantial increase in industrialisation and a decline in citriculture which favoured Jewish workers more than Arab workers). The Histadrut chose to include Arab workers through the creation of a separate Arab department and by providing separate activities, separate unions and branches. In this way, the Histadrut has been able to maintain control over Arab involvement in trade union policy making. The separate Arab branch still exists today (Shalev, 1992, p. 42).

Welfare state provision has also been considerably segmented between Arab and Jews. While universal coverage and non-discriminatory benefits were introduced in 1958, Arab citizens seldom received the same level of benefits as Jewish citizens. During the 1960s, this segregation was indirectly formalised with the establishment of separate scales for urban and rural residents. In reality, this ruling never applied to Jewish citizens in rural localities (Doron and Kramer, 1991, p. 175). Although this criterion was abolished in 1973, discrimination continued to exist with respect to income maintenance, education, employment creation, housing and personal social services for Arab citizens (Shalev, 1989, p. 104).

In pre-state Israel, trade unionism and collective bargaining were highly decentralised. After 1948, the Histadrut attempted to develop several national wage policies with limited success. While strike activity has been a constant feature over the years, white-collar educated workers, and increasingly manual and technical workers in state-owned and exclusively Jewish workplaces, have continued to push for wage differentials and union autonomy. The need to maintain centralised control required the Histadrut to sanction these wage demands, contributing to the impossibility of corporatist restraint (Grinberg, 1991; Shalev, 1992; 1989). Today, bargaining takes place at three levels: nationally; within each sector; and, at the workplace.

Despite the existence of a centralised and strong labour movement, a universal welfare state and centralised wage bargaining system have not been forthcoming in Israel. While the income gap between workers grew after the establishment of the state of Israel, this development has not led to any substantial increase in political mobilisation on the basis of class. Indeed, it appears that in the drive for nationhood, working class identification has been overshadowed by Zionism (Horowitz and Lissak, 1989, pp. 84–91). In this process, the role of trade unionism was, and has remained, marginal to the labour movement's political aspirations.

It is evident that Israel has many of the organisational features required to acquire the label corporatist, but there are also features that make the Israeli version peculiar. While the rhetoric of class struggle was initially applied in pre-state Israel, this was soon overshadowed by the rhetoric of Zionism. In the practice of politics, the Histadrut has involved itself not only in working class representation, but also in projects relevant to nation-building. In this sense, Israel's unitary labour organisation is not dependent on working class solidarity manifest through class-oriented trade unionism. Rather, the Histadrut has refused to foster comprehensive class solidarity between all workers, Arab and Jewish, focusing instead on developing a unified Jewish labour movement.

Women's Representation in the Israeli Union Movement

The creation of a new society in pre-state Israel was based on a socialist Zionist rhetoric of equality which led many women to believe that Jewish national liberation would include women's liberation. However, although women themselves sought to discourage the re-emergence of old forms of inequality, the practice of nation-building required women to maintain their traditional roles of mothers and homemakers (Bernstein, 1987b; Swirski, 1991). Women were often excluded from much of the paid work that was being undertaken; in particular, road construction work groups and agricultural communes avoided employing women and, if accepted, women were relegated to service jobs (Bernstein, 1987a, p. 456; 1987b). Women's labour force participation in these areas was also strongly resisted by the Histadrut-controlled employment exchange and frequent unemployment meant that there was little incentive for the male-dominated labour movement in pre-state Israel to promote women's full participation in the labour force (Bernstein, 1987a; Izraeli, 1992). In response, some women began organising separately in collectives, tendering for construction jobs and setting up their own agricultural training farms (Bernstein, 1987a, p. 456).

Yet unlike women in the other countries examined here, women's exclusion from certain spheres of the labour force did not exclude them from Histadrut membership. All women, paid workers and wives of workers were encouraged to become members. Despite this inclusion, few women delegates were sent to the founding convention of the Histadrut and women were under-represented on the Histadrut Council. As a result of this exclusion the Women Workers' Movement was formed. Its objective was to place the "woman question" on the Histadrut agenda and convince the labour movement that equality for women was an important issue in the creation of the new society (Bernstein, 1987a, p. 459; 1987b).

Local committees for the affairs of women workers were formed to mobilise local women and to focus on issues of concern to women. There was some debate over the level of autonomy to be provided to these women's committees. Histadrut officials sought complete integration with the labour councils (thereby bringing them under direct Histadrut control), while some women wanted the committees to be autonomously elected by women workers (Bernstein 1987a; 1987b; Izraeli, 1981; 1992).

In the end, a Histadrut resolution required that the women workers' committees be appointed by and accountable to the labour councils. This limited autonomy meant all decisions and initiatives undertaken by the committees needed the approval of the local labour councils. The women's committees thus became dependent on those organisations whose indifference had initially stimulated their creation (Bernstein, 1987a, p. 464). Histadrut control made it difficult to maintain links with women at grass-roots level, which in turn curtailed the possibility of mobilising local women around specific causes, thereby limiting the committees' impact on mainstream Histadrut policy making (Bernstein, 1987a; Izraeli 1992; Pope, 1991).

Over time, women's labour force participation has fluctuated, altering the composition of female Histadrut membership. In 1926, 32 per cent of all women members were wage earners and 66 per cent were workers' wives. By 1930, the proportion of women wage earners decreased to only 25.4 per cent and the proportion of workers' wives rose to 74 per cent. The reduction in the number of working women members was exacerbated by an employment crisis in the late 1930s, which prompted many Histadrut members to demand that only one member of each married couple be entitled to work. Although not official Histadrut policy, it was implicitly accepted that married women would be the non-workers (Bernstein, 1987a, p. 461).

Corresponding to the increase in the proportion of workers wives, the Organisation of Working Mothers was created within the Histadrut. By the late 1930s, the Organisation had become a major organ of the Women Workers' Movement, involving itself in volunteer social work among immigrants and placing considerable emphasis on the role of mothers in state building. While the concept of workers' wives gave symbolic recognition to women's domestic labour and provided a means by which women could remain socially active, it also reinforced traditional conceptions of women's activities (Bernstein 1987b; Pope, 1991).

In 1976, the Council of the Women Workers' Movement and the Organisation of Working Mothers merged and was renamed Na'amat. Today Na'amat is described as "the women's movement of the Histadrut whose aim is the advancement of women in legislation, society and at work" (Histadrut, 1994, p. 3). Na'amat maintains a network of day care centres, vocational schools, and community centres for both Jewish and Arab women. It also provides legal advice on issues of discrimination and personal status. While 100 branches exist at local level, it is argued that the structure, objectives and achievements of Na'amat have been constrained by its connection to the institutional framework of the Histadrut. Na'amat was developed as part of the Zionist movement, so at various times its objectives of equality for women have been diluted by national and partisan concerns (Pope, 1991, p. 232). Na'amat now represents over 700,000 women, but these women are seldom mobilised around issues outside of their locality.

The Department for Salaried Women within the Histadrut's Trade Union Department has the explicit role of representing the interests of working women. Established in 1959, it is a small department that liaises with women elected to union secretariats and representatives from large national workers' committees. Through regular meetings and links with local women, the Department for Salaried Women aims to organise unorganised women workers, improve working conditions and oversee implementation of relevant rules and laws passed by the Histadrut and Knesset respectively (Histadrut. 1981, p. 15).

However, the Department's resources are limited and the already marginal position of trade unionism within the Histadrut restricts its realm of influence. Indeed, neither the Department for Salaried Women nor Na'amat are considered core or powerful sections within the Histadrut. A number of women unionists expressed a concern over the lack of political power women's sections appeared to have. These women maintained that the potential power of Na'amat needed to be better harnessed, with more militant and aggressive action taken, especially with respect to the constant perception that women's issues were less important than those concerning the economy and security.

Women have remained conspicuously absent from the leadership of the Histadrut. The two top positions of Secretary General and Deputy Secretary General have always been occupied by men (Buber Agassi, 1991, p. 208). The highest committee is the Central Committee with 43 members, of which women made up 17 per cent in 1988, an increase of 5 per cent over ten years. In 1988, women made up 11.2 per cent of the 196 member executive committee. This latter figure is almost the same as ten years ago (Benson and Harverd, 1988; Status of Women, 1981).

Few women were heads of national trade unions. The Pharmaceutical Union elected its first female chairperson in 1990 and while several female-dominated unions had women chairpersons (nurses, teachers and social workers), women unionists noted that the predominance of women within an occupation did not guarantee representation by women. In male-dominated unions there were few women representatives with, for example, only one woman out of forty on the secretariat of the Metal Workers' Union. At the local level, women responsible to the Department for Salaried Women were represented in half of the 72 labour councils.

Segregation within the paid workforce appeared to have an impact on women's access to local workers' committees. Within the metal industry, women predominated in the clerical and electronics sections, whereas men were concentrated in the heavy metals areas, from whence most of the workers' committee representatives were drawn. In addition, many private sector firms in which women work remained non-unionised and without workers committees, thereby reducing women's representation in the negotiating process.

Quotas for Women

Histadrut elections are held every three or four years and delegates are elected from lists put forward by nearly all the political parties represented within the Israeli Parliament (the Knesset). In this way the industrial and political wings of the labour movement in Israel are intimately linked.

Israel

Thus, an assessment of women's representation in the Histadrut requires an examination of the way women have been represented within political parties. Here I focus primarily on women in the Labour Party because, until 1994, the Israeli Labour Party held the majority of votes in the Histadrut.

A multi-party list system of proportional representation has been found to be highly correlated with the greater representation of women in Parliament (Castles, 1981). However, in Israel, where a proportional system is used, women's representation in the Knesset has never surpassed 9.1 per cent (Azmon, 1993). Women's representation is a little higher on the Histadrut executive, but it is still far from proportional to women's membership of the Histadrut (50 per cent).

In an attempt to remedy this under-representation, Labour women pushed for a quota of 20 per cent women to be written into the Labour Party Constitution. This quota would then also apply to the Histadrut, when controlled by the Labour Party. However, women unionists noted that realising the quota required constant vigilance. A decision was taken at the most recent Histadrut conference to have a quota of 30 per cent representation of women in all Histadrut bodies, although no enforcement mechanisms were established so how this is implemented remains to be seen.

If quotas are to be successful in a list system, women must be placed in winnable positions on the party lists. A bill was put before Parliament proposing that all parties be obliged to have affirmative action strategies to promote more women onto party lists, but was not passed. While Labour's unofficial number is one woman in every ten, the Israel Women's Network (IWN is a moderate non-partisan women's organisation) has been lobbying for women to be listed in every second or third position.

In the past, an elected committee compiled these lists. Now primaries are held whereby candidates need to target 160,000 voters rather than the previous 3,000. This requires considerable campaign money and resources, and is often difficult for women candidates to find. Early IWN research has suggested that this system restricts the participation of women in the candidate selection process.

At the local level, during the 1970s, women were represented on only one-third of the workers' committees in workplaces where there were large numbers of women (Izraeli, 1982). Since this time, women trade unionists have begun to explore several quota options. Prior to 1993, a workplace with more than 300 employees and with more than 25 per cent of them women was required to elect at least one woman to the workers' committee even if she had received fewer votes than a male candidate. This measure was amended in 1993, requiring the election of at least one woman delegate where women made up 10 per cent of workers (Department for Salaried Women, 1993).

Partisanship and Women's Interests

All levels of the Histadrut, including Na'amat and the Department of Salaried Women, are administered by party nominees (Shalev, 1992). As already mentioned, the only exception to this model are the committees established at the workplace level.

Herzog (1996) has argued that, although women are often selected as representatives of women, "they are expected to prefer the general interests of the party over their so-called particularistic interests as women" (Herzog, 1996, p. 3). Several women Members of the Knesset had previously been the Head of Na'amat, but this had not guaranteed the representation of women's issues in parliament. Further, the numbers of women who made the transition from the women's sections to the mainstream political arena had been minimal.

In the past, few women in Parliament identified as feminist or sought to represent issues identified as "women's issues", and women-only lists had proved both unsuccessful and politically unacceptable (Freedman, 1990). During the 1990s, the issue of the political representation of women assumed a greater profile and several women members of the Knesset openly identified themselves as feminists working for the cause of women's equality. However, women's interests were ultimately overshadowed by party interests if a conflict arose, thereby reinforcing the notion that the common cause, whether it be security or the economy, took precedence over sectional interests (Izraeli, 1994; Weiss and Yishai, 1980).

In addition, political parties hold a near-monopoly on local organising and this has undermined the possibility for grass-roots activity by women within alternative organisations. Na'amat, as a party organisation, has helped to preserve the organisational monopoly by coopting new organisational efforts or by denying support to activities not initiated internally (Buber Agassi, 1991, p. 299). Thus, increasing women's participation in trade union politics is inherently linked to women's participation in party politics.

In response, women from the Histadrut and other organisations were recruiting more women into politics at a local level. The head of the Women's Division of the Labour Party had organised conventions around the country, some specifically targeted at drawing career women into Labour Party activities. Work was being done to encourage women who were unsuccessful the first time they stood for election, either locally or nationally, to stand again. There was also an increasing emphasis on equal representation in the youth branches of the party, with a quota of 40 per cent women being lobbied for in an effort to change the future profile of the organisation.

In 1991, a joint cross-party national campaign facilitated by the Israel Women's Network (IWN) was set up to encourage more women to join any political party. It targeted the 1992 election, and was repeated for the 1996 election. The campaign received substantial media response, primarily "because it was the first time that anyone saw right and left women sitting together and saying join a party and get active".

The IWN has also been active in running seminars and courses aimed at developing women's skills in different aspects of political life. These courses were being run nationwide and had been supplemented with a publication entitled *Politics is for Me,* which provided women with advice on how to participate and succeed in the political arena.

The Department for Salaried Women held seminars for members of the workers' committees, where issues relating to women and work were integrated with other material in order to teach men about women's concerns. A variety of women-only courses were also provided by the Department which women unionists viewed as important in encouraging women to be more active. While individual unions ran courses in union negotiation, the rights of workers, the pension system and elections, in which women were encouraged to participate, few of these were specifically aimed at women.

Na'amat and the Department for Salaried Women within the Histadrut act as the focal points for most of initiatives undertaken to increase women's representation and participation in party and union life. Through their local labour councils and women's branches, these bodies have provided a framework for the creation of informal networks amongst working women. Several women unionists acknowledged that these networks were necessary to counter the "old-boys network", which dominated Histadrut politics. While women unionists noted that women's family responsibilities hindered the increased involvement of women in party and trade union politics, no specific strategies existed to address this apart from encouragement to participate and the provision of support networks.

Several women argued that employing more women negotiators was vital to avoid agreements with potentially negative consequences being signed on their behalf. However, not all women trade unionists agreed that representation by women made a difference to the visibility of women's issues. Some maintained that the importance of having women union leaders depended on who the woman was and on her motivation. It was considered important to distinguish between whether they were women who were capable of expressing women's needs as workers or whether they were just political appointments to provide "window dressing". Others felt it made little difference having men or women negotiating on behalf of workers, although they noted that, while male colleagues were rhetorically supportive, this was not always followed up with substantive support.

Representing Diversity

Before moving on it is necessary to note that all the above material relates primarily to Jewish women. Within Na'amat, Arab women have their own section, which was headed by an Arab woman for the first time in 1978. However, in general Arab-Israeli women have limited visibility and voice in both the Histadrut and the broader political culture of Israel.

Furthermore, the Histadrut does not represent Palestinians who live in the occupied territories. Instead, Palestinian women have organised themselves in the form of grass-roots women's committees across the country (Strum, 1992). These committees have, amongst other things, encouraged Palestinian women workers to enrol in independent Palestinian trade unions. Membership by married women has depended on the attitudes of husbands, who dislike women participating in gender-integrated groups. Objections were also raised by families who did not want their unmarried daughters to join male organisations. In response, women committee leaders have set up union centres in their own homes where only women unionists meet. Approximately five per cent of Palestinian women workers from the occupied territories were unionised compared to 17 per cent of men (Strum, 1992, pp. 59–65).

The institutionalisation of a separate division for women has, over time, become the primary means by which the labour movement addresses the "woman question" in Israel. Although women's issues are provided with a political space within the labour movement in Israel, it is a space that lacks autonomy and resources. Both Na'amat and the Department for Salaried Women remain marginal to the decision-making process of the Histadrut and their role, particularly in the case of Na'amat, has often been defined in terms of the national interest rather than in reference to the interests of women workers. Channelling protests (including women's), into a manageable division is a tactic used often by the Histadrut. Its electoral system allows for internal opposition, thereby diverting workers' opposition away from expression through the formation of separate organisations. This has left the Histadrut's monopoly largely unchallenged and the women's sections have certainly proved to be no threat to Histadrut unity.

With the adoption of quotas being pushed by women unionists and women politicians alike, the numbers of women on local labour councils and workers' committees have begun to increase. Quotas have also been pursued at higher levels within the Histadrut but adherence has been less diligent. In addition, because workers' committees are not linked to the Histadrut, the women's quota implemented at worker committee level has not challenged male dominance further up the Histadrut hierarchy. Indeed, women officials within Na'amat and the Department for Salaried Women are party representatives, rather than women promoted from the shop floor through the ranks of the various trade unions. Thus, the process of interest redefinition has been dominated by those within the governing political party.

Women's Wages

Between 1954 and 1993, women's labour force participation in Israel increased from 21 per cent to 43.4 per cent (ILO, 1994). Considerable growth occurred during the 1970s in response to the expansion of financial, public and community services following the 1967 war (Izraeli, 1994, p. 304). These participation rates vary considerably according to ethnicity, with considerably more European-American Jewish women than African-Asian Jewish women in paid work. In 1985, the participation by Arab women was 11 per cent, although, once married, participation in paid work by these women becomes less acceptable (Rakba, 1991, p. 189).

Regardless of ethnicity, large numbers of women predominate in a small number of occupations, such as clerical, service and semi-professional positions. Women public employees predominate in the tertiary sector, while in the primary sector, which has considerable industrial strength, the presence of women is marginal. Even within the military, women are occupationally segregated. Of the 790 military occupational classifications, only 210 are open for women, most of them clerical and largely unskilled (Ehrlich, 1980; Yuval-Davis, 1985, p. 662).

In terms of wage equality, women do not fare well in the state of Israel. A study of gender differences in wages undertaken in 1980, indicated that women in the public sector earned 78 per cent of their male counterparts. The study also showed that, if women were paid the same as men for their human capital, their income would be two per cent more than men's (Izraeli, 1991, p. 171). In 1992, the gender-wage gap had widened to 30–35 per cent (Efroni, 1994). More generally, Histadrut figures indicate that 65 per cent of those who earn $500 (US) a month are women, while women comprise only 9 per cent of those earning $2500 (US) a month. Seventy per cent of working women earn the minimum wage (Levavi, 1991).

Collective Bargaining Strategies

Before entering a bargaining round, the trade union department formulates a wage policy, which includes a blanket increase in wages and benefits and, sometimes, additional benefits targeted toward low income earners (Brauer, 1990, p. 639). Economy-wide framework agreements are concluded every two years for each sector. A cost of living allowance is granted to workers according to a general collective agreement negotiated between the Histadrut and the Coordinating Bureau of the Economic Organisations (the employers' umbrella organisation). National level collective agreements are also made for specific industries, occupations or large firms (Shalev, 1992, p. 26).

The Minister of Labour has the legal power to extend a specific general collective agreement, or part of it, to include other workers. This practice, combined with the frequent enactment into law of key provisions of central agreements, assures that particular conditions are applied universally. It also frees the Histadrut from needing to organise all workplaces, although there has been no real need to do so with the Sick Fund providing a guaranteed membership.

Despite the appearance of centralisation, a significant degree of wage determination takes place at sub-national level. This arrangement has not always been acceptable to the Histadrut. However, its desire to represent

Israel

the totality of labour meant, by the 1980s, national wage settlements were accepted as the floor above which workers could expect to obtain additional benefits through negotiation at the plant level. Negotiation locally has also been considered by employers to provide flexibility in times of high inflation (Brauer, 1990, p. 647). Thus, workers' committees at the plant and enterprise level have become responsible for negotiating wage supplements, such as seniority pay, productivity bonuses, fringe benefits and overtime payments.

Such decentralisation is viewed as problematic for women wage earners. Anecdotal evidence suggests that the allocation of fringe benefits can sometimes account for up to 40 per cent of net earnings (Izraeli, 1991, p. 171). Within the various financial industries, fringe benefits can contribute to a gender-wage differential of up to 46 per cent for those in full-time work. In this industry, fringe benefits may include not only the standard car and overtime payments, but also loans on easy terms, bonuses and profit allocations (Efroni, 1994, p. 5). Vertical segregation has meant that few women have been entitled to these benefits and this has been exacerbated by the often arbitrary issue of lower job rankings for women (Efroni 1988 cited in Izraeli, 1991, p. 171). While the *Equal Opportunity Law* (1981) outlawed employers advertising positions or vocational training in a gender-specific manner several women unionists indicated this had not prevented the allocation of gendered job titles within the workplace. Women's work was often graded as unskilled whereas men's was graded as skilled, even when the work was similar in nature (Benson and Harverd, 1988, p. 18).

Several strategies were being employed to regulate the allocation of fringe benefits. Trade union women were collecting statistics, undertaking surveys of their members and monitoring agreements made at the workplace level to gain a clearer picture of this phenomenon. Threats of strike action had also been made in an effort to obtain a more equitable allocation of fringe benefits in collective agreements.

The Department for Salaried Women consulted monthly with women representatives from labour councils regarding the nature and implementation of collective agreements. However, a stronger representation of women and their issues at the workplace was considered necessary for any real change to occur. While the Department met regularly with groups of women at the workplace level, it did not have the resources to monitor all collective agreements signed at workplace level.

At national level, the Department for Salaried Women worked with women unionists from a variety of unions in negotiations over collective agreements. However, the ability of the Department to influence the Histadrut's stance on particular issues during the negotiation process did not appear significant. Efroni has claimed that the Histadrut failed to investigate recent research indicating a widening of the gender-wage differential (Efroni, 1994, p. 4). She argued that, while the Histadrut might have had good reasons for not publicly showing any interest in the gender-wage differential, this in itself was worrying, considering the organisation signed general wage agreements which applied to both women and men. Efroni's own research suggested that wage agreements for the years 1988–1992 had disadvantaged those at lower levels (many of whom were women). A wage increase of 23 per cent for all workers had actually translated into an increase of 32 per cent for higher level workers and an increase of only 9 per cent for those at lower levels (Efroni, 1994, p. 2).

Strike action has been used by women to pursue more general wage claims. Between 1992–94, the teachers' union (which is independent of the Histadrut), and the nurses' union, undertook several strikes over wages and conditions and, in doing so, achieved considerable gains for their women workers. Advances in wages had also been made for physiotherapists, pharmacists and social workers through strike action. In many of these cases, support from other women's organisations such as Na'amat and the Israel Women's Network had been forthcoming in the form of public demonstrations and press releases.

The use of the strikes has not been restricted to public sector unions. In early 1994, sewing workers in three textile factories went on strike over the inadequacy of minimum wages. During this strike, the Department for Salaried Women supported the union with legal advisory assistance. In 1995, women workers in a textile factory in an Arab village won a 30 per cent wage rise and improved working conditions after a three year struggle and four strikes (The Guardian, 1995). This struggle was led by a 23 year old Arab seamstress, who was hailed by trade union leaders as having achieved what most trade unions have failed to do - that is make a major industrial group comply with the minimum wage law.

While strikes were "windows of opportunity" for some workers, for others in industries not strategically placed or for those not organised, this kind of action has been less feasible. Furthermore, while economy-wide wage restraint policies were attempted by the Histadrut, its simultaneous acceptance of certain trade unions avoiding such restraint has undermined the possibility of closing the gender-wage gap.

Israel

Labour Laws and Legislative Strategies

In Israel, labour legislation has set out basic standards that apply to all workers and employers. The *Equal Pay Act* (1964) provided that women be paid a wage equal to that of their male counterparts when undertaking the same work. However, this law has not succeeded in achieving any significant reduction in the gender-wage differential. In recent years, the attention of women unionists has become focused on extending the definition of wages within this legislation to include fringe benefits.

Na'amat, the Department for Salaried Women and the Israel Women's Network viewed lobbying the government as an important strategy in the fight to acquire amendments to the *Equal Pay Act* (1964). The lobbying process was undertaken both independently and through the Parliamentary (Knesset) Committee on the Status of Women. Women unionists had held meetings with the Minister of Labour (in 1994 this post was held by a woman) and the Minister of Finance but, as at the end of 1994, petitions regarding the fringe benefits amendment had failed. While women unionists noted that "it only required adding one sentence so it reads equal pay for equal work and fringe benefits", the Minister of Finance claimed that such an amendment would be too expensive.

In addition to the issue of equal pay, women unionists raised the importance of the minimum wage. Women constitute 70 per cent of those on minimum wages in Israel. Legislation provides for a minimum wage and defines how it is to be calculated. In general, the minimum is set at 45 per cent of the average wage, does not include fringe benefits and is updated annually (Histadrut, 1994, p. 11). However, token supervision by the Histadrut at the workplace often meant workers were not paid the required minimum. This had a significant impact on many Israeli Arab women who worked jobs characterised by very low wages, no overtime pay, no social benefits and little or no recreation or sick leave (Rakba, 1991, p. 189). While many firms paid the minimum wage, some did not while others paid a daily minimum wage (based on a full working week), but then restricted the number of days available for work.

The Histadrut itself has been implicated in the exploitation of Arab women workers, who provide a cheap and often unorganised labour source for Histadrut-owned textile and electronics factories. Na'amat acknowledged the problems these women faced, but has been unable to provide any effective opposition, either through the Histadrut or as a pressure group in its own right. The role of Na'amat in this sense has been complicated by the fact that in many instances Na'amat was instrumental in bringing Jewish factories into villages to provide employers with low cost labour. At the same time, this employment provided at least some economic security for Arab women (Pope, 1991, p. 229). This highlights the contradictory solidarities being constituted - with Na'amat attempting to support both the national interest and the interest of Arab women workers.

Several women unionists argued that the implementation and enforcement of legislation remained the most pressing problem. Implementation was dependent on individual women claiming their entitlements if they were not already being provided. Workers' committees were an avenue for women's wages grievances, but a number of unionists noted that few women pursued their complaints for fear of being labelled troublemakers. Nor was it obvious that the male-dominated workers' committees were supportive of women's claims. Representatives from both Na'amat and the Department for Salaried Women have sought to encourage women to pursue issues of unequal pay and poor working conditions through the labour courts. However, with unemployment rates much higher for women than for men, and with work often being scarce in development towns and Arab villages, many women refused to lodge complaints. Arab women in particular were often hesitant to go to court, as raising their profile in public ran counter to traditional views on the behaviour of women. The Arab Section of the Histadrut had organised courses and seminars for workers' committees and had distributed literature in Arabic, to inform Arab workers, including women, of their rights to a minimum standard of wages and conditions.

Both Na'amat and the Department for Salaried Women saw their role as educating women in the workplace of their rights. They provided lectures, seminars and information leaflets on how to be "legally literate". Also significant was the legal service provided by Na'amat through 40 offices nationwide, where woman could obtain free legal advice on any matter of concern. If a case was likely to set a legal precedent, Na'amat represented the woman in the labour court. In 1994, this service was being reviewed with the hope of expansion to provide fuller services including blanket (rather than selective) legal representation at a reduced cost. While few wage cases had been decided by the labour court, precedent cases were considered by Na'amat to be important in providing benchmarks on interpreting legislation and in gaining media publicity on the role and achievements of Na'amat.

Other Strategies

The notion of comparative worth is not included in the *Equal Pay Act* (1964). Comparing wage structures has been difficult because wage data is based on average income, which included fringe benefits and overtime, the components of which differ between women and men. Detailed data has begun to be collected and several women unionists regarded this as an important step; in their view such data was necessary in testing and confirming the principles of equal pay. However, while separate wage scales exist for women and men within collective agreements, comparative worth analyses were likely to have minimal impact on women's wages.

Women's professional advancement and occupational upgrading were considered by white-collar women unionists as necessary for achieving wage equality. Seniority and promotion were important components of wage determination (including pension benefits) and in the past have accounted for between 30 and 50 percent of income (Benson and Harverd, 1988, p. 17).

Na'amat and several individual unions were concerned with the issue of professionalism offered their workers courses and seminars on the relevance of professionalism to promotion. Courses have also been offered to both Arab and Jewish women in management training, small business operation, and assertiveness, with some programs co-sponsored by business. However, Na'amat officials acknowledged that such strategies only helped those women in jobs with a career path.

While providing women workers with better access to training was considered to be an important strategy for promotion, union support for this has not always been forthcoming. Recently, a class action suit was taken by women flight attendants working for Israel's national airline (El Al). The women involved maintained they were being excluded from an all-male training course, completion of which was a necessary requirement for promotion. While the Department for Salaried Women supported the case from within the Histadrut, the union movement as a whole did not support the women, nor did their male colleagues. Indeed, male flight attendants appealed that the court allow them to participate as defendants with the employer. This right was granted, allowing the men of El Al to unite across class lines to counter women's claim to equal opportunity (Izraeli, 1994, p. 319).

Although the collective bargaining process in Israel appears centralised, with general wage policies being agreed on at national level, the most relevant negotiations take place at the local level with the Histadrut demonstrating little commitment to a solidaristic wage policy. The motivations for this are historical and related to the desire of the Histadrut to represent the totality of Jewish labour. The result has been a considerable gender-wage differential for women workers in Israel; one that is continuing to widen.

In many instances, women do not make up a critical mass in a unionised workplace and may not be unionised at all. For this reason, and because the Histadrut has failed to see equal pay for women as a significant industrial issue, women in trade unions have looked to gender-specific legislative strategies as a remedy. To date, however, implementation and enforcement mechanisms have been limited and, since little support from the Histadrut and national trade unions has been forthcoming, class actions are rare. Instead, women must pursue their grievances individually. While Na'amat provides legal advice to women, few actually take their case to the labour court, preferring low pay to the likely alternative of unemployment.

Women's Working Conditions

Several Israeli scholars have argued that Israel is a family-centred society with most women marrying and becoming mothers (Azmon and Izraeli 1992; Herzog, 1996; Izraeli, 1994). Indeed marriage and motherhood are cited to be "social imperatives" (Izraeli, 1994, p. 311). Ben Gurion, first Prime Minister of the State of Israel, noted that,

> First, women have a special mission as mothers. There is no greater mission in life ...... However, a second factor must be remembered: the woman is not only a woman, but a personality in her own right, in the same way as a man. As such, she should enjoy the same rights and responsibilities as the man, except where motherhood is concerned (cited in Yuval-Davis, 1985, p. 670).

The *Equal Rights Act* (1951) gave women formal equality, but at the same time conceived of them as mothers, preserving both national unity and traditional family life (Herzog, 1996). In terms of participation in the military, women do so only temporarily before embarking on marriage and motherhood (Yuval-Davis, 1985, p. 671).

It is not surprising, given this context, that considerable emphasis in Israeli public policy has been placed on the protection of mothers. While Israel has not had a comprehensive natal policy (partly to avoid encouraging Arab reproduction), there has existed a comprehensive health service, which for many years was supplemented with minimal information concerning family planning options (Ehrlich, 1980, p. 95). Indeed, Israel has more publicly funded *in vitro* fertilisation clinics per capita than any other country (Izraeli, 1994, p. 311).

As early as 1954, women were provided with three months paid maternity leave and were then entitled to nine months unpaid leave or could resign and receive severance pay. Employers were prevented from firing pregnant women and nursing mothers were allowed to work an hour less without pay deductions (Raday, 1991; Safir, 1991). Maternity leave began as a universal benefit, but is now linked to labour force participation. Some public and Histadrut sector collective agreements have also permitted mothers of small children to work a shorter day at the employers expense and use part of their own sick leave to care for children (Izraeli, 1994; Raday, 1991). In 1994, special provisions for women (as potential mothers) were still included in collective agreements and were seen by some unions as indicating their support of women in the paid labour force.

Izraeli has argued that women in Israel have been successful in "creating a support structure for encouraging women's labour force participation including high quality child care" (Izraeli, 1994, p. 318). A network of child care centres exists for working Jewish mothers with children aged between six months and four years. However, 90 per cent of these are provided by women's organisations including Na'amat, and are only partly subsidised by the state, with payment for these services means-tested (Pope, 1991, p. 229). Those women earning the average wage pay nearly 20 per cent of their monthly income per child in child care costs. Several women unionists argued that this expense acted as a disincentive for women to enter the paid labour force in a full-time capacity.

The notion that women should only work part-time has been reinforced by the length of the school day; four hours in the morning for primary school children. Most women unionists considered the length of the school day to be significant in the choices women made regarding labour market participation, while many educated women have chosen teaching jobs in an effort to synchronise paid work with children's school schedules (Izraeli, 1994, p. 312).

Women and Trade Unions

The Department for Salaried Women has made written and verbal policy submissions on the issue of reducing the cost of child care. The Department argued that, from an economic perspective, restricting women's labour force participation to part-time work was a waste of educational resources. Rhetorically, Government Ministers have shown an interest in the issue of child care but women unionists argued that national security and economic stability continued to be the major policy priorities, precluding further state expenditure on child care. Neither child care nor the length of the school day was seen by the Histadrut as a union issue and so support for reform in these areas has been limited.

Equal Employment Opportunities

From the mid-1970s, women argued less for legislation concerning women's responsibilities as mothers and the protection of women, focussing instead on equal opportunity provisions. The *Equal Opportunity Act* (1981) criminally prohibited discrimination on account of sex, marital or parental status. It also outlawed employers advertising jobs or vocational training unless they were described in terms addressed to both sexes (Izraeli, 1994).

After considerable lobbying from women both within and outside of the labour movement, this law was amended in 1988 to extend the provisions previously granted to working mothers to working fathers. Entitlement to severance pay when resigning to care for a new born or adopted baby can be transferred to the father; statutory leave without pay is transferable; and fathers may also use their sick leave to look after children. Under this legislation, sexual harassment is also prohibited. In addition, legislation passed in 1987 stipulated the retirement age for men and women be the same and removed the prohibition on night work, although women still have the right to refuse night work and to retire earlier than men (Raday, 1991).

While equal employment legislation bans discrimination on the basis of marital status, the issue of marriage had a heightened relevance for Arab women workers. Over 50 per cent of Arab women stop work after marriage for traditional cultural reasons. According to the law, when a worker is dismissed, or if the worker resigned under special circumstances (such as having a baby), he/she is entitled to receive one month's wages for each year of service. However, marriage is not covered under the law as a special circumstance and, as a result, individual complaints cannot be taken to the labour court for resolution. Instead, the Arab Section of the Histadrut had sought to convince the employers to provide compensation voluntarily; a strategy which was only sometimes successful.

Despite the presence of equal opportunity laws, women workers were still subject to discrimination. Sexual harassment was considered a critical issue by women unionists, particularly for women in the army, but it had yet to gain a high profile and many women were afraid to lodge complaints. Nor was it uncommon for employers to sack women workers after they returned from maternity leave. Although women were encouraged by Na'amat to make a case for unfair dismissal in the labour court, the court would seldom force an employer to reinstate a worker, preferring instead to order financial compensation, thereby leaving the woman jobless.

Women unionists viewed their laws as progressive but lamented the ineffective enforcement mechanisms. The *Equal Employment Opportunity Act* (1988) did not establish agencies to implement the principle of equality. Rather, the labour courts have remained the major means of implementation, and it has been up to women themselves, albeit with the support of Na'amat and the Department for Salaried Women, to initiate the judicial process. To date, few cases have been forthcoming. During the 1980s, judges in the labour courts were rarely supportive of the discrimination claims filed by women (Izraeli, 1994, p. 319). Furthermore, as a result of the hostile reaction of many union representatives and employers to women's actions, women have been hesitant to proceed with a case (Pope, 1991; Raday, 1991).

Until the mid-1970s, the development of supply side policies around women's labour market participation was provided more for paternalistic reasons than through an egalitarian desire to redress gender inequality. In the late 1970s, women workers began to view existing protections as restrictive and sought new legislation around equal employment opportunities. However, although family-oriented policies have been extended to include both women and men, the focus of both employers and the union movement is one which continues to view all women as "candidates for the 'mommy track'" (Izraeli, 1994, p. 318). That the Histadrut views women's interests in terms of their role as mothers, and as social rather than industrial or economic issues, suggests the labour movement in Israel is continuing to reinforce the marginalisation of gender claims.

In pursuing equal employment opportunities, women unionists have not looked to the Histadrut or the collective bargaining system for either reform or enforcement. Instead, strategies have been targeted at the judicial process and at Parliament in attempts to gain legislative remedies. However, the lack of implementation and enforcement mechanisms has resulted in little substantive change to women's labour market position. O'Connor (1994) has argued enforcement of anti-discrimination legislation is very much dependent on government and trade union support. For women in Israel, it is not evident that support has been forthcoming from workers' committees, the Histadrut or from the labour court judges.

Conclusion

The Israeli labour movement is one in which class has been overshadowed by Zionism, with the Histadrut oriented more toward the building of an independent Jewish homeland than the representation of a unified class interest. Indeed, the whole notion of a unified class interest was initially undermined both ideologically, through labourist links with Zionism, and institutionally, through the exclusion and then segregation of Arab workers by the Histadrut. To some extent, women in Israel have also been marginalised by the Histadrut. While Jewish women were never made to feel politically isolated from the labour movement in Israel, they were often excluded from the labour force. The mix of exclusion from paid work and inclusion as wives meant women (re)constituted their interests accordingly, focusing their attention through their separate organisation on voluntary work rather than on issues relevant to women in the paid labour force.

Women in pre-state Israel organised collectively but separate from their men. With the creation of the Histadrut and the need for consolidation in the process of nation building, women aligned their organisations with the centralised labour organisation. The corporatist mode of interest articulation that emerged in Israel has made women's divisions within the Histadrut dependent on political parties, thereby discouraging the establishment of an independent women's movement. While forming solidarities within existing corporatist institutions has been accepted by union women, the fact that neither the Department for Salaried Women nor Na'amat are core or powerful sections within the Histadrut, has meant women's issues have yet to gain currency in the industrial arena. Gender-specific strategies and mobilisation were deemed necessary to address the labour movement's neglect but these solidarities have never seriously challenged the overarching objective of an encompassing Jewish labour movement.

Whitehouse has argued that women's employment is by definition "a class issue where politicisation of conflict and a proclivity for interventionist strategies may facilitate more egalitarian outcomes" (Whitehouse, 1995, p. 16). Trade unionism is a necessary component in this process. However, the Histadrut's lack of focus on class interests is highlighted by the marginal role played by the trade union department within the Histadrut. The Histadrut's administration of the Sick Fund guaranteed its membership, negating the requirement to organise, or be accountable to workers.

It is not surprising, given the weakness of trade unionism in Israel, that women have seldom looked to the Histadrut *per se* to redress the equality imbalance. Rather, gender-specific legislation has been the major means through which women have sought to have gender inequality addressed. However, women's inclusion into the paid labour force and the labour movement has been specifically defined as part of the national cause rather than a class cause. To a large extent it appears that this broader solidarity created around national Jewish identity has overshadowed and undermined the usefulness of both class-based and gender-specific strategies in pursuing the claims of women.

6 Sweden

Introduction

Much of the literature on Sweden refers to a "Swedish model". There are numerous views as to what this represents: a mode of regulation (Lane, 1991); pragmatism in policy development (Heclo and Madsen, 1987); compromise, consensus and corporatism (Sainsbury, 1991); public sector expansion and a universal welfare state (Premfors, 1991). The model is also portrayed as one that has provided women with considerable gender equality. Eduards has argued that the Swedish "gender model" includes a conception of equality in the labour market, the home and the political decision-making process, which has made it easier for women to put demands onto the political agenda. But Eduards suggests this conception of equality, while appearing gender-neutral in form, has left unchallenged the possible existence of a conflict of interests between women and men (Eduards, 1991, pp. 169–170).

In this chapter I investigate the extent to which the context set by this gender model has influenced the demands and solidarities of women trade unionists. It becomes apparent that women have seen the labour movement as an ally in their efforts to further the interests of women in the labour force. However, many features of the Swedish (gender) model have come under threat with the shift to a more decentralised wage bargaining system, recent cuts to welfare state provision and increasing unemployment. This has led to the remobilisation of women around the identity of gender which, while not completely overriding class, has highlighted the particularity of what have in the past been considered gender-neutral reforms and universal class strategies.

The Labour Movement in Sweden

Due to the late arrival of industrialisation in Sweden, it was not until the 1870s that a fully-fledged trade union movement developed, and 1898 that the Swedish Confederation of Trade Unions was established. The movement was reformist in orientation, with trade unions constituting the "backbone of the Swedish Social Democratic Party from its inception in 1889" (Higgins, 1985, p. 365). The intimate connection between party and trade union continued with the party actively promoting unionisation and trade unions stressing the importance of both suffrage and economic rights (Higgins, 1985). The symbiotic relationship between both "branches" of the labour movement became the cornerstone of the hegemonic position established by the Social Democratic government between 1932 and 1976 (Olsson, 1994, p. 46). The Social Democrats governed again between 1982 and 1991 and were re-elected in 1994.

Trade unions were involved in corporatist political arrangements established for policy-making purposes at the local level long before the arrival of a Social Democratic government. For example, in 1902 both employers and the labour movement were represented on the boards that operated local labour exchanges and, by 1920, the labour movement was involved nationally in policy development and implementation through its representation on the Insurance and Labour Councils (Rothstein, 1991, pp. 157–160). The board of most significance for the labour movement has been the 16 member National Labour Market Board (set up in 1948) which, until recently, had seven trade union representatives as members (Ahrne and Clement, 1994, pp. 232–234).

Despite these corporatist developments, the first thirty years of this century were littered with class conflicts, and high unemployment in the early 1920s weakened the bargaining position of trade unions (Korpi, 1978, p. 80). The beginning of consensus politics came with the signing of the *Saltsjöbaden* Agreement in 1938 between LO and the Swedish Employers Association (SAF). The aim of the agreement was to encourage negotiation and co-operation between both parties (without state intervention), with a view to reducing industrial conflict and providing an environment conducive to sustained economic growth.

The 1938 agreement paved the way for centralised wage bargaining to emerge in the 1950s. Between 1955 and 1965, the wage negotiation process was dominated by LO and SAF and their agreements served as the norm for the rest of the labour market (Olsson, 1991, p. 39). During this period, full employment and equality were the central goals that underpinned the development of LO's economic policy program, which linked centralised wage bargaining with an active labour market policy. According to the Rehn-Meidner plan, wage solidarity would equalise wages across the economy, reducing differentials to the minimum required to adequately compensate workers. Over time this equalisation would put pressure on less efficient firms to either adapt or shut down. The provision by government of policies to facilitate full employment combined with uniform wages would further accelerate modernisation by reducing worker resistance to firm rationalisation and redundancy while avoiding inflation (Rowthorn, 1992, p. 114).

Wage solidarity involved nation-wide wage increases, and special increases for low wage earners to narrow differentials. This strategy was supplemented with highly progressive taxes designed to contribute to the redistribution process through the provision of universal social policies (Milner, 1990, p. 106). Considerable expansion in the social sector included increases in funding for existing programs and the addition of new ones. Universal benefits were provided in areas of health, education, housing and pensions (Heclo et al, 1987). Thus wage solidarity was both an instrument of economic efficiency and an expression of the egalitarian goals of Swedish social democracy, while full employment was seen by trade unions as "critical to a person's welfare and sense of belonging" (Tilton, 1991, p. 277).

One result of the rapid growth of the welfare state was an increase in public sector employment, supplemented by a parallel increase in private sector white-collar employment. This changing occupational structure enabled white-collar unionism to become a stronger force, centralisation continued as the norm. From 1952, white-collar unions began negotiating centrally with the employers and, by 1974, over 70 per cent of the white-collar employees in Sweden were organised (Olsson, 1991, p. 39). The major white-collar union confederation, the Central Organisation of Salaried Employees (TCO), established in 1944 has, over time, become quite powerful. By the end of the 1980s, its three bargaining cartels were negotiating for approximately the same wage sum as LO (Åmark, 1992). Professionals are represented through the Swedish Confederation of Professional Associations (SACO). Despite this blue/white-collar split, the trade union movement has reflected the nature of Swedish society, remaining relatively homogenous, with no major divisions along religious, ethnic or political lines (although TCO and SACO are not partisan like LO).

In the mid 1980s, employers sought to move away from centralised bargaining and began to press strongly for negotiations with individual trade unions on a decentralised basis. At the same time, the government began to indirectly intervene in public sector negotiations in an effort to emphasise its desire for low inflation. This was an unusual step since the labour market was always considered to be a designated union/employer domain. In general, the 1980s were characterised by high profits, high wage drift, inflation and industrial conflict. The combination of these factors, and the decision by employers in 1990 not to participate in centralised negotiations, suggested an end to the infamous Swedish model (Meidner, 1994, p. 341).

The labour movement in Sweden has, since its origins, been committed to creating a society where workers could participate on equal terms. In the process of implementing such equality, the trade union movement has focused on broad industrial issues while the Social Democratic government has supplemented economic outcomes with social ones. Recently however, women in Swedish trade unions have begun to challenge whether the social democratic project does indeed provide equality of participation for all citizens, both men and women.

Women's Representation in the Swedish Union Movement

The underlying basis of Swedish unionism has been an explicit class politics. While the "woman question" was highlighted in the 1880s by Clara Zetkin as a vital element of socialist politics, this position was subsumed by the general feeling that women's liberation would be resolved with working class liberation (Dahlström and Liljeström, 1983, p. 11). Claims were made for a universal, classless politics, but it was the needs of working class men that dominated the agenda of the labour movement.

Separate organising by women's groups was seen as a bourgeois threat to working class solidarity in Sweden. Women in LO and the Social Democratic Party (SAP) were loathe to call themselves feminists and instead formed support organisations to the male-run unions and parties (Hirdman, 1994). Women in blue-collar occupations initially organised themselves into women-only unions, but these were soon absorbed by male unions. Women's union membership in LO rose from ten per cent in 1920 to 17 per cent in 1930, then remained stagnant until the mid 1940s (Qvist et al, 1984). In the white-collar sector, women had created national trade unions for nurses, school teachers, women in the postal and telecommunications service and academic women. These women-only unions existed until amalgamations began around 1955, by which time women's membership in TCO had reached approximately 40 per cent

Women and Trade Unions

(Qvist, 1985).

The post-war growth in women's labour force participation was reflected in substantial increases in women's membership in both LO and TCO from 1945 onwards (see Table 6.1).

Figure 6.1 Increases in Women's Union Membership, LO and TCO

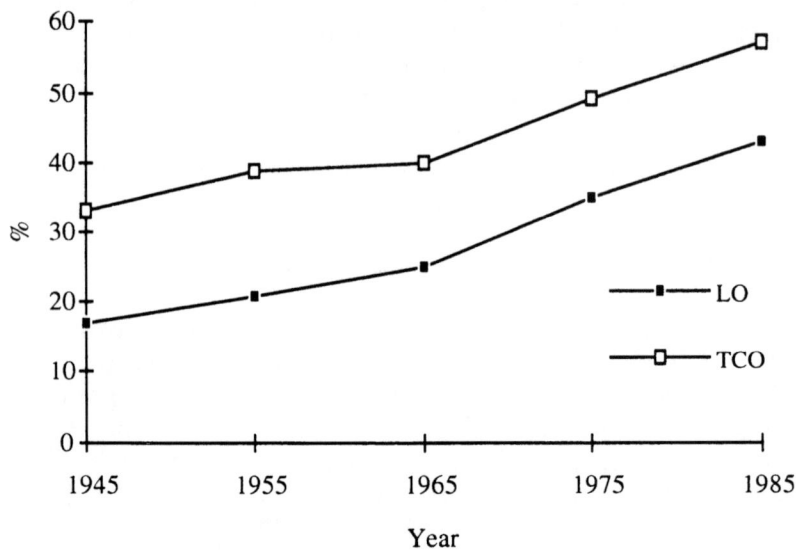

Source: Bergqvist (1991, p. 111).

These upward trends in women's union membership persuaded trade unions of the need to represent the interests of their women members. In 1947, the LO Women's Council was formed and in 1948, it initiated educational training courses for women. The founding of the Council was followed by the establishment of women's committees in LO's district organisations. In 1951, LO and SAF set up the Joint Women's Labour Council, designed to encourage the entry of more women into the labour force. In 1962, TCO followed LO's lead, establishing a Women's Council, and in 1967 joined the LO-SAF Joint Women's Council (Qvist et al, 1984, p. 264).

During the 1960s, the requirement to better accommodate women workers in the labour market, and in trade unions, stimulated a debate on the concept of sex roles. It was argued that a change in the position of women, both at home and in working life, could never be accomplished without simultaneous change in men's lives (Baude, 1978, p. 155). In 1969, the Social Democratic Party adopted a program that reflected an emerging consensus that men would have to assume equal responsibility for family life, if women were to assume equality in the workplace. Men, too, were to strive for equality - equality as parents (Qvist et al, 1984, p. 266). Thus, a new concept of equality was embraced (*jämställdhet*), representing the equal standing of both men and women in all areas of social life (Acker, 1994, p. 9).

Within the union movement, this move away from ideas of an exclusive women's interest, and toward an inclusion of men, led both the TCO and the LO to abolish their women's divisions, and establish instead equality committees or councils for family policy. The Joint Labour Women's Council was abolished in the early 1970s.

Despite the insistence on equality, women have remained under-represented in the union hierarchies in Sweden. Bergqvist's data indicate that while there has been an increase in women's representation, particularly during the period 1975-1985, compared to their proportion of membership, women remain under-represented at all three levels (see the ratio columns in Tables 6.1 and 6.2).

Table 6.1 Percentage and Representational Ratio* of Women in Upper Levels of LO

Year	LO Congress		General Assembly		Executive Board	
	%	Ratio	%	Ratio	%	Ratio
1945	1	0.06	1	0.05	0	0
1955	5	0.2	2	0.09	0	0
1965	5	0.15	1.5	0.05	0	0
1975	13	0.27	6	0.13	0	0
1985	25	0.43	14	0.22	7	0.09

* see below Table 6.2.
Source: Bergqvist (1991, pp. 112-115).

Table 6.2 Percentage and Representational Ratio* of Women in Upper Levels of TCO

Year	Congress %	Ratio	TCO General Assembly %	Ratio	Executive Board %	Ratio
1945	14	0.3	16	0.38	14	0.45
1955	19	0.37	22	0.46	22	0.46
1965	17	0.3	17	0.3	20	0.37
1975	20	0.25	16	0.2	14	0.17
1985	39	0.48	35	0.4	18	0.16

*Bergqvist labels this an index and has calculated it as follows:

$X = \dfrac{\text{Number of female representatives/number of female members}}{\text{Number of male representatives/number of male members}}$

$X = 1$ indicates proportional representation; $X>1$ indicates over representation and $X<1$ indicates under-representation.

Source: Bergqvist (1991, pp. 112–115).

Within LO, there has been a general increase in the ratio over time at Congress, Assembly and Board level, with a slight downturn occurring between 1955 and 1965. The amalgamation of several smaller unions into larger ones during the 1950s arguably resulted in the decline in women's representation in decision-making positions within LO (Qvist et al, 1984). However, in the 1960s women's representation rates began to rise again, despite continued amalgamations. It has been suggested that this may have resulted from women becoming a large minority within a new union, and increasing female membership overall (Bergqvist, 1991). As at 1994, there were two women on the LO Executive Board.

Within TCO, women's representation has increased at Congress and Assembly level over the last forty years, but this has not yet matched women's proportion of the membership. Indeed, during the 1970s, there was a drop in the ratio to below the levels reached in the 1950s.

Most remarkable is the ratio for the Executive Board in TCO where, since 1945, women's position has been consistently weakened whereas, in relation to their share of membership, men have strengthened their position. The Executive Board, while not the highest decision-making body in a formal sense, does have more power informally, in that Board members are more involved in the implementation of the union agenda

(Bergqvist 1991, p. 113).

Amalgamations have also occurred within TCO, with early all-female unions being absorbed by other unions. This process meant women's representational role within the TCO hierarchy decreased continuously until amalgamations ended after 1975 (Bergqvist, 1991). The absorption of women-only unions, while providing a greater influence for new unions generally, also allowed for a growing male influence over issues that concerned women (Nielsson, 1994; Qvist et al, 1984). This, combined with the dominance of men on the Executive Board, undermines the general assumption that TCO has been a more "woman-friendly" union confederation because its membership is predominantly female (Bergqvist, 1991, p. 114).

In addition, amalgamations may have been harmful to women's representation at lower levels of both LO and TCO hierarchies. Three-quarters of all union branches disappeared between 1960 and 1975. This led to a decrease in the proportion of women officials, since women tended to be more active at local level (Scott, 1982, p. 53). Recently, the under-representation of women at lower levels in the union hierarchy has become less pronounced. In 1994, in the Municipal Workers' Union, 80 per cent of members were women, while 60 per cent of the organisers and shop stewards were women. Within the Metal Workers' Union, 12 per cent of the members were women compared to 14 per cent female shop stewards. Several white-collar unions with approximately 50 per cent female membership manifested an almost proportional representation at the local level.

Combating Union Culture

Trade union culture has been described as particularly male and dominated by the "traditional view of a worker - a white man who works full-time". This prevailing culture was perceived by women unionists to have made it more difficult for women to combine union activities with family responsibilities. Women sometimes felt participation was difficult, with too many meetings, too late at night. Combining a union job with marriage and small children was quoted as

> a hell of a job. It involves travelling two to three days a week, and you have to live with your calendar. I still feel guilty and I worry when I am away from my children even though they are being looked after.

Several unions had sought to reorganise meetings to make them more accessible to women by changing meeting times and having smaller group meetings that were less confrontational and less hostile. Changing the type of language used was also seen as important for creating a more woman-friendly environment – "the old male union culture uses very stilted language, which is foreign to many women".

Other unions have provided support for women on boards, and have organised conferences on female leadership and assertiveness. Recently, within the Metal Workers' Union, there has been a more active policy of encouraging groups of women onto the board. This shift was based on the view that the more women were represented as a group, the easier it would become to undermine the male culture.

> If a woman is isolated, she may decide to leave if the culture is too difficult to deal with alone. Being only one woman amongst nine men is tough, but having two or three women with six men makes it much easier.

In the same vein, having women in visible positions was considered crucial to increasing women's participation and representation. Between 1989 and 1995 the largest blue-collar union in Sweden, the Municipal Workers' Union, had a woman chairperson. Women unionists saw this as important in indicating that women could actually take up leadership positions in blue-collar trade unions. While there was a female head of TCO at the time of interviewing, it was too early to assess if her appointment had made an impact on women members.

Dealing with "Women's Questions"

While the under-representation of women in trade unions was considered a problem in Sweden, the traditional emphasis on collective bargaining to settle all labour relations questions has contributed to the absence of a strong national affirmative action program. Indeed, strategies involving overt positive action for women were rarely considered. In 1987, the union representing clerical and technical workers in the private sector set the objective of proportional representation of women on the executive board, but, in general, trade unions have appeared ambivalent toward quotas. Neither SACO nor TCO provided special programs to increase women's representation, as this was the responsibility of individual affiliates, although they did undertake a monitoring role in this regard. Recently,

LO's Executive Board decided that all vacant positions within the Confederation should be filled by women. There was also a verbal commitment that, when research committees were set up, 50 per cent of the participants would be women. This was seen as a substantial step for women in an institution that had previously avoided a focus on gender-specific representation.

Several unions had concentrated on education, both as a means of involving more women and of changing both men's and women's attitudes. Within the union for clerical and technical employees, education programs were not explicitly oriented towards increasing women's union participation, but this was the implicit notion motivating the creation of the programs. Education programs were also offered by both LO and their affiliate unions. In 1992, the Metal Workers' Union moved away from technical-type training towards more communication-oriented courses. This was seen to facilitate the acceptance of different perspectives, including women's, and to encourage women to speak out. One woman unionist noted that "we felt this was one way of showing the female members that the union was interested in the same things they were interested in".

To some extent the *Equality Act* (1992) has forced unions to actively address equal access to participation and representation. An employer with more than ten employees must draw up an equality plan each year, which contains an outline of the measures the employer intends to take to facilitate the combination of employment and parenthood, to overcome sex-segregation and to eliminate discrimination with respect to promotion, training, and pay. Many trade unions employ more than ten people and so have been required to submit an annual plan. The results of the implementation process were then listed in the following year's report.

Such legislative intervention was a considerable step for Sweden. Although various labour laws were passed during the 1970s, the union movement and employers have tended to oppose legislation addressing equal employment opportunities. It was a bourgeois government that passed the *Equality Between Women and Men at Work Act* (1979). At that time, a concession was provided to trade unions and employers, preserving the priority of collective agreements, and making the Act only applicable to the few workers not covered by such agreements (Cook et al, 1992). The amended *Equality Act* (1992) had more of an impact in that it provided the Office of the Equality Ombudsman with the power to scrutinise the previously exempt collective agreements.

An official from the Equality Ombudsman's Office argued that trade unions were showing considerable interest in pursuing better strategies for achieving gender equality: "the trade unions see it as a popular issue, and they want to be seen to be working with it". Proportional representation of women was being listed as an objective in the equality plans of several unions and the means for achieving this have included reviewing the numbers of women on the boards and having training sessions for those in charge of candidate selection.

The Strategy of Separate Organising

In an institutional sense, Swedish unions have, since the sixties, avoided acknowledging the existence of a particular woman's interest and instead have concentrated on equality between the sexes as a gender-neutral issue. Equality officers rather than women's officers were the means by which equal opportunity in unions was addressed and not all equality officers within unions were women. Within the Metal Workers' Union, having both men and women working in this area was considered more effective, in that it undermined "sexist male attitudes and made equality questions relevant to men and women". Within the Factory Workers' Union, equality issues were dealt with by men for many years. It was thought that "men would be more likely to listen to other men than to women".

Both major trade union confederations had full-time equality officers, while in SACO, equality was given a third of a position. The Municipal Workers' Union, the Bank Employees' Union and the Union of Clerical and Technical Employees also had full-time equality officers, while the unions representing civil servants, police and medical professionals had delegated half a position to equality issues, which was often shared amongst several people. Between 1978 and 1989, the Metal Workers' Union had a full-time equality officer, but this was changed to become a shared responsibility between four people: two men and two women. Their role has been not only to deal with equality issues, but also to provoke all departments within the Union to consider equality questions when pursuing policy matters.

The strategy of integrating gender analysis has also been adopted by LO. All policy proposals considered by the Executive Board must include an assessment of how they will affect women in particular. To facilitate this process, all staff who work within LO attended training courses to learn how to incorporate a gender dimension into all areas of their work.

Both women and men considered these courses had been successful, while the equality officer in LO felt that not only was this strategy useful in terms of outcomes for women, it also had the potential to further change men's attitudes by providing them with a better understanding of women's position in the workforce.

In the 1980s, the political representation of women (re)surfaced as a contentious issue. In 1986, a high profile commission on women's representation reported on the gender patterns of representation in other commissions and state administrative boards. These institutions are of considerable significance in the corporatist decision-making process in Sweden. The commission found that women were rarely appointed as trade union representatives (Bergqvist, 1995, pp. 211–215).

After the defeat of the Social Democratic Government in 1991, women's representation in Parliament dropped from 38 per cent to 33.5 per cent. This under-representation, combined with the conservative government's intention reduce welfare state and municipal spending and cut public employment, led to considerable disaffection amongst women in the labour movement. Officials in LO recognised the negative consequences this disaffection could have for union membership and undertook considerable research on the extent of women's exclusion from union hierarchies. What was remarkably new about this report was not the content but the title - *Class and Sex* - representing a symbolic abandonment of subordinating gender to class.

Women themselves began to undertake political action in response to what were perceived as threats to their political representation and economic well-being. A separate women's party was touted as both an alternative and a threat to mainstream political parties and, within trade unions, the renewed emphasis on women's representation expressed itself through a substantial increase in women's networks throughout Sweden. Special women's projects were created in each of LO's 17 districts and a number of different kinds of women's groups, seminars and networks were established within several unions. These networks were informal mechanisms to encourage women's participation and facilitate the increase in women's representation within the labour movement. In 1994, women conference delegates from the Metal Workers' Union met before the conference to network for support. This was the first time that women from this Union had officially come together separately. Male unionists interpreted it as a conspiracy and forced the women to find independent funding and meet outside Union headquarters.

Perhaps the most interesting new network to develop has been *Tjejligan* (the "women's gang") established by LO women in 1991. Its objective has been to share news and bring women together to put pressure on the labour movement to address various issues concerning women. In 1994, *Tjejligan* had 14,000 members but remained an informal organisation. Much of its emphasis has been on increasing women's representation within all levels of politics, but particularly within trade unions. A large number of union women were actively involved in the Social Democrats' election campaign in 1991. The aim was to increase women's self-confidence about participation and to maintain a profile on women's issues during the campaign. This was considered a highly successful strategy as many women from *Tjejligan* went on to stand for local government and trade union election.

At the central level of the LO, acceptance of *Tjejligan* has been confirmed by substantial executive financing of *Clara*, a glossy magazine designed specifically for women. When budget cuts occurred throughout the Confederation, there were no funding cuts to women's activities. *Tjejligan* has popularised the slogan "half the power, the whole wage" throughout the union movement and has continued to use its networks to keep newly elected women delegates in touch with rank and file members. In short, *Tjejligan* has sought not only to increase women's representation in trade unions, but also to ensure that women in elected office can work effectively for women's interests (Curtin and Higgins, 1998).

Claims of a universal class politics in Sweden, which initially appeared gender-neutral in character, have been largely exclusive of women. Demands for political equality were not accepted within trade unions themselves and women's under-representation has remained conspicuous. Furthermore, because trade unions are represented on a variety of boards and commissions that participate in the corporatist policy-making process, the invisibility of women in trade union decision-making has been mirrored in these arenas.

Over the years the idea of women representing women has received mixed support within the Swedish labour movement. Although the "woman question" was dealt with in the 1950s by women's officers and women's councils, this gender-specific approach was replaced in the 1960s with a gender-neutral concept of equality between the sexes. Now the political under-representation of women has become a contentious issue and has sparked a renewed emphasis on gender-specific strategies for inclusion by women within the trade union movement.

Women's Wages

Since the 1960s, women in Sweden have been included in the drive for full employment. Women's labour force participation, whether it be in a full-time or part-time capacity, has been embraced by trade unions. In 1995, in both the blue and white-collar sectors, Swedish women were in the position of being more unionised than men: 87.1 per cent of women in the former and 86.3 per cent in the latter were unionised, as against male rates of 84 per cent and 79.8 per cent respectively (Curtin and Higgins, 1998).

As early as 1909, LO provided support, in principle, for equal pay for women but little active support was forthcoming. Implementation was left to individual unions, many of which endorsed a system of separate wages for women. Indeed, distinct female pay scales were supported by the LO secretariat until 1960 (Qvist, 1985). With the increase in women's union membership from the 1930s and the emergence of a competing white-collar confederation, LO integrated women's wages into its overall wage policy. However, because of the lack of coordination amongst LO affiliates regarding wage policy prior to the 1950s, equal pay remained a myth.

In the post-war period, equal pay for women gained a higher profile. The Social Democrats included the issue in their platform in 1944 and, in 1946, the LO Secretariat report on equal pay recommended not only the implementation of equal pay for equal work, but also raising the overall salary levels of women to those of men (Qvist, 1985). A Council of Women and a Women's Ombudsman for LO were created to provide direction for implementation (although both had advisory capacities only).

However, it was the Rehn-Meidner policy of wage solidarity, in place from the 1950s until the 1980s, which had the most significant impact on the gender-wage differential. Women were disproportionately advantaged because they were a substantial proportion of low-wage earners. By 1995, women earned 90 per cent of a man's wage in private sector industry and 84 per cent of a man's wage in the government sector (Statistics Sweden, 1995, p. 56).

Wage Solidarity and Workplace Reform

The intentions of wage solidarity were not gender-specific, and in recent years, further closing of the gender wage gap has stalled. This has been attributed partly to the breakdown in the mid-1980s of centralised wage bargaining. With wage negotiations beginning to occur at sub-national level, alternative strategies have been articulated by blue-collar women, in an effort to maintain a profile on equal pay. The Municipal Workers' Union has worked to make its own local representatives, negotiators and activists more conscious of gender-wage differences. While the equality officer at LO was quietly optimistic about such strategies, she acknowledged there could be implementation problems in industries where there were few women negotiators. As a result, getting more women active and encouraging affiliates to include more women in their negotiating teams has been targeted as the next reform.

The Swedish labour force is one of the most highly segregated in the OECD, with 41 per cent of women working in occupations that are 90 to 100 per cent female and another 35 per cent working in occupations that are 60 to 90 per cent female (Higgins, 1996). New initiatives in the area of workplace reform arguably have the potential to undermine this gender segregation. A number of industries in both the private and public sectors have undertaken organisational change, replacing the emphasis on individual output with a focus on group work and job rotation. Workers participate in direct and indirect production, supervision and are involved in decision-making on all issues related to the internal work of the group. The upgrading of skills and multi-skilling have been the main features of this change (Mahon, 1994, pp. 296–297).

Workplace reform was not initiated as a gender-specific strategy and there is a concern that a gender-neutral approach to work reorganisation will fail to recognise the gender division of labour in reproductive work, which could impinge on women's involvement in retraining programs and team-work. Several women unionists were seeking to combat this by educating men about accepting more of the domestic responsibilities and encouraging them to see the reorganisation of work as an opportunity to become more involved in family life.

While the initiative came from the Metal Workers' Union, other unions such as the Retail Workers' Union and the Factory Workers' Union have also moved in this direction. Substantial workplace reform was also undertaken by the Municipal Workers' Union in the mid-1980s in an effort to subvert restructuring and substantial job loss. This involved large-scale training and reorganisation programs to equip the rank and file with the skills to reorganise their own jobs. The Union also established its own in-house consultancy group, through which it has been granted most local government consultancies. In doing so, it has utilised autonomous work teams, skill development and democratic "bottom-up" approaches to job redesign that have benefited the largely female workforce in terms of both wages and conditions (Curtin and Higgins, 1998).

Many union women considered work reorganisation to have important potential in increasing women's wages and working conditions. Through its focus on multi-skilling, team-work could reduce horizontal and vertical divisions of labour and undermine gender segregation in the labour market. In addition, multi-skilling had made industrial work more interesting and rewarding for women by providing them with additional training, which women unionists noted could lead to an increase in women's wages relative to men's.

Gender-Specific Strategies

In terms of wage equality for women, TCO has followed a different tactic to LO. The Confederation has tended toward centralised agreements, but it has had neither the political affiliation with the Social Democrats nor the same commitment to wage solidarity as LO, viewing some pay differentials as fair. Equal pay has been pursued through job evaluation, with an emphasis on the human and social importance of work or through an individual salary system, based on individual performance and technical requirements of the job (Ruggie, 1984, p. 172). The narrowing of wage differentials within white-collared employment has been less than that achieved within blue-collared employment, particularly in the private sector.

Job evaluation has continued to be a key strategy and has been gender-specific in focus. Within the public sector, internal union research indicated that men as a group earn around 500 Swedish Crowns ($75 US) more per month than their female counterparts. As this only compared women as a group to men as a group, further research was being conducted to investigate more precisely where the differences in income were located.

Several such projects were underway in banking and other private sector industries, with additional research in this area being funded by the KOM Program (an acronym meaning "Men and Women Working Together"). Sponsored by the Swedish Work Environment Fund and supported by both the trade union movement and employers, KOM has funded various projects, several of which have investigated the gender-wage differential and the value of women's work. One project undertaken by the Municipal Workers' Union evaluated the jobs done primarily by women in eight local communities in one county and used the data during the 1992 round of wage negotiations. By drawing from the study's findings during the negotiation process, gender-wage differentials were reduced by between 25 to 30 per cent (KOM, 1994, p. 30).

Evaluation projects alone were not considered to be sufficient to undermine unequal pay. Rather, women unionists thought these should be supplemented with investigations into who was undertaking negotiations on behalf of female members and how this was being done. Similarly to LO, TCO was looking to provide training for negotiators to encourage them to revalue women's work and negotiate wages accordingly. Access to vocational training and education was also highlighted as a means to increasing women's wages.

One strategy providing more immediate outcomes has involved the negotiation for additional money targeted specifically at closing the wage gap. This was initiated by public sector women in 1989. Apart from the general increase given to both men and women, 60 million Swedish Crowns ($8 million US) was allocated to improve women's salaries. This money was not immediately passed on to women but invested, with the interest paying for special training courses for women to increase their skills, buy books and attend seminars.

Following this successful bid, "a significantly more radical" claim was made in the name of women. Women unionists requested that women workers be given an additional one per cent increase in salary every year, until the gender-wage gap was completely removed. This strategy was overwhelmingly rejected by male members and the union hierarchy. While women unionists argued that the extra money would not be extracted from men's wages, the proposal remained unacceptable, with both men and women divided over the idea of giving women such explicit special treatment.

The traditional LO focus on the provision of general increases to low wage earners was recently challenged by a number of women in blue-collar unions. In 1994, pressure on LO to give a higher priority to women's wages resulted in one per cent of the margin for wage increases earmarked for women's wages. Women unionists acknowledged that having a woman on the LO executive was critical in achieving this outcome.

Finally, there has been an increasing emphasis on the role of legislation in the pursuit of gender-wage equality. The *Equality Act* (1992) requires employers to provide equal pay. Where a wage gap between men and women exists employers have to provide evidence to show it is not based on gender differences and are required to stipulate measures they will undertake to reduce the gap. Breaches of the legislation are heard in the labour court but, in the past, equal pay cases have been rare. More recently, there has been a shift in behaviour, with more women seeking redress through the labour court and the Equality Ombudsman's Office experiencing an increased workload with respect to equal pay complaints.

The labour movement in Sweden has had an inclusive and egalitarian commitment to wage equality through centralised wage bargaining and, in the case of LO, a solidaristic wage policy. However, equal pay was never viewed as a woman's right but as part of a broader set of reforms required for better functioning of the labour market. For many years this gender-neutral approach was acceptable to women trade unionists since it fitted with the more gender-neutral discourse of equality between the sexes and because women, as the majority of low paid workers, were beneficiaries of the wage solidarity approach.

Since the breakdown of centralised wage bargaining, closure of the gender-wage gap has stalled and in some sectors has begun to widen. As a result, women unionists have redefined equal pay as a woman's right and with this has come a renewed desire to focus on the gender-specific impact of labour movement initiatives. Thus, while the class-based strategy of workplace reform in blue-collar industries has the potential to benefit women through job rotation and multi-skilling, the possible negative impacts on women have also been identified by women trade unionists.

While women in blue and white-collar trade unions have approached the issue of wage equality differently in the past, of late, there has been something of a convergence in the types of strategies adopted, all of which have been gender-specific. Perhaps, the most radical proposal yet has been the explicit request by both LO and TCO unions for an extra one per cent increase in the wages of women in an effort to close the wage gap. This gender-specific wage claim is an acknowledgment by women trade unionists of the particularity of previous class strategies, which have failed to view participation in the labour market as intersected by both gender and class.

Women's Working Conditions

While women in Sweden were granted permission to work in trades and sales occupations as early as 1810 (Kaplan, 1992, p. 69), it was well over a century later before women's labour force participation, particularly that of married women, became acceptable. During the 1930s, Swedish women's organisations put up a considerable fight for the right of married women to undertake paid work and in 1938, they were successful in having a law passed which prohibited the firing of women who were married, pregnant, or single with children (Hobson, 1993). From the late 1930s onwards, the number of married women entering the labour force began to increase. Between 1950 and 1965, the participation rate of married women rose from 15.7 per cent to 36.7 per cent (Hirdman, 1994, p. 25).

This trend continued during the 1960s and 1970s. Between 1960 and 1990, women's labour force participation increased from 51 per cent to 81 per cent (OECD, 1991a), entrenching women's position in the labour market as permanent. This dramatic increase can be attributed to the substantial growth in government employment, which increased by an average of four percentage points per decade between 1960 and 1989 (OECD, 1991a, p. 34), with the majority of this increase occurring before 1980. The service sector share of total employment also rose from 29 to 35 per cent between 1972 and 1980 (Scharpf, 1984, p. 266). Much of this employment was picked up by married women, largely as a result of growth in part-time work. By 1974, part-time employment was 24 per cent of total employment (OECD, 1995).

The focus of welfare policy during the 1930s and 1940s had been on women's role as wife and mother, which fitted with the vision of the "People's Home" articulated by Per Albin Hansson in the 1930s (Hirdman, 1994). This began to change during the 1960s, although the increase in women's labour force participation had not been motivated primarily by a desire for increased equality for women. Rather, women were seen as an acceptable alternative to immigrant labour in a tight labour market situation (Cook et al, 1992). This phenomenon served to highlight and politicise the obstacles facing married women's entry into paid work (Qvist, 1985, p. 159) and provided a political space for what became known as the "sex-roles" debate. During the 1960s and 1970s, the Social Democratic government, with the support of the trade union movement, initiated a number of programs to enhance women's right to work (Baude, 1978, pp. 153–161).

Taxation reform in 1971 provided for individual tax returns without regard for partners' earnings. This removed the financial disadvantage married women had previously faced when entering employment. In 1974, maternity leave was replaced with parental leave, with either parent able to take leave with insurance compensating 90 per cent of pay (Scott, 1982). The number of places in child care also rose rapidly from the late 1960s, although demand for these still outweighs supply. Such facilities have been heavily subsidised by the state (Gelb, 1989, p. 169).

Trade union support for the development of this "woman-friendly welfare state" (Hernes, 1987) was largely a result of the labour movement's emphasis on growth, with women's labour force participation seen as essential to this growth. Eduards has noted that the element of woman-friendliness was driven by "productivity, pragmatism and paternalism" rather than any sense of gender equity (Eduards, 1991, p. 169). The existence of such policies explains why women trade unionists have made comparatively fewer demands for supply-side policies to support women's labour market participation.

Although comparatively utopian, the conditions of women's employment have remained contested in Sweden. Women are concentrated in a few occupations and are the majority of low-status workers. It is predominantly women who interrupt their labour force participation, take up part-time work and receive considerably less earnings-related superannuation, which supplements the basic flat-rate aged pension. Thirty six per cent of women pensioners, as opposed to just four per cent of their male counterparts are entirely dependent on the basic pension (Curtin and Higgins, 1998).

Thus, the widely held expectation, espoused by social democrats and feminists alike, that labour market participation in itself would lead to gender equality, has not been fulfilled. As a result, women trade unionists have begun to emphasise how gender has remained a fundamental organising principle in working life. Women unionists do not deny the gains made for women through their entry into the labour market. Rather, there has occurred a questioning of the ability of gender-neutral strategies to challenge the explicitly gendered character of the labour market. In this vein, the KOM program funded approximately 100 projects to look specifically at applying a gender-specific perspective to the organisation of work. These projects ranged from gendering local government working environments and developing a mentor scheme to the establishment of women's co-operatives and occupational networks (KOM, 1994).

The juxtaposition of family and work responsibilities was seen by women trade unionists as problematic for women, particularly those in male-dominated occupations where bosses often viewed women with children as a burden. Equality officers in unions were trying to change this view with education and information, emphasising, for example, that "women were good policemen even when they had children".

While comprehensive family policies have substantially ameliorated the combination of paid and unpaid work, women trade unionists noted, and statistics show, that the revolutionising of men's roles is an ideal that has yet to be realised. Mothers continued to assume most of the responsibility for their children, while only 7.5 per cent of parental insurance benefit periods have been claimed by fathers (Eduards, 1991, p. 173). This statistic stimulated the introduction of the "daddy month" whereby 90 days were reserved for the second parent - usually the father. Special dispensation is required if the second parent cannot take up this leave. Officials in LO have called on affiliate unions to undertake active work to alter the negative attitude of employers toward fathers who take parental leave.

Changing the conditions of women's working life in Sweden was still seen as inherently linked to a change in the attitudes and behaviour of working men and trade unions were accepted as having a legitimate role to pay in stimulating such change.

Part-time Work and Unemployment

It has been women who predominantly work part-time in Sweden, a high percentage of whom are unionised. Union demands on behalf of part-time workers have included limiting the minimum number of hours worked per week, lowering the limit of hours to qualify for social insurance and forcing employers to better inform part-time workers of their rights (Cook et al, 1992, p. 210).

Within the Municipal Workers' Union, 80 per cent of the membership are women, 60 per cent of who worked part-time. A number of these women wanted to work part-time, but there were some that did not. Much of the involuntary part-time work has been an effect of cutbacks in public sector spending and meant some women received insufficient wages to maintain their standard of living. In response, the Union had adopted the long-term goal of having the status of "part-time" abolished. Workers instead have gained the right to cut down work hours in favour of family responsibilities, without losing full-time status or the right to return to full-time work.

In general, however, the union movement has pursued few strategies that challenge the traditional structure of employment. Organisation of the labour market is still oriented toward full-time work, despite women's demands for a six hour working day (Blomqvist, 1990). In 1990, the LO leadership was given the choice between shorter working days (favoured by women) and longer holidays (favoured by men). Priority was given to longer holidays (Åmark, 1992, p. 435).

Historically, the right to work has been considered sacred in Sweden and the continued emphasis on full employment across party lines is a tribute to this (Rollen, 1978). Thus, recent increases in unemployment were cited as an issue for concern by many women unionists. While these women noted that men had a higher rate of unemployment than women did, many of new jobs created were in export industries where few white-collar women were employed. There was a fear that less well-educated women between the ages of 40 and 50 in particular, would be unable to re-enter the labour market.

In response to this fear, TCO had organised workshops with government officials, other trade unions and employers to discuss specific measures to deal with women's unemployment – a strategy well suited to a corporatist environment. In addition, it was considered important to monitor the way government targeted money to employment schemes. While it was accepted that women and men got equal opportunities in retraining, the male-dominated programs tended to be more expensive and, as such, received a bigger part of the budget.

Perhaps least well addressed has been the issue of sexual harassment. In 1987, the Swedish government estimated that sexual harassment affected around 20 per cent of working women and argued it was used "to keep women out of male-dominated jobs" (cited in Elman, 1993, p. 515). The labour court heard its first sexual harassment case in 1995 and found no specific legal provision against it. The union involved had to rely on extending the boundaries of non-specific principles to establish that an offence existed in law (Elman, 1993).

Several women unionists noted that minimal acknowledgment of the issue of sexual harassment had been made by their trade unions. The Equality Ombudsman's Office had begun work on projects that would force both unions and employers to address the issue. A booklet on how to deal with harassment complaints had been compiled and distributed and several courses and information seminars had been designed to educate unionists and employers on how to address harassment in their equality plans. The Ombudsman's Office argued that the issue warranted further attention if "women workers were to believe their trade unions viewed them as full members of these organisations". However, the labour movement's long-time refusal to support sex discrimination legislation has meant sexual harassment has been largely ignored, receiving little or no attention in the collective bargaining arena.

Trade unions in Sweden have encouraged women's labour force participation and have provided considerable support for the development of supply-side policies to further encourage and facilitate the position of women in the labour market. In recent years, the quality of this labour market participation has come under increasing scrutiny by women in trade unions and feminist academics over the last decade. Women's employment is still biased towards repetitive jobs in industry, low-level office jobs and health and child care (KOM, 1994). While the gender-neutral notion of equality between the sexes has highlighted the disadvantages incurred by men by their lack of participation in the home, there has been little change in the take-up rate by men of parental leave and women continue to undertake most of the domestic responsibilities.

Women trade unionists have begun to accept that, while the gender-neutral approach has provided women with many benefits, it has also served to hide the gender-specific structure of the labour market. In response, work is being undertaken to change the attitudes of male workers and employers to men's involvement in domestic life. Women unionists have also sought to include a more gender-specific perspective in the development of active labour market policies, the organisation of part-time work and in addressing the previously hidden issue of sexual harassment.

Conclusion

Women have not been well represented within trade union hierarchies in Sweden. Both the white-collar and blue-collar confederations have a history of their executives being heavily dominated by men. Despite this lack of a women's presence, the policy directions developed within the Swedish corporatist model have substantially improved the economic and social position of working women in Sweden. Initially, this did not come about as part of a particular interest by unions in women's rights, but had more to do with how the position of women might affect the labour market and the overall state of the economy (Cook et al, 1992; Eduards, 1991; Qvist, 1985; Ruggie, 1984). During the 1960s, gender equality did become an independent political issue on the trade union agenda, but in gender-neutral rather than gender-specific terms. Women have benefited substantially from measures generated by such a strategy, evident by the lack of claims made by women unionists in recent years around issues of child care and parental leave provisions. In addition, the gender-neutral discourse has sought to incorporate men into the domestic sphere and encourage them to participate more fully in what was traditionally seen as women's work. In this sense, the focus on class has led to solutions for both the working class and for working women.

The insistence by the labour movement that the class interest was the major concern for both sexes has had a considerable impact on the way women themselves have organised their interests, working within both the Social Democratic Party and the trade union movement. Women in unions affiliated to LO accepted that general class strategies, such as centralised wage bargaining and workplace reorganisation, had provided positive outcomes for women. While more individualistic strategies had been pursued within white-collar industries, these too have been undertaken in ways that include rather than exclude men.

More recently, the focus on equality between the sexes and working alongside men has been supplemented with women organising with other women and articulating strategies around wages and conditions in explicitly gender-specific terms. This renewed emphasis on the gender-specific has been women unionists' response to a shift to the right in public policy rhetoric and to a belief that the gender-neutral strategy has failed to challenge the explicitly gender-specific nature of paid work. Furthermore, while Swedish conceptions of equality include equal status in the political decision-making process, this has eluded Swedish trade union confederations. The resurgence in women's collective action is a significant change in an environment where the social democratic strategy has been predicated on a universal, (gender-neutral), encompassing class politics.

7 Concluding with Comparisons

Introduction

The previous accounts of strategies undertaken by women trade unionists in Australia, Austria, Israel and Sweden provide a profile of how women have tried to make working class representation more inclusive of women and their interests. In this chapter, I revisit the historical and contemporary experiences of women trade unionists from an explicitly comparative perspective, examining the similarities and differences in women's solidarities. In doing so, I draw the distinction between strategies which invoke notions of "class" and "woman". It becomes evident that, while universal claims can be made on behalf of the working class and/or women, the definition of interests is necessarily selective and exclusive. Examination of the commonalities and contrasts in strategies deployed by women unionists within this framework allows for a reconsideration of women's collective actions as contingent, rather than fixed around a specific class or gender identity.

The first three sections of this chapter examine the cross-national similarities and differences in the strategies pursued by women trade unionists in their quest for increased representation within union hierarchies, wage equality and better working conditions, particularly with respect to mixing paid work with family responsibilities. In the final section, I evaluate the usefulness of the notion of contingent solidarities in interpreting these strategies.

The Representation of Women within Trade Unions

Despite the different ideological origins of the labour movements in Australia, Austria and Sweden, women workers were initially excluded from trade union membership in these countries. Only in Israel were women included from the beginning as part of the trade union movement, although this was on the basis of their being Jewish, rather than workers. Indeed, in Israel, as in the other three countries at the turn of the century, women's labour force participation was often discouraged and viewed as a threat to male wages. Thus, from the very inception of trade unionism in the modern era, and despite Marx's call for the overriding of sectional interests, the notion of working class representation was not universal but harnessed a masculine norm of inclusion.

The inclusion of women as trade union members came only after considerable struggle, with women workers establishing their own separate trade unions in Austria, Sweden and Australia. Since those early days, and more recently with the increase in women's labour force participation, women's trade union membership has increased substantially. It is argued that with these increases in labour force participation and trade union membership there should also be an increase in the number of women in trade union hierarchies (Lovenduski, 1986, p. 166). However, just as trade unions were slow to include women as members, so too have they been reticent in electing and appointing women to decision-making positions.

The importance of women representing women was, and is, an issue for women in trade unions cross-nationally, both as an end in itself and as a means for making trade union agenda more inclusive of the interests of women workers. Attempts to increase the representation of women have required women trade unionists to appeal to their identity as women. Yet the ways in which this identity has been invoked has varied both across the four countries under investigation and within these countries over time. The measures employed include encouraging women to become more active as union members, the formation of separate organisations and programs that provide women with special representation.

Theoretically, by virtue of their union membership, every member has the right to attend meetings, voice their opinions and vote on relevant issues. In terms of equal access to participation, however, women trade unionists in all four countries identified a number of barriers that prevented women from participating. These included domestic commitments, negative attitudes held by men regarding women's capabilities to undertake union work and a general lack of confidence on the part of women. In an effort to dismantle these barriers, women unionists have lobbied for the provision of child care at meetings, holding meetings during working hours and educating women workers on union politics and practices.

Participation in union activities at the workplace, while not the same as representation, is important, since advancement in union office tends to begin with this type of political experience. Furthermore, without equal access to political participation, the democratic nature of trade unions comes into question. That women trade unionists in Australia, Austria, Israel and Sweden have used similar strategies to increase women's participation suggests trade union politics continues to be a male domain. Women trade unionists have sought to reveal it as such through the deployment of gender-specific strategies.

At various times since their acceptance as trade union members around the turn of the century, women have sought to have their interests addressed through the creation of separate spaces within trade unions. Although separate organising and women representing women are strategies which are gender-specific in character, they have not become permanently entrenched or pre-determined and are often contested by both men and women in trade unions.

In Sweden, although women's councils existed during the 1950s, in the 1960s through until the early 1990s, gender equality was redefined as equality between the sexes. Women's representation by women was no longer considered to be a fruitful approach in this context. As a result, women's councils were renamed equality councils and attempts were made to integrate women's officers and women's issues within a gender-neutral environment. Such an approach was considered appropriate since class strategies were thought to guarantee universal outcomes and had provided women with comparatively high levels of gender equality. More recently, with threatened cuts to the welfare state and continuing barriers to an equal political presence for women, a new feminist rhetoric has emerged within Swedish trade unions to stand beside the previously dominant class discourse.

In Australia, the increase in women's labour force participation and the emergence of a high profile women's movement in the 1970s highlighted the numerous barriers undermining the achievement of gender equality in the workplace. During this period, the specific representation of women's interests through separate organisation began to flourish, with women unionists organising committees, networks and conferences at federal, state and local levels. While the ACTU executive is not required to formally consult the ACTU Women's Committee, the Committee has provided both visibility and voice for women workers and their interests. With the recent reshaping of the union movement through amalgamations and declining union membership in Australia, the issue of gendered representation has taken on new significance, especially with respect to the recruitment of women.

In contrast to both Sweden and Australia, women's divisions have existed in Austria and Israel since the incorporation of women as members. This has provided women with token representation in the upper echelons of the trade union confederations, but in neither country have the women's divisions any considerable power, with many of the issues of concern to women workers yet to gain currency in the industrial arena. In Israel, Na'amat has a female constituency of over 700,000, yet its role is to provide women with social services, not to organise women nor to politicise issues of concern to women as workers.

Women's divisions have been an acceptable means of incorporating and addressing the "woman question" without undermining the overriding cause of national or labour unity. While this has often led to women's concerns being subordinated to those of class, it is not a process in which women were necessarily passive. In many cases, women chose to prioritise the generic working class political interest over the gender-specific, since it was thought that benefits would flow to both men and women with the arrival of socialism. Moreover, women's power resources were limited and establishing regulated wages and working conditions was difficult without the support of their male colleagues.

In addition, the entrenched corporatist frameworks in Sweden, Austria and Israel have reinforced the efficacy of women linking their interests to those of labour. Corporatist policy making is based on the capital-labour nexus and groups that are considered peripheral to this nexus are seldom provided with official access to this closed environment. Thus, there is little space for independent women's organisations to have their interests represented. Indeed, it could be argued that the dominance of corporatist decision-making arrangements has stifled the development of an independent women's movement in these three countries, making the labour movement the primary means of representation for women. Under these circumstances, the creation of separate spaces for women workers within trade unions has facilitated the required redefinition of the diverse interests of workers into a unified representable working class interest.

The case of Australia contrasts with these three nations in that it was not until the 1970s that women's sections and committees in trade unions began to burgeon. No formal corporatist framework came into existence until 1983, with the arrival of a Labor government that remained in power for 13 years. Up until that time, the Australian Labor Party had not been the dominant party of government. This lack of hegemonic presence and the existence of a more pluralist policy-making environment provided women activists with little incentive to pursue their demands solely in terms of class. While women were active in trade unions, they were also organising their interests outside of the labour movement. By the late 1970s a visible women's movement had developed which often applied explicitly feminist discourses in its interaction with, and demands on, the state. This heightened feminist consciousness, combined with the increases in women's labour force participation had an influence on women's organising in trade unions, leading them to openly challenge the masculine character of union structures and policy agendas.

In this sense, creating separate spaces for the representation of women's interests, whether or not it is within an entrenched corporatist framework, has not been a fixed strategy. The disappearance and reappearance of gender-specific strategies by women unionists in Sweden and the creation of women's spaces in Australian unions over the last two decades suggests that trade unions have been perceived by women unionists as remiss in addressing the interests of women workers. While accountability is an important facet of representative democracy within trade unions, as in other political institutions, this does not appear sufficient if particular needs of a group of workers, in this case women's, are being ignored.

Although the structural positioning of women's representative spaces is relevant to the discursive integration of women's interests in industrial relations, the marginal status of such spaces does not necessarily equate with powerlessness. Nor does the fact that women's divisions are seldom accorded institutional power within the trade union hierarchy foreclose women's collective action as a possible strategy for empowerment. Indeed, conceiving of women's collective actions as without power precludes the identification of more local, partial and emerging acts of empowerment. At various times, women's sections in all four countries have facilitated contact with women at the grass-roots level and have proven an important contact for women working in isolated or unorganised occupations. Women's committees and officers have also been critical in the gathering and dissemination of information, in politicising women's claims and, along with women's conferences, have provided a space for women to discuss policies and formulate strategies in an effort to further feminise trade union agenda. In environments, such as

Israel, discursive space in the public arena is dominated by issues of "national" and "economic security". This has limited the avenues available for the representation of working women's interests to those located within the Histadrut. Labelling these women's sections as essentially without power could lead to "political disappointment and exhaustion" amongst women workers in Israel (cf Gibson-Graham, 1995, p. 175). However, viewing women's sections as spaces where a variety of possible strategies might be invented and enacted, locally or nationally, highlights the political potential of such spaces.

In their quest for gendered representation, women unionists have looked for strategies to promote individual women into positions of power within trade union hierarchies. Such measures include affirmative action, proportional representation and reserved seats for women. These strategies have received a mixed response from women trade unionists. In Sweden, the class tradition has permeated any discussion of special representation of women by women, with such strategies viewed as feminist and divisive to class solidarity. Similarly, in Austria, despite the existence of a reserved seat on the executive, the issue of quotas and affirmative action measures remains contested, with women unionists instead actively seeking to recruit more women as negotiators and shop stewards. In Israel, a reserved seat exists on the board of the Histadrut for the female head of Na'amat, while the Labour Party, which has in the past dominated the Histadrut's leadership, has accepted quotas for women. However, implementation of quota targets has been limited, with success only at the lowest level of work council.

It is in Australia that affirmative action strategies have been most actively embraced as necessary to increase women's representation within trade unions. In 1991, the ACTU set a target of 50 per cent female representation by the turn of the century and as a first step established three affirmative action places on its executive. This, combined with the recent election of a woman president and women leaders representing several female-dominated unions, has led to a substantial increase over the last ten years in the number of women present at executive level.

Of the four countries examined here, the ACTU has the highest level of female representation, 29 per cent, compared to the female unionisation rate of 33 per cent. In Sweden, Austria and Israel women's representation at confederation level in 1993 was less than 20 per cent, hardly a critical mass, and a long way from being proportional to women's membership levels. It would seem, then, that at least in the short term, affirmative action strategies are necessary if the representation of women is to become more than a token presence. However, as an explicitly feminist strategy, affirmative action remains difficult to accept in Sweden and Austria where class discourse continues to dominate. In Austria, a conservative attitude to women's labour force participation has also precluded such feminist challenges to date.

The under-representation of women in the hierarchies of trade union movements takes on an added significance in the four countries examined in that trade unions have played and continue to play (except in the case of Australia) a crucial role in the public policy-making arena. Within these corporatist environments, the patterns of representation are fixed, reinforcing the systematic exclusion of women from these elites (Bergqvist, 1991; Hernes, 1987; Lovenduski, 1986). Schmitter (1981) suggests that interests are formulated within the corporatist decision-making environment itself, independent of the expressed concerns of trade union membership. If this is the case, then without women's presence within corporatist elites, women's interests as workers will continue to be ignored when defining and constructing public policy.

Women unionists in all four countries acknowledged that the presence of women in the upper echelons of trade unions does not guarantee the representation of all interests important to all women workers. Nor has the strategy of gendered representation come with the assumption that there exists an overarching and fixed common interest between women workers. Rather, there is an explicit acceptance that women's class and gender interests are intersected by interests stemming from ethnicity, occupational status, number of hours worked and numerous other factors. Nevertheless, having women in decision-making positions was considered by most women unionists as necessary to provide a gender perspective to the process of interest representation undertaken by trade unions.

Women's Wages

Similarities exist in Australia, Austria, Israel and Sweden with respect to early union resistance in accepting women as equal participants in the paid labour force. For many years, the role of women as mothers took precedence over their role as workers. Women were regarded as secondary participants in the labour force and trade unions were seldom forthcoming in actively seeking equal pay for women. The socialist leanings of early trade unionism in Sweden, Austria and Israel encouraged rhetorical support for equal pay but no implementation measures emerged. Rather, the opposite occurred, with trade unions in these three countries supporting the existence of separate wage scales and agreements for women workers. In Australia, the establishment of a family wage provided a basic income for a male worker, his wife and three children. This ruling reinforced the notion that women should work only if they were single. Married women were provided for in their husbands' wages, so equal pay was not required. It was not until the 1950s and 1960s that women workers in these four countries were able to force trade unions to explicitly acknowledge the issue of the gender-wage differential.

Despite these cross-national similarities, variations exist in the mix of class and gender-specific strategies pursued by women trade unionists in Australia, Israel, Sweden and Austria around equal pay. To account for these similarities and differences, emphasis must be given to the different wage bargaining structures and wage policy objectives evident in each country. Also important is the extent to which class-based initiatives have been considered effective in ameliorating the specifically gendered features of the labour force such as occupational segregation, skill acquisition and the valuation of women's work.

Although Australia, Israel, Sweden and Austria have centralised trade union organisations, not all have centralised wage bargaining, nor have they exhibited a commitment to wage solidarity. Yet it is the existence of centralised wage bargaining which can be demonstrated to have a considerable impact on reducing the gender-wage differential (Whitehouse, 1992).

Of the four countries examined here, Sweden exhibits the smallest gap in the female/male pay ratio, with women earning around 90 per cent of a man's wage in the private sector and 84 per cent in the public sector. A reduction in the gender-wage differential of 15 per cent occurred between 1959 and 1972 as a direct result of the solidaristic wage policy adopted by LO and implemented through the centralised wage bargaining framework established in the late 1930s. The strategies pursued by women trade unionists during the same period were marked by a strong commitment to wage solidarity and, from the early 1960s, by a gender-neutral discourse of equality, which sat well with LO's focus on class before sex. Women workers benefited substantially from the goal of wage compression, because they were the majority of low paid workers and women trade unionists within LO continued to support a gender-neutral approach to wage equality until the early 1990s.

However, the Swedish example confirms that centralised wage bargaining alone is insufficient in reducing the gender-wage differential. The TCO in Sweden, although participating in centralised bargaining with employers, has never displayed the same commitment to wage solidarity as LO, arguing that wage differentials are a necessary return for skill. As a result, women in white-collar work have not benefited from an encompassing class politics. Women unionists in TCO-affiliated unions have focused instead on gender-specific strategies of job evaluation and upgrading women's skill base.

In Australia, centralised wage bargaining did not, in itself, reduce the gender-wage differential. There existed no formal commitment by the labour movement to wage solidarity, although national wage cases did deliver regular and uniform wage increases across the market and the existence of comparative wage justice curbed excesses in wage disparities. In addition, the regulation of minimum wages through awards benefited women as low paid workers. However, for many years the differences in earnings between women and men were formalised by the arbitration system through the under valuation of women's work and the establishment of the family wage. The existence of the latter was regularly used to deny women equal pay (Macintyre, 1985, p. 43). It was women's upfront demand for wage equality and the resulting equal pay decisions handed down by the Australian Industrial Relations Commission in 1969 and 1972, which made a significant contribution to closing the wage gap. By 1991, women in full-time work were earning approximately 84 per cent of their male counterparts.

Although gender-wage equality was not an explicit objective of the wage fixing system in Australia, the centralised framework has been an effective mechanism in the implementation of the equal pay provisions. While trade unions were required to present a case on behalf of workers covered by each award, this was more encompassing than an individual complaints system. Furthermore, the principles were integrated into the wage fixing system and were applied across industries thereby extending its coverage (Whitehouse, 1995, p. 256). In this way, women unionists were able to use the traditional class-oriented strategy of centralised wage fixing to pursue a gender-specific outcome.

The cases of the TCO in Sweden and the ACTU in Australia, prior to the equal pay decisions, reinforce Therborn's argument that similar sorts of labour market institutions can have significantly different outcomes. Therborn maintains different outcomes are dependent upon the objectives set and whether or not these objectives are institutionalised (Therborn, 1992, p. 39). Women unionists in Sweden and Australia have been aware of the utility of the centralised wage bargaining system when it is directed toward the objective of wage solidarity or pay equity and, for this reason, their deployment of legislative strategies has been limited. In Sweden, equal treatment legislation has existed since 1980, and was introduced by a bourgeois government without the support of trade unions. In Australia, the *Sex Discrimination Act* (1984) and the *Affirmative Action (Equal Employment Opportunity for Women) Act* (1986) had not been used in the context of equal pay.

In contrast to Sweden and Australia, the trade union movements in Austria and Israel have not embraced a centralised wage bargaining system. Although wage policy targets are set at the central level, the majority of bargaining in both countries takes place at sub-national level, and in neither country has the notion of a unified working class interest led to a commitment to wage solidarity. Without these two factors, women trade unionists in Austria and Israel have been limited in their ability to rely on class-based strategies to undermine the gender-wage differential. In Austria, the political coalition between left and right led to the sanctioning of status-oriented wage benefits and, in an effort to maintain full employment and appease capital, wage increases were based on productivity and economic growth. In Austria, wage disparities are comparatively high and this is reflected in the female/male pay ratio of 70 per cent, with women represented disproportionately amongst workers earning less than the minimum wage.

Like Austria, the wage gap between men and women in Israel is comparatively wide, with women (in full-time work) earning approximately 71 per cent of their male counterparts. Wage disparities have been sustained through the negotiation of a variety of fringe benefits at sub-national, local or individual level. The Histadrut has tolerated wage disparities in an effort to preserve a unified and encompassing Jewish trade union confederation and so has exhibited little explicit concern over gender-wage differentials. Thus, the combination of decentralised wage bargaining and the lack of commitment to wage compression has disproportionately harmed women workers in both Austria and Israel.

Women trade unionists in both Austria and Israel have focused their attention on legislative strategies. In Austria, the *Equal Treatment Act* (1979) prohibited wage discrimination in collective agreements, while in Israel, the *Equal Pay Act* (1964) required women and men to be paid the same wages for the same work. However, occupational segregation has meant that few women actually undertake the same work as men and, in both Austria and Israel, women are often issued lower job rankings or gendered job titles. Furthermore, implementation has been dependent on individual grievance procedures rather than class action and trade union support for grievances is not guaranteed. In an effort to combat the inaction by trade unions on the issue of discrimination in collective agreements and job descriptions, women trade unionists in Austria have supported legislative amendments which have resulted in an Equal Treatment Officer being appointed and an office which provides legal advice for individual women. A similar service is provided by Na'amat in Israel. Women unionists in Israel are also attempting to have the arbitrary allocation of fringe benefits addressed through legislation. Thus, it appears that when the wage bargaining system is decentralised and the trade union movement lacks an encompassing solidaristic wage policy, women unionists construct solidarities around legislative strategies that are gender-specific in focus.

The existence of decentralised wage bargaining environments has also stimulated strategies that focus on the need for gendered representation. Active recruitment of women negotiators in Austria, and the implementation of quotas for women on work councils in Israel, indicate women unionists do not view class solidarities as sufficient in accounting for the interests of women workers in wage negotiations. The connection between decentralisation and gendering representation is also attested to by the increased attention being given by women unionists in Sweden and Australia to strategies that provide women with an explicit voice in wage negotiations. In both these countries, shifts to a more decentralised wage bargaining system have been interpreted by women unionists as having the potential to undermine the push for gender-wage equality. In this sense, the utility of class strategies and solidarities is undermined when the objective of wage equity is either threatened or does not exist.

In Sweden, class strategies have been pursued most often by women in blue-collar unions. Recent workplace reform initiatives have been seen as having the potential to improve women's wages by providing women with an increase in skills and experience through job rotation and increased training, thereby undermining, albeit indirectly, occupational segregation. Women unionists in blue-collar industries in Australia have supported similar reforms.

Support for class strategies has not been limited to women in blue-collar unions. Both blue-collar and white-collar women in Australia have attempted, through the process of award reclassification, to formally revalue women's skills and rectify the institutionalised gender bias in the categorisation of skill. In Israel, nurses, teachers and public service workers have all undertaken militant industrial action in an effort to gain wage increases, as have bank and municipal workers in Sweden, and nurses in Australia. By contrast, while it was white-collar women in Sweden who traditionally employed gender-specific strategies, there has been a recent acknowledgment by LO women that class strategies were a necessary, but not sufficient, means of addressing the gender-wage differential. As a result, both white and blue-collar women unionists have sought extra wage increases specifically targeted at women.

In general, women unionists in all four countries acknowledged that the gendered structure of the labour market limits the potential of class strategies to address occupational segregation, skill revaluation and equal access to training; factors which continue to constrain the attainment of equal pay for women. As a result, women unionists cross-nationally have harnessed similar gender-specific strategies including job evaluation, comparative worth and professionalisation.

Cross-national analyses indicate that corporatist institutional arrangements, such as those exhibited in the countries examined here, have been useful in their control over market forces, providing benefits to workers through increased employment and economic growth. With these analyses comes an assumption that such outcomes equally benefit all workers. However, in examining the similarities and differences between women's choices of strategies, it is evident that in terms of wage outcomes, corporatist arrangements do not necessarily benefit all workers equally. Unless wage bargaining is centralised and wage policy objectives incorporate a notion of wage equality, class-based solidarities have a limited impact in reducing the gender-wage differential. Even with centralised wage bargaining mechanisms, women's solidarities are contingent in that the gendered character of the labour market necessarily demands the construction and reconstruction of gender-specific strategies at various times to supplement or replace class strategies which have not accounted for the intersectional identities of workers.

Women's Working Conditions

Women unionists in Australia, Austria, Israel and Sweden agree that the representation of women and wage equality are issues that continue to be of concern to women workers. With respect to women's working conditions there are some striking contrasts in the claims made on behalf of women. One crucial factor influencing the focus of women's fight for better working conditions is the variation in how women's inclusion in the labour market has been defined and supported by the state and trade unions. Also relevant to the selection of strategies is the breadth of each trade union movement's agenda and the extent to which trade unions involve themselves in action beyond traditional notions of wages and working conditions. What trade unions perceive as the parameters of working conditions is influenced by attitudes to women's labour force participation and the existence of a broad "political" unionism.

The most pressing concern for the majority of women workers in Australia, Austria and Israel is combining paid work with family responsibilities. In Austria and Israel, maternity leave provisions are relatively generous in both payment and duration of leave. However, in neither country has this been supplemented with adequate state funded child care. While Na'amat provides a day care service, this is not always available or affordable. In Austria, most child care centres exist in Vienna and the number of places is considered by women unionists to be insufficient. In addition, in both countries, primary school children attend school for only half a day.

In Austria and Israel, a traditional sexual division of labour is reflected in public policy concerns, with a strong emphasis being placed on women as mothers. In Austria, the participation of married women in the labour market has not been actively encouraged, with little increase evident in part-time employment or public sector employment over the last three decades. In Israel, while women's labour force participation has increased, the exemption of married women from military service has reinforced traditional notions of women's role as mothers. This sexual division of labour has been largely accepted by the trade union movement in both countries, with women trade unionists unable to push for child care or school reform through trade union channels, focusing instead on lobbying government ministers for change. In Austria, increases to the duration of maternity leave have received constant support from the labour movement. Many women unionists however, have been reluctant to support such reform, arguing that it would be detrimental to women's careers and wage equality, acknowledging the difficulties that come with strategies that focus first on women's role as mothers not workers.

In Australia, maternity leave and child care have also been issues of concern to women workers. However, because welfare state benefits were based on need and wives were provided for in the family wage, maternity leave conditions have been less generous compared with Austria and Israel. Women unionists in Australia have recently been able to use corporatist channels to negotiate extensions to maternity leave provisions and increased funding for child care. It appears there is now an acceptance by the Australian labour movement of women as permanent residents in the labour market. In addition, women unionists have been able to place an increasing emphasis on workers as parents, using the traditional test case mechanism to provide parents with sick children access to carer's leave.

Part-time work is a common means by which women have sought to combine paid work and family responsibilities. The conditions of part-time workers continue to be an issue of concern to women unionists in both Australia and Israel. Many women who work part-time have less access to training and promotion and therefore lower wages and trade unions have been reluctant and slow to show an interest in the needs of these workers. Although many part-time workers are now entitled to *pro rata* benefits, many are not unionised and work in small workplaces or at home, making it difficult for unions to monitor their conditions.

In Austria, trade unions have refused to support the increase in part-time work. Using traditional arguments about the threat part-time work poses to the existence of full-time work, this strategy has also served to hinder the growth in women's labour force participation. Interestingly, women unionists have supported the conventional trade union stance, arguing that part-time work would not benefit women, aligning themselves instead with the general class position of demanding an overall decrease in the working week.

In all three countries, women workers have at various times been granted protection from particular kinds of work. In many cases, women themselves campaigned for these protections. More recently, campaigns for equal employment opportunity (EEO) have challenged protective measures. In Israel, EEO has been pursued through legislative channels and, as with equal pay, has been dependent on individual grievances for implementation. In contrast, women unionists in Australia have been able to draw on both legislative and industrial strategies. Legislation has required employers to monitor and establish mechanisms to undermine equal employment opportunity, while within the wage bargaining arena, EEO requirements have been written into awards. The maintenance of EEO conditions in the new decentralised environment of enterprise bargaining is considered to require diligence on the part of union negotiators to ensure such conditions are not traded off for wage gains. As a result there has been an increased emphasis on including more women on bargaining teams and educating male officials as to the value of EEO.

Again Austria differs from both Israel and Australia in that protection of women workers continued to exist until very recently, with women denied access to most night work and required to retire five years earlier than men. It took entry into the European Union to overturn the ban on night work and a Constitutional Court ruling to remove the gender-specific retirement age. Since then, trade union women in Austria have argued for better night work conditions using gender-neutral terms in a tactical effort to gain the support of their male colleagues.

Engels argued that the liberation of both workers and women required drawing women into the labour market and involving them in the struggle for socialism, while advocates of social democracy maintained that the goal of full employment was crucial to equality. Yet trade union support for including women as equal participants in the labour force has varied across countries. Moreover, the definition of women's inclusion, whether it be considered as transitional or permanent, has in turn affected the extent to which trade unions view the concerns of women workers as industrial. The definition of what does and does not constitute a legitimate industrial issue necessarily has an impact on the usefulness of class strategies and solidarities formulated by women trade unionists in the pursuit of child care, equal employment opportunity and parental leave.

The breadth of the bargaining agenda is also a factor in deciding the perceived utility of class strategies in pursuing gender-specific claims. Trade unions in Israel, Austria and Australia (up until the early 1980s), defined industrial issues in a narrow sense, maintaining a distinct separation between what is dealt with through collective bargaining and what is dealt with at a political level. In Israel and Austria, women's working conditions have been primarily defined as social issues and the responsibility of the political domain. In Israel, the Histadrut's ambivalence to trade unionism generally, despite it being the major trade union confederation, has not encouraged women workers to view the institution as one through which to pursue gender-specific claims. In Australia, the definition of women's issues as social began to be undermined with the activity of women unionists during the late 1970s and early 1980s. The shift was enhanced with the adoption of the Accord, whereby the linking of wage restraint to social wage outcomes blurred the line between industrial and political outcomes. This enabled women trade unionists to lobby around women's working conditions using both political and industrial channels.

Unlike these three countries, the labour movement in Sweden has explicitly encouraged women's labour force participation; first in the 1930s and more significantly in the 1960s. Although instrumentalist in their motives, trade unions and consecutive social democratic governments have facilitated the inclusion of women through tax reform, universal maternity and later parental leave benefits, state-funded child care and the unionisation of part-time workers. Because the goal of full employment included women, class strategies that were aimed at this goal included women. As a result, from the 1960s until the 1990s, women unionists in Sweden were able to utilise a universal class politics to provide for women workers.

The Swedish case, according to Higgins, is an exceptional model of political unionism in that its major union confederation has accepted its role is not just to defend workers rights but to "change working life from the bottom up, ... to democratize society and the economy and make work itself valuable and meaningful" (LO cited in Higgins, 1985, p. 349). This broadening of what constitutes class interests has allowed for claims around child care provision, welfare benefits and equal employment opportunity to be defined as within the boundaries of capital/labour nexus. With the exception of equal employment opportunity, implementation of these claims has largely been the domain of the parliamentary branch of the labour movement, albeit with the unequivocal support of the trade union movement.

Despite espousing a universal basis to its claims, the trade union movement in Sweden has been unable to produce full equality for women. An unintended consequence of the major equality gains made through the labour movement is the incentive provided to women workers to demand total equality. Women unionists have begun to question the utility of a gender-neutral class approach in a labour market that remains gendered in structure. A renewed focus has been placed on highlighting the particularity of the universal, with new strategies constructed to explicitly reveal the male bias at both work and within trade unions.

The issue that most challenges the utility of class strategies is sexual harassment. By seeking to de-gender the labour market, as was the case in Sweden, problems have arisen in politicising issues such as sexual harassment, which are relevant to women with sex specific bodies (cf Sullivan, 1990). While it is not always women who are subject to sexual harassment, women trade unionists in all four countries viewed it as a major concern for women workers. To deal with sexual harassment women unionists in Sweden have had to re-gender the politics of the workplace and reintroduce gender-specific strategies accordingly.

Sexual harassment is also an issue in Austria and Israel, with women unionists working to highlight its relevance as an industrial issue. But perhaps the greatest contrast to Sweden is the case of Australia, where sexual harassment has received considerable attention by trade unions. Numerous courses have been offered, publications produced and comprehensive policy positions adopted, while trade union officials are expected to bargain with employers for policies on combating sexual harassment. The acceptance of sexual harassment as an industrial issue by both trade unions and employers in Australia is largely a result of women within and outside the labour movement actively employing gender-specific strategies and often explicitly feminist arguments to politicise such issues.

Contingent Solidarities

This examination of the variety of similarities and differences in the choice of strategies made by women in unions cross-nationally offers a challenge to the notion that interests are fixed or unified around either gender or class (or national) identities. Corporatist practice implies that a unified class interest can, and for the success of the corporatist policy-making process must, be provided by trade union confederations. This position has had an impact on the representation of women's interests as workers in several ways.

First, the fixed patterns of representation applied by corporatist partners continue to exclude women, who are seldom elected as heads of trade union confederations. Theoretically this should not be a problem if, as is assumed in the literature, the internal workings of trade unions allow for adequate representation of the variety of workers' interests and if the redefinition of these into a single unified interest occurs in a democratic manner. Second, there is an assumption that outcomes resulting from corporatist representation equally benefit all workers.

Material presented in the previous chapters indicates that representation by women is seen by women trade unionists to be crucial at particular times and around particular claims. Arguments for an increase in representation by women within union hierarchies and in the negotiation process, and invoking the identity of women in the formulation of claims suggests that the existing process of interest redefinition has not been sufficiently inclusive of women's concerns. A universal class politics, as best displayed by the labour movement in Sweden, has provided women with tangible outcomes in terms of wages and welfare benefits. Yet women trade unionists in Sweden have highlighted the particularity of this universal in their pursuit of gender-specific strategies for representation and closure of the wage gap. It is also apparent that in Australia, Austria and Israel, a unified working class interest was seldom sought, with the working class interest represented as masculine, conservative or Jewish respectively.

The identities and interests of workers are not only influenced by class and gender. They are affected by the numerous ways in which workers are situated: as blue-collar or white-collar workers, in the public or private sector, in full-time or part-time employment, with or without family responsibilities. No one strategy or solidarity, whether it is based on class or gender, is ever able to include the interests of all workers. While equal employment opportunity may be pursued through gender-specific claims by some women unionists, simultaneously, other women may be more interested in deploying class strategies that focus instead on increasing minimum wages and conditions. The relevance of each strategy is also affected by the particular historical and discursive context within which the claim is formulated. In Austria, the utility of separate, explicitly feminist demands is constrained by corporatist dynamics, as is strike activity, while dialogue within corporatist channels is extremely useful. In contrast, in Australia, overt feminist claims both within and outside of the corporatist environment are an acceptable and often effective mode of interest representation.

Conventional notions of solidarity based on the opposition between capital and labour have precluded the acknowledgment of differences between workers. By providing a comparative examination of how women in trade unions have acted collectively with each other and with other groups of workers, this analysis suggests it is possible to think more creatively about the formation of solidarities. Sectional interests amongst workers are inevitable, but the conflicts that arise from these differences need not be seen as negative or detrimental to trade unionism. Rather, the formation of solidarities around class or gender could be viewed as dynamic and fluid, with the changing boundaries of those included and excluded in the process of interest formation and redefinition, creating new claims and new solidarities: contingent solidarities.

The concept of contingent solidarities is a useful way of interpreting both women's collective actions and class-based actions. The concept provides a framework for analysis of class-based and gender-specific strategies in a manner that reveals women's agency regarding the (re)formulating of interests; that is, we can identify how and why women have defined themselves and their concerns in the way that they have. In particular, it allows for a cross-national analysis of the ways in which class, welfare state, labour market and cultural discourses have included or excluded women and how women trade unionists' themselves have influenced the construction and formulation of claims, strategies and solidarities.

What implications does this interpretation of women's collective actions have for trade union policy-making, the democratic nature of trade unions and for union strength in general? The introduction reviewed the increase in women's trade union membership that has occurred over the last thirty years. Despite this increase, in three of the four countries examined here, women continue to make up a large proportion of potential

Concluding with Comparisons

union members. Having trade unions appear more "women friendly", through better representation of the interests of working women and of women themselves, could be seen as a means by which these potential members become actual members and thereby increase union strength.

It is not self-evident that corporatist institutional arrangements will survive the increasing demand for smaller government, the challenge to trade union legitimacy and the dominance of the global market. Thus, it may be that trade union confederations will need to attract different coalitions of support to maintain their presence in the policy-making arena. This may in turn require an increased presence for women (amongst others) in decision-making elites, especially as women's labour force participation continues to increase. Accepting, acknowledging and providing voice for different groups of workers within trade unions becomes increasingly necessary if unions are to continue to be viewed by governments and employers as representing "the working class" in the public policy-making arena.

Trade unionism is predicated on a collective identity formed around the commonality of working life. Trade union confederations, particularly those within corporatist environments, also seek to represent a unified working class interest. The experience of women unionists in Australia, Austria, Israel and Sweden, as represented here, challenges the usefulness of assuming a unified working class interest can include all workers. This does not mean that workers of both sexes do not share common work experiences. Rather, contesting notions of conventional solidarity may encourage trade union movements to reconceptualise workers as having diverse interests which are not fixed but fluid and, in doing so, become more representative of their membership.

Appendix One: Interview Sources

Australia

Australian Council of Trade Unions.
Australian Education Union.
Australian Nurses' Federation, Australian Capital Territory Branch.
Australian Nursing Federation, National Office.
Australian Services Union.
Automotive, Food, Metals and Engineering Union.
Community and Public Sector Union (2 officials).
Construction, Forestry, Mining and Energy Union.
Finance Sector Union of Australia.
Miscellaneous Workers' Division of the Liquor, Hospitality and Miscellaneous Workers' Union (2 officials).
National Union of Workers.
Shop, Distributive and Allied Employees' Association.
Textile, Clothing and Footwear Union of Australia, Victorian Branch.
Trades and Labour Council, Australian Capital Territory.
Transport Workers' Union of Australia.
Vehicle Division of Automotive, Food, Metals and Engineering Union, Victorian State Office.
Victorian Clerical and Administrative Branch of the Australian Services Union.

Austria

Austrian Chamber of Labour, Vienna.
Banking Section, Union of Salaried Employees in Private Employment.
Economic Policy Section, Union of Salaried Employees in Private Employment.
Equal Treatment Officer, Equality Commission.
Industry Sector, Union of Salaried Employees in Private Employment.
Labour Law Section, Federal Ministry of Social and Labour Affairs.
Ministry of Women's Affairs.

Appendix One

Union of Employees in Public Services.
Union of Hotel, Restaurant and Personal Services Workers.
Union of Metal, Mining and Power Supply Workers.
Union of Textile, Clothing and Leather Workers.
Women's Division, Austrian Confederation of Trade Unions.
Women's Division, Union of Salaried Employees in Private Employment.

Israel

Arab Workers' Section of the Histadrut.
Clerical Workers' Committee within Metal Industry.
Department of Salaried Women, Histadrut.
Head Office, Na'amat.
Israel Women's Network, Jerusalem.
Legal Section, Na'amat
Mapam Party.
National Association of Nurses.
National Union of Clerical, Administrative and Public Service Employees.
National Union of Textile, Garment and Leather Workers.
National Union of Workers in the Metal, Electrical, Electronics and Plastics Industries.
Overseas Department, Na'amat.
Women's Section, Israeli Labour Party.
Youth Section of the Histadrut.

Sweden

Central Organisation of Salaried Employees.
Federation of Civil Servants (2 officials).
Office of the Equal Opportunities Ombudsman.
Swedish Bank Employees' Union.
Swedish Confederation of Academics.
Swedish Confederation of Trade Unions.
Swedish Factory Workers' Union.
Swedish Medical Association.
Swedish Metal Workers' Union (3 officials).
Swedish Municipal Workers' Union.

Swedish Union of Clerical and Technical Employees.
Union of Swedish Policemen (2 officials).

Appendix Two: Data Sources

Female and Male Trade Union Density

Trade union density refers to actual union members as a percentage of potential union members. When looking at union density data, a number of difficulties arise. Union membership figures can be both overstated due to the inclusion of retired members and the unemployed and understated since small non-aligned unions may be excluded (Wallerstein, 1989, p. 497). The time periods referred to with respect to union reporting of membership varies between the average in a calendar year, the average in a financial year and on a specific day within that year. Furthermore, data is gathered from union records and/or labour force or household surveys (Bain and Price, 1980, p. 3).

However, Bain and Price (1980), Visser (1989) and Ebbinghaus and Visser (1999) have tried to account for these problems and present trade union membership figures in the most consistent manner possible. Union density and membership data for Austria, Denmark, Germany, Ireland, Netherlands, Sweden and the United Kingdom for the years 1960, 1970, 1980, 1989 and 1993–95 were taken from the DUES data set and additional data kindly supplied to me by Jelle Visser and Bernhard Ebbinghaus. Data for Canada and the United States were taken from Labour Canada and Bureau of Labor Statistics publications (see also Bain and Price, 1980; OECD, 1991b). Data for Australia was drawn from the Australian Bureau of Statistics, Catalogue Number 6323.0.

Bibliography

Acker, J. (1994), 'Two Discourses of Reform: Women in the Future Swedish Welfare State', Department of Sociology, University of Oregon.
Affirmative Action Agency (AAA), (1997), 'Policy for Waiving Affirmative Action Reporting Requirements', AAA, Sydney.
Ahrne, G. and Clement, W. (1994), 'A New Regime?: Class Representation within the Swedish State', in W. Clement and R. Mahon (eds), *Swedish Social Democracy: A Model in Transition,* Canadian Scholars Press, Toronto, pp. 223–244.
Anderson, H. (1990), 'Feminism as a Vocation: Motives for Joining the Austrian Women's Movement', in E. Timms and R. Robertson (eds), *Vienna 1900: From Altenberg to Wittgenstein,* Edinburgh University Press, Edinburgh, pp. 73–86.
Anderson, H. (1992), *Utopian Feminism: Women's Movements in fin-de-siècle Vienna,* Yale University Press, New Haven.
Ang, I. (1995), 'I'm a feminist but ...... "Other" Women and Post-National Feminism', in B. Caine and R. Pringle (eds), *Transitions. New Australian Feminisms,* Allen and Unwin, St Leonards, pp. 57–73.
Anon, (1992), 'Austria: Industrial Relations Background', *European Industrial Relations Review,* vol. 222, pp. 23–29.
Archer, R. (1992), 'The Unexpected Emergence of Australian Corporatism', in J. Pekkarinen, M. Pohjola and B. Rowthorn (eds), *Social Corporatism: A Superior Economic System?,* Clarendon Press, Oxford, pp. 377–417.
Arian, A. (1989), *Politics and Government in Israel,* Chatham House Publishers, Chatham.
Australian Bureau of Statistics (ABS), (1992), *Trade Union Statistics, Australia,* Catalogue No. 6323.0, ABS, Canberra.
Australian Bureau of Statistics (ABS), (1998), *Trade Union Statistics, Australia,* Catalogue No. 6323.0, ABS, Canberra.
Australian Council of Trade Unions (ACTU), (1987), *Future Strategies for the Trade Union Movement,* ACTU, Melbourne.
ACTU, (1990), *Restructuring Awards: Issues for Women Workers,* ACTU, Melbourne.
ACTU, (1991), *Parental Leave Test Case,* ACTU, Melbourne.
ACTU, (1995a), *The 1995 National Union Directory and Diary,* ACTU, Melbourne.

Bibliography

ACTU, (1995b), *Advances in Equal Pay Under the Accord: Further Progress*, ACTU, Melbourne.
ACTU/Trade Development Corporation (TDC), (1987), *Australia Reconstructed*, Australian Government Publishing Service, Canberra.
Australian Industrial Relations Commission, (1994), *Family Leave Test Case*, November.
Azmon, Y. (1993), 'Women and Politics: The Case of Israel', in Y. Azmon and D. Izraeli (eds), *Women in Israel*, Transaction, New Brunswick, pp. 253–267.
Åmark, K. (1992), 'Sweden', in Joan Campbell (ed), *European Labor Unions*, Greenwood Press, Westport, pp. 429–444.
Bacchi, C. L. (1990), *Same Difference: Feminism and Sexual Difference*, Allen and Unwin, Sydney.
Bader-Zaar, B. (1996), 'Women in Austrian Politics, 1890–1934: Goals and Visions', in D.F. Good, M. Grandner and M.J. Maynes (eds), *Austrian Women in the Nineteenth and Twentieth Centuries*, Berghahn, Providence, pp. 59–90.
Bain, G.S. and Price, R. (1980), *Profiles of Union Growth*, Basil Blackwell, Oxford.
Bain, G.S. and Price, R. (1983), 'Union Growth: Dimensions, Determinants and Destiny', in G. S. Bain (ed), *Industrial Relations in Britain*, Basil Blackwell, Oxford, pp. 3–34.
Bakker, I. (1988), 'Women's Employment in Comparative Perspective', in J. Jenson, E. Hagen and C. Reddy (eds), *Feminization of the Labour Force*, Polity Press, Cambridge, pp. 17–44.
Balser, D. (1987), *Sisterhood and Solidarity: Feminism and Labor in Modern Times*, South End Press, Boston.
Barrett, M. (1980), *Women's Oppression Today: Problems in Marxist Feminist Analysis*, NBL, London.
Baude, A. (1978), 'Public Policy and Changing Family Patterns in Sweden 1930–1977', in J. Lipman Blumen and J. Bernard (eds), *Sex Roles and Social Policy: A Complex Science Equation*, Sage Publications, London, pp. 145–175.
Bebel, A. (1904), *Woman under Socialism*, New York Labor News Press, New York.
Bei, N. (1990), 'Women and Social Institutions', Paper presented to the International Council on Social Welfare, February, Vienna.
Benard C. and Schlaffer, E. (1984), 'Austria: Benevolent Despotism Versus the Contemporary Feminist Movement', in R. Morgan (ed), *Sisterhood is Global*, Doubleday, New York, pp. 72–76.
Benson, M. and Harverd, D. (1988), *The Status of Women in Israel*, Israeli Women's Network, Jerusalem.
Berger, I. (1992), 'Categories and Contexts: Reflections on the Politics of Identity in South Africa', *Feminist Studies*, vol. 18, no. 2, pp. 284–294.

Bergqvist, C. (1991), 'Corporatism and Gender Equality: A Comparative Study of Two Swedish Labour Market Organisations', *European Journal of Political Research*, vol. 20, no. 2, pp. 107-125.

Bergqvist, C. (1995), 'The Declining Corporatist State and the Political Gender Dimension', in L. Karvonen and P. Selle (eds), *Women in Nordic Politics: Closing the Gap,* Dartmouth, Aldershot, pp. 205-228.

Bernstein, D. (1987a), 'The Women Workers' Movement in Pre-State Israel, 1919-1939', *Signs*, vol. 12, no. 3, pp. 454-470.

Bernstein, D. (1987b), *The Struggle for Equality: Urban Women Workers in Pre-State Israeli Society,* Praeger, New York.

Bernstein, E. (1909), *Evolutionary Socialism,* Schocken Books, New York.

Biffl, G. (1996), 'Women and their Work in the Labour Market and in the Household', in D.F. Good, M. Grandner and M.J. Maynes (eds), *Austrian Women in the Nineteenth and Twentieth Centuries,* Berghahn, Providence, pp. 133-156.

Blomqvist, M. (1990), 'Work Beyond Measure', Paper presented to Women's Directorate's 5th Annual Conference: *Work, Work, Work: Women in the Nineties,* 18-19 October, Sydney.

Booth, A. and Rubenstein, L. (1990), 'Women in Trade Unions in Australia', in S. Watson (ed), *Playing the State,* Allen and Unwin, Sydney, pp. 121-135.

Boreham P. and Compston, H. (1992), 'Labour Movement Organisation and Political Intervention', *European Journal of Political Research*, vol. 22, pp. 143-170.

Boreham, P., Hall, R. and Leet, M. (1993), 'Labour and Citizenship: the Development of Welfare State Regimes', Paper Presented to the Australasian Political Studies Association Conference, 29 September-1 October, Monash University.

Boreham, P., Hall, R., Harley B. and Whitehouse, G. (1996), 'Trade Unions - Enterprise Bargaining and Control at Work: Evidence from the First Wave of Enterprise Agreements', *Policy, Organisation and Society,* vol. 11, pp. 46-66.

Boston, S. (1987), *Women Workers and the Trade Unions,* Lawrence and Wishart, London.

Brauer, D.A. (1990), 'Does Centralised Collective Bargaining Promote Wage Restraint? The Case of Israel', *Industrial and Labor Relations Review,* vol. 43, no. 5, pp. 636-649.

Brennan, D. (1998), *The Politics of Australian Child Care,* Cambridge University Press, Melbourne.

Briskin, L. (1993), 'Union Women and Separate Organising', in L. Briskin and P. McDermott (eds), *Women Challenging Unions: Feminism, Democracy and Militancy,* University of Toronto Press, Toronto, pp. 89-108.

Bibliography

Brown, W. (1991), 'Feminist Hesitations, Postmodern Exposures', *Differences: A Journal of Feminist Cultural Studies,* vol. 3, no. 1, pp. 63–84.
Bryson, L. (1992), *Welfare and the State*, Macmillan Press, Basingstoke.
Bryson, L. (1994), 'Women, Paid Work and Social Policy', in N. Grieve and A. Burns (eds), *Australian Women: Contemporary Feminist Thought,* Oxford University Press, Melbourne, pp. 179–193.
Bryson, L. (1995), 'Two welfare states: One for Women, One for Men', in A. Edwards and S. Magarey (eds), *Women in a Restructuring Australia,* Allen and Unwin, St Leonards, pp. 60–76.
Buber Agassi, J. (1991), 'How Much Political Power do Israeli Women Have?', in B. Swirski and M.P. Safir (eds), *Calling the Equality Bluff,* Pergamon Press, New York, pp. 203–212.
Butler, J. (1992), 'Contingent Foundations: Feminism and the Question of "Postmodernism"', in J. Butler and J.W. Scott (eds), *Feminists Theorize the Political,* Routledge, New York, pp. 3–21.
Calhoun, C. (1995), 'The Gender Closet: Lesbian Disappearance under the Sign "Women"', *Feminist Studies,* vol. 21, no. 1, pp. 7–31.
Cameron, D. (1984), 'Social Democracy, Corporatism, Labour Quiescence and the Representation of Economic Interest in Advanced Capitalist Society', in J. Goldthorpe (ed), *Order and Conflict in Contemporary Capitalism,* Clarendon Press, Oxford, pp. 143–178.
Carney, S. (1988), *Australia in Accord: Politics and Industrial Relations under the Hawke Government,* Sun Books, South Melbourne.
Castles, F.G. (1978), *The Social Democratic Image of Society,* Routledge and Kegan Paul, London.
Castles, F.G. (1981), 'Female Legislative Representation and the Electoral System', *Politics,* vol. 1, no. 2, pp. 21–27.
Castles, F.G. (1985), *The Working Class and Welfare,* Allen and Unwin, Sydney.
Castles, F.G. (1988), 'Realism and Reality: Australia's Trade Union Movement Seeks a New Policy Strategy', *Australian Quarterly,* vol. 60, no. 3, pp. 308–316.
Castles, F.G. (1989), 'Introduction. Puzzles of Political Economy', in F.G. Castles (ed), *The Comparative History of Public Policy,* Polity Press, Cambridge, pp. 1–15.
Castles, F.G. (1991), 'A Century of Parliamentary Socialism - A Comparative Overview', *Legislative Studies,* vol. 5, no. 2, pp. 3–10.
Castles, F.G. and Mitchell, D. (1993), 'Worlds of Welfare and Families of Nations', in F.G. Castles (ed), *Families of Nations: Patterns of Public Policy in Western Democracies,* Dartmouth, Aldershot, pp. 93–129.
Cobble, D.S. (1990), 'Rethinking Troubled Relations between Women and Unions: Craft Unionism and Female Activism', *Feminist Studies,* vol. 16,

no. 3, pp. 519–544.
Cobble, D.S. (1993), 'Introduction: Remaking the Unions for the New Majority', in D.S. Cobble (ed), *Women and Unions: Forging A Partnership*, ILR Press, Ithaca, pp. 1–18.
Cockburn, C. (1997), 'Gender in an International Space: Trade Union Women as European Social Actors', *Women's Studies International Forum*, vol. 20, no. 4, pp. 459–470.
Collette, C. (1989), *For Labour and for Women*, Manchester University Press, Manchester.
Compston, H. (1992), 'Trade Union Participation in EC Economic Policy-Making', Papers on Government and Politics, No. 90, University of Strathclyde.
Compston, H. (1994), 'Union Participation in Economic Policy-Making in Austria, Switzerland, The Netherlands, Belgium and Ireland, 1970–1992', *West European Politics*, vol. 17, no. 1, pp. 123–145.
Cook, A. (1984), 'Introduction', in A. Cook, V. Lorwin and A.K. Daniels (eds), *Women and Trade Unions in Eleven Industrialised Countries*, Temple University Press, Philadelphia, pp. 3–33.
Cook, A. (1991), 'Women and Minorities', in G. Strauss, D.G. Gallagher and J. Fiorito (eds), *The State of the Unions*, Industrial Relations Research Association, Wisconsin, pp. 237–258.
Cook, A., Lorwin V. and Daniels A.K. (eds), (1984), *Women and Trade Unions in Eleven Industrialised Countries*, Temple University Press, Philadelphia.
Cook, A., Lorwin V. and Daniels, A.K. (1992), *The Most Difficult Revolution*, Cornell University Press, Ithaca.
Coote, A. and Campbell, B. (1982), *Sweet Freedom*, Basil Blackwell, Oxford.
Cott, N.F. (1987), *The Grounding of Modern Feminism*, Yale University Press, New Haven.
Curtin, J. (1997), 'Engendering Union Democracy: Comparing Sweden and Australia', in M. Sverke (ed), *The Future of Unionism. International Perspectives on Emerging Union Structures*, Ashgate, Aldershot, pp. 195–210.
Curtin, J and Higgins, W. (1998), 'Feminism and Unionism in Sweden', *Politics and Society*, vol. 26, no. 1, pp. 69–94.
Curtin, J. and Sawer, M. (1996), 'Gender Equity in the Shrinking State: Women and the Great Experiment', in F.G. Castles, R. Gerritsen and J. Vowles (eds), *The Great Experiment: Labour Parties and Public Policy Transformation in Australia and New Zealand*, Allen and Unwin, Sydney, pp. 149–169.
Dahlström, E. and Liljeström, R. (1983), 'The Patriarchal Heritage and the Working Class Women', *Acta Sociologica*, vol. 26, no. 1, pp. 3–20.

Deery, S.J. and Plowman, D.H. (1991), *Australian Industrial Relations*, McGraw-Hill, Sydney.
Department for Salaried Women, (1993), 'Information for the Working Woman', Histadrut, Tel Aviv.
Diamond, I. and Harstock, N. (1981), 'Beyond Interests in Politics: A Comment on Virginia Sapiro's "When are Interests Interesting? The Problem of Political Representation of Women"', *American Political Science Review*, vol. 75, no. 3, pp. 717–721.
Dill, B.T. 1983, 'Race, Class, and Gender: Prospects for an all-inclusive Sisterhood', *Feminist Studies*, vol. 9, no. 1, pp. 131–150.
Donaldson, Mike, 1991, *Time of our Lives. Labour and Love in the Working Class*, Allen and Unwin, Sydney.
Doron, A. and Kramer, R.M. (1991), *The Welfare State in Israel: The Evolution of Social Security Policy and Practice*, Westview Press, Boulder.
Dow, G., Clegg, S. and Boreham, P. (1984), 'From the Politics of Production to the Production of Politics', *Thesis Eleven*, vol. 9, pp. 16–32.
Drake, B. (1920), *Women in Trade Unions*, Virago, London.
Dye, N. S. (1980), *As Equals and as Sisters: Feminism, the Labor Movement, and the Women's Trade Union League of New York*, University of Missouri Press, Colombia.
Ebbinghaus, B. and Visser, J. (forthcoming 1999), *The Development of Trade Unions in Western Europe, 1945–95*, Campus Verlag, Frankfurt.
Eduards, M. (1991), 'The Swedish Gender Model: Productivity, Pragmatism and Paternalism', *West European Politics*, vol. 14, no. 3, pp. 166–181.
Efroni, L. (1994), 'The Wage Differential between the Sexes', Paper presented to the International Seminar on Women, Family and Society, April, Haifa.
Ehrlich, A. (1980), 'Zionism, Demography and Women's Work', *Khamsin*, vol. 7, pp. 87–105.
Eisenstein, H. (1991), *Gender Shock. Practising Feminism on Two Continents*, Allen and Unwin, Sydney.
Ellem, B. (1992), 'Organising Strategies for the 1990s: Targeting Particular Groups: Women, Migrants, Youth', in M. Crosby and M. Easson (eds), *What Should Unions Do?*, Pluto Press, Sydney, pp. 347–361.
Elman, A.R. (1993), 'Debunking the Social Democrats and the Myth of Equality', *Women's Studies International Forum*, vol. 16, no. 3, pp. 513–522.
Engels, F. (1950), *The Condition of the Working Class in England in 1844*, Basil Blackwell, Oxford.
Engels, F. (1972), *The Origins of the Family, Private Property and the State*, Pathfinder Press, New York.
Equal Pay Unit, (1992), *A Guide to the Minimum Rates Adjustment Process*, Department of Industrial Relations, Canberra.

Esping-Andersen, G. (1985), *Politics against Markets,* Princeton University Press, New Jersey.
Esping-Andersen, G. (1990), *The Three Worlds of Welfare Capitalism,* Polity Press, Cambridge.
Esping-Andersen, G. and Korpi, W. (1984), 'Social Policy as Class Politics in Post War Capitalism: Scandinavia, Austria and Germany', in J. Goldthorpe (ed), *Order and Conflict in Contemporary Capitalism,* Clarendon Press, Oxford, pp. 179–208.
ETUC, (1983), *Women's Representation in Trade Unions,* ETUC, Brussels.
ETUC, (1994), *Women in Decision-Making in Trade Unions,* ETUC, Brussels.
Evans, R.J. (1977), *The Feminists: Women's Emancipation Movements in Europe, America, and Australasia, 1840–1920,* Croom Helm, London.
Evatt Foundation, (1995), *Unions 2001: A Blueprint for Trade Union Activism,* Evatt Foundation, Sydney.
Falkner, G. and Tálos, E. (1994), 'The Role of the State within Social Policy', *West European Politics,* vol. 17, no. 3, pp. 52–76.
Ferguson, A. (1989), *Blood at the Root: Motherhood, Sexuality and Male Dominance,* Pandora, London.
Fischer-Kowalski, M. (1994), 'Social Change in the Kreisky Era', in G. Bischof and A. Pelinka, *The Kreisky Era in Austria,* Transaction, New Brunswick, pp. 96–115.
Frances, R. (1991), 'Marginal Matters: Gender, Skill, Unions and the Commonwealth Arbitration Court - A Case Study of the Australian Printing Industry, 1925–1937', in R. Frances and B. Scates (eds), *Women, Work and the Labour Movement in Australia and Aotearoa/New Zealand,* Australian Society for the Study of Labour History, Sydney, pp. 17–29.
Freedman, M. (1990), *Exile in the Promised Land,* Firebrand Books, Ithaca.
Gabin, N. (1990), *Feminism in the Labor Movement: Women and the United Auto Workers,* Cornell University Press, Ithaca.
Gardner, M. (1983), 'Women Workers, Trade Union Government and Strategies: The New South Wales Nurses' Association and Teachers' Federation', PhD thesis, University of Sydney.
Gardner, M. (1986), 'The "Fateful Meridian": Trade Union Strategies and Women Workers', in M. Bray and V. Taylor (eds), *Managing Labour? Essays in the Political Economy of Australian Industrial Relations,* McGraw-Hill, Sydney, pp. 168–194.
Gardner, M. and Palmer, G. (1992), *Employment Relations: Industrial Relations and Human Resource Management in Australia,* Macmillan, Melbourne.
Gatens, M. (1996), *Imaginary Bodies: Ethics, Power and Corporeality,* Routledge, London.
Gay, P. (1979), *The Dilemma of Democratic Socialism: Eduard Bernstein's*

Challenge to Marx, Octagon Books, New York.
Gelb, J. (1989), *Feminism and Politics: A Comparative Perspective*, University of California Press, Berkeley.
Gerlich, P. (1992), 'A Farewell to Corporatism', in K.R. Luther and W.C. Müller (eds), *Politics in Austria: Still a Case of Consociationalism?*, Frank Cass, London, pp. 132–146.
Gerritsen, R. (1986), 'The Necessity of "Corporatism": The Case of Hawke Labor Government', *Politics*, vol. 21, no. 1, pp. 45–54.
Gibson-Graham, J.K. (1995), 'Beyond Patriarchy and Capitalism: Reflections on Political Subjectivity', in B. Caine and R. Pringle (eds), *Transitions. New Australian Feminisms*, Allen and Unwin, St Leonards, pp. 172–183.
Gramsci, A. (1919), *Selections from Political Writings*, Lawrence and Wishart, London.
Gregory, R.G. and Daly, A.E. (1990), 'Can economic theory explain why Australian women are so well paid relative to their U.S. counterparts?', Centre for Economic Policy Research, Discussion Paper No. 226, Australian National University.
Griffin, G. and Benson, J. (1989), 'Barriers to Female Membership Participation in Trade Union Activities', *Labour and Industry*, vol. 2, no. 1, pp. 85–96.
Grinberg, L.L (1991), *Split Corporatism in Israel*, State University of New York Press, Albany.
Gruber, H. (1991), *Red Vienna: Experiment in Working-Class Culture 1919–1934*, Oxford University Press, Oxford.
Guardian, The (1995), 'We got what was due to us - but it is also a victory as Israeli Arabs and as Arab women', *The Guardian*, 21 June, London.
Guger, A. (1992), 'Corporatism: Success or Failure? Austrian Experiences', in J. Pekkarinen, M. Pohjola and B. Rowthorn (eds), *Social Corporatism: A Superior Economic System?*, Clarendon Press, Oxford, pp. 338–362.
Haavio-Mannila, E., Dahlerup, D., Eduards, M et al., (1985), *Unfinished Democracy: Women in Nordic Politics*, Pergamon Press, Oxford.
Hampson, I. (1997), 'The End of the Experiment: Corporatism Collapses in Australia', *Economic and Industrial Democracy*, vol. 18, no. 4, pp. 539–566.
Harding, S. (1991), 'The Instability of the Analytical Categories of Feminist Theory', in M.R. Malson, J.F. O'Barr, S. Westphal-Wihl and M. Wyer (eds), *Feminist Theory in Practice and Process*, University of Chicago Press, Chicago, pp. 15–34.
Hargreaves, K. (1982), *Women at Work*, Penguin Books, Ringwood.
Hartmann, H. (1981), 'The Unhappy Marriage of Marxism and Feminism: Toward a More Progressive Union', in L. Sargent (ed), *Women and Revolution: A Discussion of the Unhappy Marriage of Marxism and Feminism*, Pluto Press, London, pp. 1–42.

Heclo, H. and Madsen, H. (1987), *Policy and Politics in Sweden: Principled Pragmatism*, Temple University Press, Philadelphia.
Heery, E. and Kelly, J. (1988), 'Do Female Representatives Make a Difference', *Work, Employment and Society*, vol. 2, no. 4, pp. 487–505.
Henry, A. (1923), *Women and the Labor Movement*, George H. Doran, New York.
Henry, M. and Franzway, S. (1993), 'Gender, Unions and the New Workplace: Realising the Promise?', in B. Probert and B.W. Wilson (eds), *Pink Collar Blues: Work, Gender and Technology*, Melbourne University Press, Melbourne, pp. 126–153.
Hernes, H. (1987), *Welfare State and Woman Power*, Norwegian University Press, Oslo.
Hernes, H. and Voje K. (1980), 'Women in the Corporate Channel in Norway: A Process of Natural Exclusion', *Scandinavian Political Studies*, vol. 3, no. 2, pp. 163–186.
Herzog, H. (1996), 'Why so Few? The Political Culture of Gender in Israel', *International Review of Women in Leadership*, vol. 2, no. 1, pp. 1–18.
Hicks, A. (1991), 'Unions, Social Democracy, Welfare and Growth', *Research in Political Sociology*, vol. 5, pp. 209–234.
Higgins, W. (1985), 'Political Unionism and the Corporatist Thesis', *Economic and Industrial Democracy*, vol. 6, no. 3, pp. 349–381.
Higgins, W. (1996), 'The Swedish Municipal Workers Union: A Study in the New Political Unionism', *Economic and Industrial Democracy*, vol. 17, no. 2, pp. 167–197.
Hirdman, Y. (1994), 'Women-From Possibility to Problem?', Arbetslivscentrum, Research Report No. 3, Stockholm.
Histadrut, (1981), 'The Working Woman in Israel', International Department, Tel Aviv.
Histadrut, (1993), 'Histadrut-General Federation of Labour in Israel', International Department, Tel Aviv.
Histadrut, (1994), 'Labour Laws and Collective Agreements', International Department, Tel Aviv.
Hobson, B. (1993), 'Feminist Strategies and Gendered Discourses in Welfare States: Married Women's Right to Work in the U.S. and Sweden in the 1930s', in S. Koven and S. Michel (eds), *Mothers of a New World, Maternalist Politics and the Origins of Welfare States*, Routledge and Kegan Paul, New York, pp. 396–429.
Hooks, B. (1984), *Feminist Theory from Margin to Center*, South End Press, Boston.
Horowitz, D. and Lissak, M. (1989), *Trouble In Utopia. The Overburdened Polity of Israel*, State University of New York Press, Albany.
Human Rights and Equal Opportunity Commission (HREOC), (1992), *"Just rewards": A Report of the Inquiry into Sex Discrimination in Overaward*

Payments, Australian Government Printing Service, Canberra.
Hyman, C.A. (1985), 'Labor Organizing and Female Institution-Building: The Chicago Women's Trade Union League, 1904–24', in R. Milkman (ed), *Women, Work and Protest. A Century of US Women's Labor History,* Routledge and Kegan Paul, Boston, pp. 22–41.
Hyman, R. (1971), *Marxism and the Sociology of Trade Unionism,* Pluto Press, London.
International Confederation of Free Trade Unions (ICFTU), (1991), *Equality: The Continuing Challenge - Strategies for Success,* ICFTU, Brussels.
International Labour Office (ILO), (1986), *The Trade Union Situation and Industrial Relations in Austria,* ILO, Geneva.
International Labour Office, (1994), *Yearbook of Labour Statistics,* ILO, Geneva.
International Labour Office, (1997), *World Labour Report. Industrial Relations, Democracy and Social Stability,* ILO, Geneva.
Izraeli, D. (1981), 'The Zionist Women's Movement in Palestine, 1911–1927: A Sociological Analysis', *Signs,* vol. 7, no. 1, pp. 87–114.
Izraeli, D. (1982), 'Avenues into Leadership for Women: The Case of Union Officers in Israel', *Economic and Industrial Democracy,* vol. 3, no. 4, pp. 515–529.
Izraeli, D. (1984), 'The Attitudinal Effects of the Gender Mix in Union Committees', *Industrial and Labor Relations Review,* vol. 37, no. 2, pp. 212–221.
Izraeli, D. (1991), 'Women and Work: From Collective to Career', in B. Swirski and M.P. Safir (eds), *Calling the Equality Bluff,* Pergamon Press, New York, pp. 165–177.
Izraeli, D. (1992), 'The Women Workers' Movement: First Wave Feminism in Pre-State Israel', in Deborah Bernstein (ed), *Pioneers and Homemakers: Jewish Women in Pre-State Israel,* State University of New York Press, Albany, pp. 183–210.
Izraeli, D. (1994), 'Outsiders in the Promised Land: Women Managers in Israel', in N.J. Adler and D.N. Izraeli (eds), *Competitive Frontiers: Women Managers in a Global Economy,* Basil Blackwell, Cambridge, pp. 301–324.
Jaggar, A. (1988), *Feminist Politics and Human Nature,* Rowman and Littlefield, New Jersey.
Jonasdottir, A.G. (1988), 'On the Concept of Interest, Women's Interests, and the Limitations of Interest Theory', in K.B. Jones and A.G. Jonasdottir (eds), *The Political Interests of Gender,* Sage, London, pp. 33–65.
Kaplan, G. (1992), *Contemporary Western European Feminism,* Allen and Unwin, Sydney.
Katzenstein, P. (1984), *Corporatism and Change: Austria, Switzerland, and the*

Politics of Industry, Cornell University Press, Ithaca.
Katzenstein, P. (1985), *Small States in World Markets: Industrial Policy in Europe,* Cornell University Press, Ithaca.
Kautsky, K. (1910), *The Class Struggle,* Charles Kerr and Co, Chicago.
Kelly, J. (1988), *Trade Unions and Socialist Politics,* Verso, London.
Kelty, B. (1989), *The Age,* 25 September, Melbourne.
Kollontai, A. (1909), 'The Social Basis of the Woman Question', in A. Holt (ed), *Selected Writings of Alexandra Kollontai,* Allison and Busby, London, pp. 58-72.
KOM, (1994), *Men and Women Working Together: The KOM Programme,* The Swedish Work Environment Fund, Stockholm.
Korpi, W. (1978), *The Working Class in Welfare Capitalism: Work, Unions, and Politics in Sweden,* Routledge and Kegan Paul, London.
Korpi, W. (1983), *The Democratic Class Struggle,* Routledge and Kegan Paul, London.
Krebs, E. (1975), 'Women Workers and the Trade Unions in Austria: an Interim Report', *International Labour Review,* vol. 112, no. 4, pp. 265-278.
Kunkel, C, and Pontusson, J. (1998), 'Corporatism versus Social Democracy: Divergent Fortunes of the Austrian and Swedish Labour Movements', *West European Politics,* vol. 21, no. 2, pp. 1-31.
Lafleur, I. (1978), 'Five Socialist Women: Traditionalist Conflicts and Socialist Visions in Austria, 1893-1934', in M.J. Boxer and J.H. Quataert (eds), *Socialist Women: European Socialist Feminism in the Nineteenth and Early Twentieth Centuries,* Elsevier North-Holland, New York, pp. 215-248.
Lake, M. (1986), 'Socialism and Manhood: the Case of William Lane', *Labour History,* vol. 50, pp. 54-62.
Lane, J. (1991), 'Interpretations of the Swedish Model', *West European Politics,* vol. 14, no. 3, pp. 1-7.
Lawrence, E. (1994), *Gender and Trade Unions,* Taylor and Francis, London.
Lenin, V. (1902), *What is to be Done,* Martin Lawrence Ltd, London.
Levavi, L. (1991), 'Women's Situation Worse Than Before', *Jerusalem Post,* 1 January.
Levin, N. (1978), *Jewish Socialist Movements, 1871-1917,* Routledge and Kegan Paul, London.
Lewenhak, S. (1977), *Women and Trade Unions: An Outline History of Women in the British Trade Union Movement,* Benn, London.
Loane, S. (1994), 'Unionists Crash Through Glass Ceiling', *Sydney Morning Herald,* 17 March, p. 13.
Lovenduski, J. (1986), *Women and European Politics,* Wheatsheaf Books Ltd, Brighton.

Luxemburg, R. (1906), *The Mass Strike, the Political Party and the Trade Unions*, A Young Socialist Publication, Colombo.
Macintyre, S. (1985), *Winners and Losers: The Pursuit of Social Justice in Australian History*, Allen and Unwin, Sydney.
Macintyre, S. (1989), *The Labour Experiment*, McPhee Gribble Publishers, Melbourne.
Macintyre, S. and Mitchell, R. (1989), 'Introduction', in S. Macintyre and R. Mitchell (eds), *Foundations of Arbitration: The Origins and Effects of State Compulsory Arbitration 1890–1914*, Oxford University Press, Melbourne, pp. 1–24.
Mahon, R. (1994), 'From Solidaristic Wages to Solidaristic Work: A Post-Fordist Historic Compromise for Sweden?', in W. Clement and R. Mahon (eds), *Swedish Social Democracy: A Model in Transition*, Canadian Scholars Press, Toronto, pp. 285–314.
Manning, H. (1992), 'The ALP and the Union Movement: "Catch-All" Party or Maintaining Tradition?', *Australian Journal of Political Science*, vol. 27, no. 1, pp. 12–30.
Martin, R. (1975), *Trade Unions in Australia*, Penguin Books/University of Queensland Press, Ringwood.
Marx, K. (1955), *The Poverty of Philosophy*, Martin Lawrence Ltd, London.
Matthews, T. (1991), 'Interest Group Politics: Corporatism without Business?', in F.G. Castles (ed), *Australia Compared*, Allen and Unwin, Sydney, pp. 191–218.
McBride, T. (1985), 'French Women and Trade Unionism: The First Hundred Years', in N.C. Soldon (ed), *The World of Women's Trade Unionism*, Greenwood Press, Westport, pp. 35–56.
Meidner, R. (1994), 'The Rise and Fall of the Swedish Model', in W. Clement and R. Mahon (eds), *Swedish Social Democracy: A Model in Transition*, Canadian Scholars Press, Toronto, pp. 337–346.
Meidner, R. (1995), 'Swedish Trade Unionism: Threats and Challenges', in M. Sverke (ed), *The Future of Unionism. International Perspectives on Emerging Union Structures*, Ashgate, Aldershot, pp. 37–46.
Metzker, M. (1980), 'Overt and Disguised Discrimination against Women in Collective Agreements: Findings of an Austrian Survey', *International Labour Review*, vol. 119, no. 2, pp. 243–253.
Meyerowitz, R. (1985), 'Organizing the United Automobile Workers: Women Workers at the Ternstedt General Motors Parts Plant', in R. Milkman (ed), *Women, Work and Protest. A Century of US Women's Labor History*, Routledge and Kegan Paul, Boston, pp. 235–258.
Milkman, R. (1985), 'Editors Preface', in R. Milkman (ed), *Women, Work and Protest. A Century of US Women's Labor History*, Routledge and Kegan

Paul, Boston, pp. xi–xiv.
Milkman, R. (1986), 'Women's History and the Sears Case', *Feminist Studies,* vol. 12, no. 2, pp. 375–400.
Milkman, R. (1990), 'Gender and Trade Unionism in Historical Perspective', in L.A. Tilly and P. Gurin (eds), *Women, Politics and Change,* Russell Sage Foundation, New York, pp. 87–108.
Milner, H. (1990), *Sweden: Social Democracy in Practice,* Oxford University Press, Oxford.
Milner, H. (1994), *Social Democracy and Rational Choice,* Routledge, London.
Neumann, G., Pedersen, P.J. and Westergard-Nielsen, N. (1989), 'Long-run International Trends in Aggregate Unionisation', Centre for Labour Economics, Working Paper 90-4, University of Aarhus and Aarhus School of Business.
New South Wales Department of Industrial Relations, Employment, Training and Further Education (DIRETFE), (1993), *Women and Enterprise Bargaining: A Review of New South Wales Enterprise Agreements,* DIRETFE, Sydney.
Neyer, G. (1996), 'Women in the Austrian Parliament: Opportunities and Barriers', in D.F. Good, M. Grandner and M.J. Maynes (eds), *Austrian Women in the Nineteenth and Twentieth Centuries,* Berghahn, Providence, pp. 91–114.
Nicholson, L.J. (1990), 'Introduction', in L.J. Nicholson (ed), *Feminism/Postmodernism,* Routledge, New York, pp. 1–18.
Nielsson, B. (1994), Personal correspondence, History Department, University of Uppsala.
Nightingale, M. (1991), *Facing the Challenge,* Victorian Trades Hall Council, Melbourne
Norris, P. (1989), *Politics and Sexual Equality: The Comparative Position of Women in Western Democracies,* Wheatsheaf Books, Boulder.
Nowotny, E. (1993), 'The Austrian Social Partnership and Democracy', Center for Austrian Studies, Working Paper 93-1, University of Minnesota.
Nowotny, H. (1981), 'Austria: Women in Public Life', in C. Fuchs Epstein and R. Laub Coser (eds), *Access to Power: Cross-National Studies of Women and Elites,* Allen and Unwin, London, pp. 147–156.
O'Connor, J. (1993), 'Gender, Class and Citizenship in the Comparative Analysis of Welfare State Regimes: Theoretical and Methodological Issues', *British Journal of Sociology,* vol. 44, no. 3, pp. 502–518.
O'Connor, J. (1994), 'Employment Equality Strategies and Citizenship Rights in Liberal Welfare State Regimes', Paper Presented to the Political Science Program, Australian National University.
O'Donnell, C. and Hall, P. (1988), *Getting Equal,* Allen and Unwin, Sydney.

OECD, (1982), *Employment in the Public Sector,* OECD, Paris.
OECD, (1984), *The Employment and Unemployment of Women in OECD Countries,* OECD, Paris.
OECD, (1988), 'Women's Activity, Employment and Earnings: A Review of Recent Developments', *Employment Outlook,* OECD, Paris, pp. 129–172.
OECD, (1991a), *OECD Historical Statistics 1960–1990,* OECD, Paris.
OECD, (1991b), 'Trends in Trade Union Membership', *Employment Outlook,* OECD, Paris, pp. 97–134.
OECD, (1992), *Employment Outlook,* OECD, Paris.
OECD, (1995), *Employment Outlook,* OECD, Paris.
OECD, (1996), *Employment Outlook,* OECD, Paris.
O'Farrell, B. and Kornbluh, J.L. (eds), (1996), *Rocking the Boat: Union Women's Voices,* Rutgers University Press, New Brunswick.
Offe, C. and Wiesenthal, H. (1980), 'Two Logics of Collective Action: Theoretical Notes on Social Class and Organisational Form', *Political Power and Social Theory,* vol. 1, no. 1, pp. 67–115.
Offe, C. (1985), *Disorganized Capitalism. Contemporary Transformations of Work and Politics,* Polity Press, Cambridge.
Olsson, A.S. (1991), *The Swedish Wage Negotiation System,* Dartmouth, Aldershot.
Olsson, U. (1994), 'Planning in the Swedish Welfare State', in W. Clement and R. Mahon (eds), *Swedish Social Democracy: A Model in Transition,* Canadian Scholars Press, Toronto, pp. 45–64.
Orloff, A.S. (1993), 'Gender and the Social Rights of Citizenship: The Comparative Analysis of Gender Relations and Welfare States', *American Sociological Review,* vol. 58, pp. 303–328.
Orloff, A.S. (1996) 'Gendering the Analysis of Welfare States' in B. Sullivan and G. Whitehouse (eds), *Gender, Politics and Citizenship in the 1990s,* University of New South Wales Press, Sydney, pp. 81–99.
Pateman, C. (1986), 'Introduction: The Theoretical Subversiveness of Feminism', in C. Pateman and E. Gross (eds), *Feminist Challenges: Social and Political Theory,* Allen and Unwin, Sydney, pp. 1–12.
Pateman, C. (1988), 'The Patriarchal Welfare State', in A. Gutmann (ed), *Democracy and the Welfare State,* Princeton University Press, Princeton, pp. 233–260.
Patmore, G. (1992), 'The Future of Trade Unionism - An Australian Perspective', *The International Journal of Human Resource Management,* vol. 3, no. 2, pp. 225–245.
Peattie, L. and Rein, M. (1983), *Women's Claims,* Oxford University Press, Oxford.
Peetz, D. (1990), 'Declining Union Density', *Journal of Industrial Relations,* vol.

32, no. 2, pp. 197-223.
Peetz, D. (1995), 'Union Membership, Labour, Management and the Accord', PhD Thesis, University of New South Wales.
Phillips, A. (1983), *Hidden Hands. Women and Economic Policies*, Pluto Press, London.
Phillips, A. (1987a), *Divided Loyalties: Dilemmas of Sex and Class*, Virago, London.
Phillips, A. (1987b), 'Introduction', in A. Phillips (ed), *Feminism and Equality*, Basil Blackwell, Oxford, pp. 1-23.
Phillips, A. (1991), *Engendering Democracy*, Polity Press, Cambridge.
Phillips, A. (1993), *Democracy and Difference*, Polity Press, Cambridge.
Phillips, A. (1994), 'Democracy and Representation', Paper presented to the Political Science Department, Australian National University.
Phillips, A. (1995), *The Politics of Presence*, Clarendon Press, Oxford.
Pocock, B. (1994), *Raising our Voices,* Centre for Labour Studies, University of Adelaide, Adelaide.
Pocock, B. (1995a), 'Women in Unions: What Progress in South Australia?', *Journal of Industrial Relations*, vol. 37, no. 1, pp. 3-23.
Pocock, B. (1995b), 'Women's Work and Wages', in A. Edwards and S. Magarey (eds), *Women in a Restructuring Australia*, Allen and Unwin, Sydney, pp. 95-120.
Pocock, B. (ed), (1997), *Strife. Sex and Politics in Labour Unions*, Allen and Unwin, Sydney.
Pope, J.J. (1991), 'Conflict of Interests: A Case Study of Na'amat', in B. Swirski and M.P. Safir (eds), *Calling the Equality Bluff,* Pergamon Press, New York, pp. 225-233.
Premfors, R. (1991), 'The "Swedish Model" and Public Sector Reform', *West European Politics*, vol. 14, no. 3, pp. 83-95.
Pringle, R. and Watson, S. (1992), '"Women's Interests" and the Post-Structuralist State', in M. Barrett and A. Phillips (eds), *Destabilising Theory*, Polity Press, Cambridge, pp. 53-73.
Prisching, M. (1993), 'The Transformation of Austria in the Context of Europe', in G. Bischof and A. Pelinka (eds), *Austria in the New Europe,* Transaction, New Brunswick, pp. 81-106.
Przeworski, A. and Tuene, H. (1970), *The Logic of Comparative Social Inquiry*, Wiley-Interscience, New York.
Quataert, J.H. (1985), 'Women's Work and Worth: The Persistence of Stereotype Attitudes in the German Free Trade Unions, 1890-1929', in N.C. Soldon (ed), *The World of Women's Trade Unionism*, Greenwood Press, Westport, pp. 93-124.
Qvist, G.V. (1985), 'Women and the Swedish Federation of Labor, 1898-1973', in

N.C. Soldon (ed), *The World of Women's Trade Unionism*, Greenwood Press, Westport, pp. 153–163.
Qvist, G., Acker J. and Lorwin, V.R. (1984), 'Sweden', in A. Cook, V. Lorwin and A.K. Daniels (eds), *Women and Trade Unions in Eleven Industrialised Countries*, Temple University Press, Philadelphia, pp. 261–285.
Raday, F. (1991), 'Women. Work and the Law', in B. Swirski and M.P. Safir (eds), *Calling the Equality Bluff*, Pergamon Press, New York, pp. 178–186.
Rakba, S.A. (1991), 'Arab Women in the Israeli Labour Market', in B. Swirski and M.P. Safir (eds), *Calling the Equality Bluff*, Pergamon Press, New York, pp. 187–191.
Rawson, D.W. (1978), *Unions and Unionists in Australia*, Allen and Unwin, Sydney.
Rawson, D.W. (1988), 'Is Unionism Everywhere in Decline?', Paper presented to the Australasian Political Studies Association Conference, 26–28 August University of New England.
Riley, D. (1988), *"Am I That Name?" Feminism and the Category of "Women" in History*, Macmillan, Basingstoke.
Rollen, B. (1978), 'Equality between Men and Women in the Labor Market: The Swedish National Labor Market Board', in R. Steinberg Ratner (ed), *Equal Employment Policy for Women*, Temple University Press, Philadelphia, pp. 179–198.
Rose, R. (1985), *Public Employment in Western Nations*, Cambridge University Press, Cambridge.
Rothstein, B. (1991), 'State Structure and Variations in Corporatism: The Swedish Case', *Scandinavian Political Studies*, vol. 14, no. 2, pp. 149–171.
Rothstein, B. (1992), 'Labor-Market Institutions and Working-Class Strength', in S. Steinmo, K. Thelen and F. Longstreth (eds), *Structuring Politics*, Cambridge University Press, Cambridge, pp. 33–56.
Rowthorn, B. (1992), 'Corporatism and Labour Market Performance', in J. Pekkarinen, M. Pohjola, and B. Rowthorn (eds), *Social Corporatism: A Superior Economic System?*, Clarendon Press, Oxford, pp. 82–131.
Ruggie, M. (1984), *The State and Working Women: A Comparative Study of Britain and Sweden*, Princeton University Press, Princeton.
Ruggie, M. (1988), 'Gender, Work and Social Progress', in J. Jenson, E. Hagen and C. Reddy (eds), *Feminization of the Labour Force*, Polity Press, Cambridge, pp. 173–188.
Ryan, E. and Conlon, A. (1989), *Gentle Invaders*, Penguin, Ringwood.
Ryan, E. and Prendergast, H. (1982), 'Unions are for Women Too!', in K. Cole (ed), *Power, Conflict and Control in Australian Trade Unions*, Pelican

Books, Melbourne, pp. 261–278.
Safir, M.P. (1991), 'Religion, Tradition and Public Policy Give Family First Priority', in B. Swirski and M.P. Safir (eds), *Calling the Equality Bluff*, Pergamon Press, New York, pp. 57–65.
Sainsbury, D. (1991), 'Swedish Social Democracy in Transition: The Party's Record in the 1980s and the Challenge of the 1990s', *West European Politics*, vol. 14, no. 3, pp. 31–57.
Sapiro, V. (1981), 'When are Interests Interesting? The Problem of Political Representation of Women', *American Political Science Review*, vol. 75, no. 3, pp. 701–716.
Sawer, M. (1990), *Sisters in Suits*, Allen and Unwin, Sydney.
Sawer, M. and Simms, M. (1993), *A Woman's Place*, Allen and Unwin, Sydney.
Scharpf, F.W. (1984), 'Economic and Institutional Constraints of Full-Employment Strategies: Sweden, Austria and West Germany, 1973–1982', in J. Goldthorpe (ed), *Order and Conflict in Contemporary Capitalism*, Clarendon Press, Oxford, pp. 257–290.
Schmidt, M.G. (1982), 'The Role of the Parties in Shaping Macroeconomic Policy' in F.G. Castles (ed), *The Impact of Parties*, Sage Publications, London, pp. 97–166.
Schmidt, M.G. (1993), 'Gendered Labour Force Participation', in F.G. Castles (ed), *Families of Nations: Patterns of Public Policy in Western Democracies*, Dartmouth, Aldershot, pp. 179–238.
Schmitter, P.C. (1981), 'Interest Intermediation and Regime Governability in Contemporary Western Europe and North America', in S. Berger (ed), *Organising Interests in Western Europe: Pluralism, Corporatism and the Transformation of Politics*, Cambridge University Press, Cambridge, pp. 285–327.
Scott, H. (1982), *Sweden's "Right to be Human"*, M.E. Sharpe, Armonk.
Scott, J. (1990), 'Deconstructing Equality-Versus-Difference: Or, the Uses of Poststructuralist Theory for Feminism', in M. Hirsche and E. Fox Keller (eds), *Conflicts in Feminism*, Routledge, New York, pp. 134–148.
Shalev, M. (1989), 'Israel's Domestic Policy Regime: Zionism, Dualism and the Rise of Capital', in F.G. Castles (ed), *The Comparative History of Public Policy*, Polity Press, Oxford, pp. 100–148.
Shalev, M. (1992), *Labour and the Political Economy in Israel*, Oxford University Press, Oxford.
Shalev, M. and Korpi, W. (1980), 'Working Class Mobilisation and American Exceptionalism', *Economic and Industrial Democracy*, vol. 1, no. 1, pp. 31–61.
Shute, C. (1994), 'Unequal Partners: Women, Power and the Trade Union Movement', in N. Grieve and A. Burns (eds), *Australian Women:*

Contemporary Feminist Thought, Oxford University Press, Melbourne, pp. 166–178.
Simms, M. (1987), *Militant Public Servants*, Macmillan, Melbourne.
Singleton, G. (1995), 'Accord VII: Collective Bargaining in a Labourist Framework', *Policy, Organisation and Society*, vol. 10, pp. 98–115.
Smith, M. and Ewer, P. (1995), 'The Position of Women in the National Training Reform Agenda and Enterprise Bargaining', Report of the Project funded by the Women's Research and Employment Initiatives Program, Melbourne.
Soldon, N.C. (1985), 'British Women and Trade Unionism: Opportunities Made and Missed', in N.C. Soldon (ed), *The World of Women's Trade Unionism*, Greenwood Press, Westport, pp. 11–34.
State Secretariat for the General Concerns of Women (SSGCW), (1991), *Women in Austria 1985–1990*, SSGCW, Vienna.
Statistics Sweden, (1995), *Women and Men in Sweden*, Gender Statistics Unit, Stockholm.
Status of Women Bureau, (1981), *The Status of Women*, Bureau of the Advisor to the Prime Minister on the Status of Women, Jerusalem.
Steinberg Ratner, R. (1978), 'The Policy and Problem: Overview of Seven Countries', in R. Steinberg Ratner (ed), *Equal Employment Policy for Women*, Temple University Press, Philadelphia, pp. 1–52.
Stephen, D. (1995), 'Women's Relative Earnings Under Enterprise Bargaining', Centre for Economic Policy Research, Discussion Paper no. 327, Australian National University.
Stephens, J. (1990), 'Explaining Cross-National Differences in Union Strength in Bargaining and Welfare', Paper Presented to the XIIth World Congress of Sociology, 9-13 July, Madrid.
Stilwell, F. (1986), *The Accord - and Beyond: the Political Economy of the Labor Government*, Pluto Press, Sydney.
Street, M. (1994), 'Working Women and Trade Unions in New Zealand 1889–1906', in P. Walsh (ed), *Trade Unions, Work and Society: The Centenary of the Arbitration System*, Dunmore Press, Palmerston North, pp. 39–68.
Ströer, A. and Sweeney, J. (1988), 'The Austrian Trade Union Movement', in J. Sweeney and J. Weidenholzer (eds), *Austria: A Study in Modern Achievement*, Avebury, Aldershot, pp. 123–146.
Strum, P. (1992), *The Women are Marching*, Lawrence Hill Books, New York.
Sullivan, B. (1990), 'Sex Equality and the Australian Body Politic', in S. Watson (ed), *Playing the State*, Allen and Unwin, Sydney, pp. 173–189.
Sullivan, B. (1994), 'Contemporary Australian Feminism: A Critical Review', in G. Stokes (ed), *Australian Political Ideas*, University of New South Wales Press, Kensington, pp. 152–167.

Sully, M. (1982), *Continuity and Change in Austrian Socialism: The Eternal Quest for the Third Way*, Colombia University Press, Boulder.
Sully, M. (1988), 'The Socialist Party of Austria', in J. Sweeney and J. Weidenholzer (eds), *Austria: A Study in Modern Achievement*, Avebury, Aldershot, pp. 55-66.
Sundström, M. (1982), 'Part-time work and trade union activities among women', *Economic and Industrial Democracy*, vol. 3, no. 4, pp. 561-567.
Sweeney, J. (1988), 'The Austrian Social Partnership', in J. Sweeney and J. Weidenholzer (eds), *Austria: A Study in Modern Achievement*, Avebury, Aldershot, pp. 182-193.
Swirski, B. (1991), 'Israeli Feminism New and Old', in B. Swirski and M.P. Safir (eds), *Calling the Equality Bluff*, Pergamon Press, New York, pp. 285-302.
Tálos, E. and Kittel, B. (1996), 'Roots of Austro-Corporatism: Institutional Preconditions and Cooperation Before and After 1945', in G. Bischoff and A. Pelinka (eds), *Austro-Corporatism: Past, Present, Future*, Transaction, New Brunswick, pp. 21-52.
Textile, Clothing and Footwear Union of Australia (TCFUA), (1995), *The Hidden Cost of Fashion*, TCFUA, Sydney.
Therborn, G. (1992), 'Lessons from Corporatist Theorizations', in J. Pekkarinen, M. Pohjola, and B. Rowthorn (eds), *Social Corporatism: A Superior Economic System?*, Clarendon Press, Oxford, pp. 24-43.
Tilton, T. (1991), *The Political Theory of Swedish Social Democracy*, Clarendon Press, Oxford.
Traxler, F. (1992), 'Austria: Still the Country of Corporatism', in A. Ferner and R. Hyman (eds), *Industrial Relations in the New Europe*, Basil Blackwell Ltd, Oxford, pp. 270-297.
Traxler, F. (1994), 'From Demand-Side to Supply-Side Corporatism?: Austria's Labor Relations in a Process of Change', Paper prepared for the XVIth World Congress of the International Political Science Association, 20-24 August, Berlin.
Trebilcock, A. (1991), 'Strategies for Strengthening Women's Participation in Trade Union Leadership', *International Labour Review*, vol. 130, no. 4, pp. 407-426.
Visser, J. (1987), *In Search of Inclusive Unionism*, University of Amsterdam, Amsterdam.
Visser, J. (1989), *European Trade Unions in Figures*, Kluwer Law and Taxation Publishers, Deventer.
Visser, J. (1992), 'Union Organisation: Why Countries Differ', Paper presented at

the International Industrial Relations Association 9th World Congress, 30 August-3 September, Sydney.
Vogel, L. (1983), *Marxism and the Oppression of Women: Toward a Unitary Theory*, Rutgers University Press, New Brunswick.
Wallerstein, M. (1989), 'Union Organization in Advanced Industrial Democracies', *American Political Science Review*, vol. 83, no. 2, pp. 481–501.
Weiss, S. and Yishai, Y. (1980), 'Women's Representation in Israeli Political Elites', *Jewish Social Studies*, vol. 42, pp. 165–176.
Whitehouse, G. (1992), 'Legislation and Labour Market Gender Inequality: An Analysis of OECD Countries', *Work, Employment and Society*, vol. 6, no. 1, pp. 65–86.
Whitehouse, G. (1995), 'Employment Equity and Labour Organisation: The Comparative Political Economy of Women and Work', PhD Thesis, University of Queensland.
Whitehouse, G., Boreham P. and Lafferty, G. (1995), 'Casual or Permanent Part-Time? Women, Enterprise Bargaining and Service Sector Employment', Paper Presented to the 5th Women and Labour Conference, 29 September-1 October, Macquarie University.
Wilkinson, J. (1983), 'Unions and Women Workers', in B. Ford and D. Plowman (eds), *Australian Unions: An Industrial Relations Perspective*, Macmillan, Melbourne, pp. 350–365.
Wilson, P. (1994), 'Gender Agenda', *The Australian*, 8 March, p. 9.
Wolf, I. and Wolf, W. (1991), *How Much Less...? Earnings Disparities between Women and Men in Austria*, Austrian Federal Ministry of Labour and Social Affairs, Vienna.
Women's Trade Union Commission (WTUC), (1976), 'Unions are for Women Too!', A Report of the First Australian Women's Trade Union Conference, WTUC, Sydney.
Yeatman, A. (1990), *Bureaucrats, Technocrats, Femocrats*, Allen and Unwin, Sydney.
Yeatman, A. (1993), 'Voice and Representation in the Politics of Difference', in S. Gunew and A. Yeatman (eds), *Feminism and the Politics of Difference*, Allen and Unwin, St Leonards, pp. 229–245.
Yeatman, A. (1995), 'Interlocking Oppressions', in B. Caine and R. Pringle (eds), *Transitions. New Australian Feminisms*, Allen and Unwin, St Leonards, pp. 42–56.
Young, I.M. (1994), 'Gender as Seriality: Thinking about Women as a Social Collective', *Signs*, vol. 19, no. 3, pp. 713–738.
Yuval-Davis, N. (1985), '"Front and rear": The Sexual Division of Labor in the Israeli Army', *Feminist Studies*, vol. 11, no. 3, pp. 649–676.

Zetkin, K. (1929), *Reminiscences of Lenin: Dealing with Lenin's Views on the Position of Women and other Questions*, Modern Books, London.

Index

Accord, 3, 39, 40, 59, 60, 63, 157
ACTU, 12, 13, 37, 39, 40, 43–55, 58–61, 144, 147
affirmative action, 43, 44, 48, 49, 56, 64, 76, 101, 126, 147, 148
amalgamation, 45, 50, 65, 124
Arab, 93, 95–97, 99, 104, 105, 108–111, 113, 114, 116
arbitration, 22, 37, 38, 40, 42, 52, 56, 63, 64, 150
Australian Labor Party, 2, 39, 145
award, 39, 41, 51, 52, 53, 54, 56, 57, 58, 60, 64, 150, 153

blue-collar, 39, 50, 121, 126, 132, 134, 135, 140, 153, 159

Canada, 8, 10
centralised wage bargaining, 22, 97, 119, 131–132, 135, 141, 149–154
Chamber of Labour, 68, 69, 71–73, 76, 77, 86
child care, 22, 23, 46, 53, 54, 57, 59, 60, 75, 86, 87, 90, 91, 113, 114, 137, 140, 141, 143, 154–157
collective bargaining, 12, 14, 18, 19, 22, 55, 69, 74, 78, 82, 83, 86, 91, 95, 96, 112, 116, 126, 140, 157
committees, 12, 32, 47–50, 57, 62, 64, 73, 74, 79, 94, 98–105, 107, 110, 116, 122, 123, 127, 144–146
conciliation, 37, 38, 40, 56
conferences, 32, 48, 50, 64, 72, 73, 126, 144, 146
consciousness, 17, 18, 32, 47, 49, 53, 72, 146
consensus, 44, 66, 67, 69, 70, 76, 84, 91, 118, 119, 123
corporatist, 2–4, 6, 20, 23, 37, 41, 66, 69, 76–78, 84, 91–93, 96, 97, 116, 119, 129, 130, 139, 140, 145, 146, 148, 153, 155, 159–161

Denmark, 8, 10, 13
Department for Salaried Women, 99, 100, 102, 103, 105, 107–111, 114–116

Education, 45, 62, 87, 127
Engels, 17, 20, 23, 156
enterprise bargaining, 40, 46, 51, 55, 56, 60–62, 65, 156
equal employment opportunity, 15, 23, 50, 57, 89, 156, 157, 159
equal pay, 14, 22, 34, 42, 49, 52, 53, 56, 57, 64, 72, 80, 82, 84, 108, 109, 111, 112, 131, 132, 134, 135, 149, 150, 151, 153, 156
Equality Commission, 82, 89
Equality Ombudsman, 82, 83, 84, 127
equality package, 86
ethnicity, 25, 35, 50, 105, 148
European Union, 89, 91, 156

family leave, 49, 57, 58, 60, 63
family responsibilities, 15, 58, 75, 86, 103, 125, 138, 142, 154, 155, 159
family wage, 34, 39, 52, 63, 149, 150, 155
female union density, 8, 9, 11
feminist, 5, 8, 14, 17, 20, 23, 26–30, 32–35, 37, 41, 63, 64, 71, 102, 140, 144, 146, 147, 148, 158, 160
fringe benefits, 107, 109, 111, 151, 152

gender-wage, 22, 51, 57, 78–81, 83, 84, 106–109, 112, 131, 133, 135, 149–154
Germany, 8, 10, 13, 84
globalisation, 7

Histadrut, 94–106, 108–117, 147, 151
Human Rights and Equal Opportunity Commission, 53

Industrial Relations Commission, 41, 52, 53, 54, 59, 150
Ireland, 10, 13
Italy, 12, 13
Israel Women's Network, 101, 103, 108

Jewish, 93, 95–97, 99, 104, 105, 110–113, 116, 117, 142, 151, 159
job rotation, 57, 132, 135, 153

labour court, 110, 112, 115, 116, 135, 139
labour force participation, 10, 11, 51, 66, 71, 77, 78, 81, 86, 90, 91, 97, 98, 105, 113, 114, 122, 131, 136, 137, 140, 143, 144, 146, 148, 154, 155, 157, 161
labour market, 3, 4, 7, 11, 15, 17, 30, 34, 40, 51, 58, 63, 69, 82, 87, 88, 90, 91, 113, 115, 116, 118, 119, 123, 135–137, 139, 140, 151, 153–156, 158, 160
Labour Party, 94, 101, 103, 147
Lander, 87
legal advice, 69, 99, 110, 112, 152
legislative, 4, 17, 23, 30, 33, 34, 40, 62, 83, 85, 90, 112, 116, 127, 151, 152, 156
Leichter, 71
Lenin, 17, 18, 23
LO, 13, 119–125, 127–135, 138, 139, 141, 149, 150, 153, 157

married women, 90, 99, 104, 136, 154
Marx, 16, 17, 20, 23, 143
masculine, 22, 26, 37, 49, 63, 143, 146, 159
maternity leave, 28, 58, 59, 60, 85, 86, 87, 90, 92, 113, 115, 137, 154, 155
membership, 1, 3, 7, 8, 10, 12, 13, 21, 23, 31, 41, 46, 47, 50, 68–74, 91, 93–95, 98, 101, 106, 117, 121, 122–125, 131, 138, 142–144, 147, 148, 160, 161
militancy, 18, 22
military, 95, 106, 112, 155
minimum wages, 41, 52, 80, 108, 109, 150, 160
mothers, 28, 58, 85, 86, 87, 97, 99, 112, 113–115, 148, 154

Na'amat, 99, 102–105, 108–113, 115, 116, 145, 147, 152, 154
Netherlands, 8, 10, 13
networks, 32, 48, 50, 61, 64, 69, 73, 75, 77, 103, 129, 130, 137, 144
night work, 33, 88, 89, 92, 114, 156

ÖGB, 68, 69, 72, 73, 74, 75, 76, 78, 79, 82, 84, 86, 89, 90, 94
outwork, 54, 61

Palestinian, 104
parental leave, 50, 58, 64, 82, 88, 90, 137, 138, 140, 141, 156, 157
part-time, 10, 34, 47, 51, 55, 56, 60, 61, 63, 78, 79, 86–88, 90, 113, 114, 131, 136–138, 154, 155, 157, 159
pensions, 58, 59, 81, 89, 120
political unionism, 19, 157
pregnant, 33, 58, 85, 113, 136
private sector, 10, 50, 58, 59, 74, 95, 100, 107, 120, 126, 131, 133, 149, 159
promotion, 40, 54, 81, 83, 84, 88, 89, 94, 111, 127, 155
public sector, 9, 10, 11, 23, 41, 50, 59, 90, 106, 108, 118, 120, 133, 134, 138, 149, 154

Race, 25
recruitment, 10, 18, 22, 46, 47, 48, 50, 61, 77, 145, 152
representation, 1–5, 7, 12, 14, 16, 17, 20, 23–25, 30–32, 34, 36, 41–50, 57, 64, 66–70, 72–75, 77, 83, 84, 93–95, 97, 100–104, 107, 110, 116, 119, 123–130, 142–148, 152, 154, 159–161

Index

reserved seats, 12, 13, 32, 147

SACO, 120, 126, 128
school, 19, 86, 113, 121, 154, 155
Sears, 27
segregation, 22, 42, 55, 80, 96, 107, 116, 127, 132, 149, 152, 153
sex discrimination, 27, 51, 140
sex segregation, 22
sexual difference, 21, 27, 33
sexual harassment, 15, 61, 62, 63, 64, 89, 90, 114, 139, 140, 158
Sick Fund, 94, 117
social democratic, 16, 18, 19, 35, 67, 121, 141, 157
social partnership, 67, 69, 70, 76–78, 91
solidaristic wage policy, 78, 84, 91, 112, 135, 149, 152
solidarity, 5–7, 16, 20, 23, 24, 30, 38, 51, 56, 63, 64, 79, 93, 97, 117, 119, 120, 121, 131, 133, 135, 147, 149–151, 159, 160, 161
strike, 17, 18, 96, 107, 108, 160

TCO, 12, 13, 120–126, 133–135, 139, 150, 151
test case, 52, 53, 57, 58, 59, 64, 155
Tjejligan, 130
training, 47, 48, 53, 56, 57, 62, 69, 70, 75, 83, 84, 98, 107, 111, 114, 122, 127, 128, 132, 133, 134, 153, 155

UK, 10, 13
unemployment, 3, 19, 40, 66, 78, 97, 110, 112, 118, 119, 139
United Kingdom, 12
United States, 8, 22, 27, 29

welfare, 3, 9, 19, 20, 39, 40, 58, 63, 91, 94, 97, 118, 120, 129, 136, 137, 144, 155, 157, 159, 160
white-collar, 22, 23, 39, 50, 74, 78, 120, 121, 125, 131, 135, 139–141, 150, 153, 159
Women Workers' Movement, 98, 99
women's divisions, 11, 72–76, 90, 92, 116, 145, 146
women's interests, 5, 14, 16, 20, 23, 28–31, 33, 35, 36, 64, 66, 93, 102, 115, 130, 144, 146, 148, 159
work council, 68, 83, 147
working conditions, 14, 17, 18, 19, 22, 29, 33, 38, 53, 63, 71, 89–99, 108, 110, 133, 142, 145, 154, 157
Working Women's Charter, 43, 46, 49

Zionist, 93, 94, 97, 99